The Poverty Debate

**Recent Titles in
Contributions in Sociology**

Time, Memory, and Society
Franco Ferrarotti

Homelessness in the United States. Volume II: Data and Issues
Jamshid A. Momeni, editor

Promises in Promised Land: Mobility and Inequality in Israel
Vered Kraus and Robert W. Hodge

Switzerland in Perspective
Janet Eve Hilowitz, editor

Rethinking Today's Minorities
Vincent N. Parrillo, editor

Beyond Ethnocentrism: A Reconstruction of Marx's Concept of Science
Charles McKelvey

The Community in Rural America
Kenneth P. Wilkinson

The Next Three Futures: Paradigms of Things to Come
W. Warren Wager

Changing Jewish Life: Service Delivery and Planning in the 1990s
Lawrence I. Sternberg, Gary A. Tobin, and Sylvia Barack Fishman, editors

Alienation, Community, and Work
Andrew Oldenquist and Menachem Rosner, editors

High Risk and High Stakes: Health Professionals, Politics, and Policy
Earl Wysong

Immigration and Ethnicity: American Society—"Melting Pot" or "Salad Bowl"?
Michael D'Innocenzo and Josef P. Sirefman, editors

THE
POVERTY
DEBATE

Politics and the Poor in America

C. EMORY BURTON

Contributions in Sociology, Number 102

GREENWOOD PRESS
Westport, Connecticut • London

Library of Congress Cataloging-in-Publication Data

Burton, C. Emory.
    The poverty debate : politics and the poor in America / C. Emory
Burton.
        p. cm.—(Contributions in sociology, ISSN 0084–9278 ; no.
102)
    Includes bibliographical references and indexes.
    ISBN 0–313–28594–2 (alk. paper)
    1. Poor—United States. 2. Welfare recipients—Employment—United
States. 3. Poor—United States—Social conditions. I. Title.
II. Series.
HC110.P6B87   1992
362.5′8′0973—dc20   92–14353

British Library Cataloguing in Publication Data is available.

A paperback edition of *The Poverty Debate: Politics and the Poor in America*
is available from the Praeger Publishers imprint of Greenwood Publishing Group, Inc.
(ISBN: 0-275-94436-0).

Library of Congress Catalog Card Number: 92–14353
ISBN: 0–313–28594–2
ISSN: 0084–9278

First published in 1992

Greenwood Press, 88 Post Road West, Westport, CT 06881
An imprint of Greenwood Publishing Group, Inc.

Printed in the United States of America

The paper used in this book complies with the
Permanent Paper Standard issued by the National
Information Standards Organization (Z39.48–1984).

10 9 8 7 6 5 4 3 2 1

Copyright Acknowledgement

The author and publisher are grateful to the following for allowing the use
of material:

Paul West, "31 States Lack the Funds for Health, Welfare Costs," *The Baltimore
Sun*, January 3, 1991, 1A. Copyright 1992 The Baltimore Sun Co., reprinted
with permission.

This is for Dorothy

Contents

Preface		ix
Introduction		1
1	The Measurement and Extent of Poverty	5
2	The Culture of Poverty	21
3	The Underclass	39
4	The Homeless	57
5	Welfare	71
6	Welfare Dependency	89
7	Workfare	99
8	Toward a Solution	113
9	Political Implications	131
10	A Theory for Reform	149
Appendix A: 1990 Poverty Data		161
Appendix B: Percentage of Persons in Poverty, by State, 1990		165
Bibliography		167
Name Index		185
Subject Index		195

Preface

I first became interested in poverty while observing the slum areas of my home city of Birmingham, Alabama. In the process of obtaining a seminary degree in the Chicago area, I became aware of the ghetto poor in that often-studied city. My several years in the ministry led me to observe and reflect upon the human suffering that so many of our citizens experienced.

Turning to the study of sociology, I gradually began to think again about poverty, teaching several courses on this subject. While I had some experiences with poverty through working with community organizations, most of my awareness has come through reading. Of the books listed in the bibliography, I would like to single out a few.

Leonard Beeghley's *Living Poorly in America* (1983) is a vigorous defense of the poor and an underrated analysis of the situation of being impoverished in this country. William Julius Wilson's *The Truly Disadvantaged* (1987), a cogent statement of the problems of the underclass in our society, may be the most significant work on this subject in the last decade. Lisbeth Schorr's *Within Our Reach: Breaking the Cycle of Disadvantage* (1988) is an important, rather optimistic book that shows that progress against the most severe problems is possible.

Although it deals only partly with poverty, Frances Moore Lappé's *Rediscovering America's Values* (1989) is a thought-provoking, often brilliant examination of the personal and social values that inform our lives. I should also mention help provided by H. Paul Chalfant's annotated bibliography on the sociology of poverty (Chalfant 1985), including his introductory material.

Of the numerous articles examined in preparation for this work, one seems to stand out. Cynthia Duncan and Ann R. Tickamyer's long piece (Duncan and Tickamyer 1988), ostensibly on rural poverty, is actually an excellent discussion of poverty in general, and a particularly strong assessment of various poverty theories. A first-rate article on the causes and persistence of poverty by Mary Corcoran and colleagues (Corcoran et al. 1985) proved most helpful. Naomi Farber's study of unmarried adolescent mothers (Farber 1989) has a strange appeal that makes one remember it.

Even though much of this book is an argument against conservative ideas, it would be appropriate for me to mention some of the conservatives, particularly Milton and Rose Friedman, George Gilder, Charles Murray, and Lawrence Mead. Reading some of their works has motivated me to study the subject more carefully. Reading them should also caution one not to be too quick to label and dismiss those with whom one tends to disagree.

Several individuals have helped in the writing of this book. Eleanor Baugher of the Poverty and Wealth Branch of the U.S. Bureau of the Census provided up-to-date census data. Leonard Beeghley of the University of Florida read and made valuable suggestions on chapter 2. William Julius Wilson read and commented favorably on chapter 3. James Farmer of the School of Social Work at the University of Texas in Arlington gave valuable comments on chapter 4. Edward Harpham of the University of Texas at Dallas read and offered helpful suggestions on chapter 9. Susan Hoahan read the entire manuscript and made many constructive suggestions. And Lori Lewis-Traywick compiled much of the Name Index.

To Dorothy, my wife of 36 years, thanks should be offered for her patience while the manuscript was in process. And to a former teacher from the University of Tennessee, Thomas C. Hood, goes thanks for his encouragement to always work toward productive goals.

The
Poverty
Debate

Introduction

As the nation approaches the end of the twentieth century, poverty has re-emerged as a subject of inquiry. Figures from 1990 indicate that 13.5 percent of the population lives below the poverty level (U.S. Bureau of the Census 1991), and particular concern has been expressed about poor children (Johnson et al. 1991). While scholars and other writers seemed to turn their attention elsewhere for a time, writing on poverty-related issues in the last several years has been extensive.

Poverty is a major subject of study in undergraduate and graduate departments of sociology, urban affairs, and social work, and to a certain extent in economics and political science. Many seminars and task forces have issued reports on the subject (Haveman 1988: 18). There is at least a faint sign that poverty is gaining the attention of policymakers once more. Following the Los Angeles riots in the spring of 1992, recognition was made that the poverty of the region was an important underlying cause of the disturbances.

The National Conference of Catholic Bishops wrote in 1986, "That so many people are poor in a nation as rich as ours is a social and moral scandal that we cannot ignore." They established moral criteria for how we care for the poor, sick, hungry, and homeless, and how our economic system and its structures of power generate and sustain patterns of inequality, unemployment, poverty, hunger, exploitation, and what they called "marginalization" of people (Rosen 1988).

Leslie Dunbar claims that no society can be considered just that allows its citizens to live in desperate need; it is unfair for some to be rich while others suffer. Opportunity ought to be an entitlement of citizenship (cited in Lynn 1990a). The lifestyle and life chances of the poor represent an inconsistency that cannot be accommodated comfortably to our ideals (Chalfant 1985: xxii).

A person has a right in justice, not merely in charity, to at least minimal support from the society because he or she is a human being. The humane society must guarantee its citizens a decent standard of living, including education, health care, and livable housing (Walch 1973: 32–33; also see Thurow 1980: 155).

If ever there were a country where there should be no poor, it would be the United States of America. With a gross national product (GNP) in the trillions, 70 percent of the largest economic corporations in the world, and its overabundance of foodstuffs found in warehouses throughout its agricultural heartland, America is indeed rich. But it is also poor (Burghardt and Fabricant 1987: 7).

The advancement of liberty and equality defines not only the U.S. view of itself but its image of its role in the world. Poverty is the blemish on the American model. Nothing undermines our self-image more than the 33 million who cannot maintain an adequate standard of living in this land of plenty (Riemer 1988: 104–105). The physical and emotional deterioration associated with homelessness, recent unemployment, or hunger is an affront in a land as affluent as ours (Burghardt and Fabricant 1987: 11–12).

This rich nation, according to Robert Haveman, can effectively combat the intolerable and persistent poverty among a portion of its population. The image of the poor and homeless living in the midst of affluence has long plagued both our national conscience and our international esteem (Haveman 1988: 15, 29).

We quite agree with Beeghley, who feels that economic life in the United States should be less unequal than it is today, so that it would become "a more just society, more true to its heritage, more economically productive, and a more enjoyable place . . . to live" (Beeghley 1983: vii). This viewpoint informs this book and this value should be explicit from the outset.

While this approach will be interpreted as a liberal one by most observers, a word should be said about the word "conservative." In most of the literature, a conservative is one inclined to a far right or even reactionary position, one who would likely identify with *National Review* and with the Heritage Foundation. In the field of poverty, a conservative is likely to downplay the extent of poverty, emphasize its cultural causes, disparage welfare and emphasize the dependency it can lead to, and disapprove of major new policies to eliminate the problem, particularly at the governmental level. It is in this sense that we use the word, conservative, in most of this book.

But in fairness, conservative writers have often complained about poverty. "Few can fail to be moved by the contrast between the luxury enjoyed by some and the grinding poverty suffered by others" (Friedman and Friedman 1979: 146). "The moral imperative to do something to correct the situation of poor people and especially the minority poor is at least as powerful now as when Lyndon Johnson took office" (Murray 1984: 219).

In chapters 9 and 10, we recognize that some conservatives, particularly more moderate ones, are alarmed at the rate of poverty and would like to take steps to diminish it. For at least some conservatives, this might include more than a passive role for the government. While they would likely disagree with the more activist liberals, they may have ideas that should not be summarily dismissed.

This does not imply that there is now an overall consensus on the subject of poverty. On the contrary, there is enormous disagreement as to how widespread poverty is, what are its causes, the role of welfare, the question of dependency, "workfare," what ought to be done about the problem, the role of the government in such a task, and numerous other issues. It is this controversy that this book addresses.

This work is not intended as a comprehensive treatment of the entire range of poverty in the United States. It centers on issues on which there has been considerable disagreement. (Marxist theories about poverty are not considered for lack of space.) Because of the range of sources used, it may be considered as a review of recent literature in the field, particularly from a sociological perspective. Considerable literature has been included from economics and social work, and (to a lesser extent) from history and political science.

The book has three main divisions: the first four chapters consider the extent and nature of poverty, including the culture of poverty, the underclass, and the homeless. Chapters 5–7 examine welfare and related issues. Chapters 8–10 look at some of the proposals to reduce poverty, including the political implications, and propose a theory that emphasizes the urgency of reform.

One excellent article on poverty ends with these words: "The failure of sociologists to engage in poverty research has left a vacuum. The uniquely sociological imagination has produced the best work on poverty and holds out the best hope for further progress" (Duncan and Tickamyer 1988). This work seeks to employ some of that imagination on a crucially important subject.

1

The Measurement and Extent of Poverty

It might seem curious that the very existence of poverty in the United States would be a controversial issue, but the truth is that the existence, the definition, and particularly the measurement of the phenomenon are matters of considerable debate.

Defining poverty, at least subjectively, is not so difficult: it can be described as a situation in which a person or family is not able to maintain an adequate level of living by the standards of their society (Chalfant 1985: ix). Another definition is "not having sufficient resources to pay for the essentials of life—food, shelter, and medical care" (Nasar 1986). Being poor means lacking money and other things taken for granted in American society; by common consent, a family is not considered poor merely because its members live at a standard below the average.

THE MEASUREMENT OF POVERTY

The actual measurement of poverty by the census bureau and other agencies has been extremely controversial. The poverty line was first set by the government in 1964, when it was determined that an income of $3,000 for the year was considered adequate to meet the needs of an urban family of four. Since it was believed that food required about one-third of a family's budget, a total budget was set by multiplying the minimum amount required to purchase food ($1,000 for a family of four in 1964) by three. No independent calculations were made of the dollar amounts actually required to meet minimal shelter, clothing, transportation, and other needs.

The food plan upon which this was based was intended by the Social Security Administration strictly as an emergency plan and was considered inadequate for day-to-day subsistence over long periods of time. Further, goods and commodities listed in the food plan could be obtained for $1,000 in 1964 only if the shopper were exceptionally skillful and had access to the least expensive sources of food (Chalfant 1985: xi; Wilson 1987: 171).

Beeghley is probably correct when he claims that many poor households actually spend up to half their income on food. He also shows that it would take a family of nutritionists with perfect knowledge to obtain an adequate diet with the specified plan (Beeghley 1983: 24–25, 29). One author believes we could multiply the food budget by four rather than by three (Levitan 1985: 4). If some argue that the poor receive food stamps, it is worth noting that only 18 percent of food stamp recipients receive the full amount (Nasar 1986).

Mollie Orshansky, the economist who computed the first poverty line, has pointed out that the actual poverty line published in 1968 was set at 75 to 80 percent of the dollar value reflecting the cost of the United States Department of Agriculture economy budget. Orshansky herself claimed that the poverty line (in 1982) was at least 40 percent too low because of outright reductions in nutrition standards, among other things (Chambers 1982).

For the last thirty years, the poverty line for a family of four has been consistently lower than the median amount that Americans, according to Gallup polls, believe a family of four needs to "get along" in this country (Riemer 1988: 18). In 1989 pollsters asked a national sample of Americans how much weekly income they would use as a poverty line for a family of four. The figure, converted to an annual amount, given by the respondents was $15,017, nearly $3,000 above the official poverty line (Wilson 1991a).

Further, the poverty line is drawn on the basis of income, and some believe that this underestimates poverty because overall wealth is not taken into account. Oliver and Shapiro (1990) report that aggregate shares of wealth held by households are distributed far more unevenly than income shares, with higher concentration at the upper extremes. At least one-third of American households are wealth poor, and home ownership (the major source of wealth for most Americans) is becoming increasingly less available to more and more Americans. Income alone, they conclude, seriously underestimates the problems. Sherraden (1988) is another who finds that asset distribution is much more unequal than income distribution.

While a good case could be made that the poverty level is too low, we can agree with William Julius Wilson when he says that "on balance, it appears that the extent of poverty is not exaggerated by the official poverty formula" (Wilson 1987: 171).

Several observers, including many conservatives, have strenuously objected to the definition of poverty because it does not count all "in-kind" benefits as income. (While some noncash benefits are counted, others, like Medicaid, food stamps, and school lunch programs, are not.) Writers from the Heritage Foundation claim that if the missing welfare spending were counted, the number of poor would be down to only a small fraction of the current estimate (Rector et al. 1990).

Two well-known economists believe that the census count of the poor is a gross overestimate because in-kind income is neglected (Friedman and Friedman 1979: 108). One observer estimates that when in-kind food, housing, and medical care transfers are included at their cash equivalent value the 1972 poverty count is reduced to half its reported size (Smeeding 1972). Conservative Charles Murray has claimed that the many overlapping cash and in-kind benefit programs "made it possible for almost anyone to place themselves (*sic*) above the official poverty level" (Murray 1982: 64). Elsewhere Murray (1988) argues that with a free apartment, free food, free medical care, and a cash grant, many of the (alleged) poor are well above the poverty line.

George Gilder actually claims that there are poor families who receive comparable value from welfare and other programs, plus time for leisure or undocumented work, who are in fact getting a package of benefits as valuable as a middle-class job. He goes on to argue that poor families alone received average benefits that brought them some 30 percent above the official poverty line (Gilder 1981: 89, 112). As we shall see, claims like this are unsupported if not ridiculous.

One assumption made by those who make this point is that practically all poor people receive every conceivable benefit available. But most social scientists agree that there are many poor who are eligible for assistance who do not receive it—they may be unaware of the assistance, they may be repelled by the stigma, or they may be denied help (Waxman 1983: 110). Only 40 percent of households under the poverty line receive Aid to Families With Dependent Children (AFDC), and another 40 percent get by without food stamps (Nasar 1986). About 41.8 percent of persons below the poverty level in 1990 received cash assistance in that year, and

28.4 percent of the poor received no benefits of any sort in 1990 (U.S. Bureau of the Census 1991: 10).

A recent estimate is that about three-fourths of all poor families do not get any type of housing assistance, and the average poor family with children got only $141 worth of food and housing benefits per month in 1989 (Johnson et al. 1991). Zick and Smith (1991) report that almost 60 percent of the poor were not eligible for Medicaid, and the number of the poor covered by this program dropped significantly in the early 1980s (Schorr 1988: 120). Two-parent families with a full-time worker are eligible for almost nothing except food stamps (Ellwood 1988: 100). Only about 60 percent of the eligible elderly participate in supplemental security income, and in many cases these benefits do not boost them above the poverty line (Haveman 1988: 83).

One analysis showed that less than 50 percent of those eligible for enrollment in public assistance programs are actually enrolled. Some are eligible for only a short time and so do not seek aid. However, many (including those with the lowest incomes) are not able to obtain assistance because of the inaccessibility of aid. Included here are programs that are ineffective in outreach, unmanageable application forms, and offices which are not geographically available (Bendick 1980).

Riemer has good basis for claiming that even with assistance the poor would still almost all end up below the poverty line. In 1987 the median state combined benefit for a three-person family was only 74 percent of the poverty line (in Alabama and Mississippi, the percentage was 46 percent). In only two states did it exceed the poverty line (Riemer 1988: 78). Schiller says that even after receiving assistance, the poor remain "pitifully below acceptable standards of living" (Schiller 1984: 188).

After a careful analysis of AFDC, Dear (1989) found that no state provides enough cash income to bring a mother with one or two children up to the poverty line. The larger the family, the lower the per capita grants. Nasar (1986) shows that the median AFDC benefit is less than half the poverty line for a family of three.

The "market value" approach attempts to place the value of the goods or services the government benefit would command in the open market, but this becomes difficult to do, especially for a service like Medicaid. Based on such a method, it would be virtually impossible for a sixty-five–year old to be classified below the poverty level if the market value of his medical assistance from the government was added in as part of his or her income (Binford et al. 1990: 18–20).

A reasonable inference is that poor families who receive government benefits are somewhat less impoverished than they were before. One study of AFDC recipients found that 92 percent of families were poor without the welfare check, and 76 percent were still poor after it arrived (Bell and Bushe 1975). (This particular study accurately predicts a decline in the real value of AFDC benefits.) Another study found that in 1987, only one in ten of otherwise poor families was lifted from poverty by government programs (Johnson 1991: 23). Chambers (1982) found that with the possible exception of food stamps, most benefit programs left people well below the poverty line.

Perhaps the best discussion of this subject is provided by Beeghley, who shows that public assistance requires continuing destitution in order for households to retain their eligibility. Much of the money actually goes to vendors who provide services, such as Medicaid funds to the health industry. Paupers who receive Medicaid are still poor: its recipients do not become economically independent as a result. In-kind benefits reduce the suffering associated with being poor; they do not eliminate poverty (Beeghley 1983: 33–34, 67).

It is also interesting that those who emphasize the counting of noncash income seldom use the same principle when counting the income of the nonpoor. Health and life insurance plans, pension plans, expense allowances, and the like are surely much greater for the middle and upper classes than government in-kind benefits for the poor. In fact, most noncash income goes to people who are not poor and it decisively affects their economic situation (Beeghley 1983: 36).

Some conservative analysts depict the poor as relatively well-off primarily because of noncash benefits. But in a money economy, housing, food, and medical care are not substitutes for things for which people must have cash. Any family can testify that, merely on a survival basis, there are numerous items for which some cash is essential.

Another argument sometimes made by conservatives is that the poor underreport their income; that is, they have income "off the books." This is undoubtedly true to some extent: survival at this class level may make this almost essential. Jobs "off the books" usually do not last very long, and they pay minimim wage or less. And it has been repeatedly found that the higher the socioeconomic status, the higher the rate of underreporting of income, such as the dividends and other hidden income taken by the rich (Beeghley 1983: 31).

Finally, one wonders how many poor are missed by the census figures. It is widely believed that the 1990 census missed about five million people, many of them minorities. Since minorities are more likely to be poor, it is reasonable to believe that large numbers of the poor were not counted. In the crannies and alleys of the slums, in the isolated rural areas, and among the illegal aliens must be considerable numbers of poor who do not appear as statistics.

Some analysts are critical of the use of a relative definition of poverty, claiming (with perhaps some justification) that even if hardship were done away with, the bottom fraction of the population would be considered "poor" in that they had less than others (Banfield 1970: 124–125). But as Beeghley says, the poverty line is a realistic indicator of the amount of impoverishment in the United States because those who live below this level are poor in an absolute sense; that is, they have consistent and persistent difficulty surviving in the United States (Beeghley 1984).

As Wilson shows, the official poverty formula provides an accurate account of gross trends over time; has wide recognition, public access, and extensive use; and provides a rich array of trends (Wilson 1987: 171). The poverty threshold is a very useful indicator of the extent of impoverishment in the United States because it identifies people who live in dire economic straits and because it is simple to understand and has a sense of legitimacy with the public. It has served the country reasonably well (Beeghley 1983: 38; Ellwood 1988: 83).

THE EXTENT OF POVERTY

Regardless of the manner in which poverty is measured, many conservatives argue that the census bureau's figures "dramatically understate the living standards of low income Americans" (Rector et al. 1990). One observer argues that considering growth of disposable income, rising educational qualifications, and advances in health, there has been "overall progress toward greater affluence and prosperity" (Eberstadt 1988). He doubts that there are large pockets of nutritional deprivation in modern America, and believes that poverty is less physically harsh and punishing than it was in the past.

A writer for the Heritage Foundation, speaking of hunger in this country, claims "there is no reason to believe the problem is any worse now than it was in the late 1970s, and the likelihood is that it has improved." The degree of hunger here, she says, is comparatively tiny, and persistent hunger is related more to dietary ignorance than the lack of federal assistance. Dietary surveys find that the majority of the poor have perfectly adequate diets (Kondratas 1988).

The ultra-conservative Henry Hazlitt finds poverty to be a residual problem affecting only a minority, and that minority is being steadily reduced. He believes that official estimates of "poverty-threshold" income by federal bureaus are unrealistically high (Hazlitt 1973: 18, 35). Murray says that poverty is not equivalent to destitution; its victims are not necessarily malnourished, ill-clothed, in despair, without dignity, or unhappy (Murray 1988). Another conservative believes that "most of those who report income below the poverty line are not undergoing hardship" (Banfield 1970: 116).

However, the extreme vulnerability of the poor in this country has been underscored by many writers. Beeghley (1983: 25) paints a description of the often desperate lives of the poor; even those relatively well-off may be one emergency or one accident from dire straits. In describing poor two-parent families, Ellwood (1988: 96) shows that theirs is largely a picture of families who are struggling to provide for themselves and who are sharply affected by the availability of jobs and the wages being paid.

Beeghley (1983: 23–25) has devised a household budget for a family at the poverty line. The allowance for food would be $59.48 per week, or $2.12 per person per day. There would be insufficient money to meet basic expenses inherent in living in the United States. His figures were computed in the early 1980s, but there is no reason to believe things would be any easier for such families today. Further, most poor persons are well below the poverty line and their situation would be even more strained.

A more recent estimate (Johnson et al. 1991: 14) concluded that expenses for just food and shelter would consume virtually all of the income available to a family of three at the poverty line. They would have $33 left over for all other expenses!

A writer in *Fortune* magazine concludes that life at the poverty line is just get-by existence, and "many of the poor have an increasingly difficult time getting adequate amounts of food" (Nasar 1986). How many poor people go to bed hungry, live in dilapidated housing, risk having their gas or electricity cut off, allow a toothache or other problem to go untreated? Chalfant is surely correct when he says that for most of those in poverty there appears little chance to get anything good out of life (Chalfant 1985: xiv).

Wilkie (1991) discusses the severe adverse consequences of economic hard times on families. She mentions the increased risk of marital dissolution, family disorganization, physical abuse, and child neglect. Sarri and Russell document the considerable health and financial burden on families who were victims of welfare termination in Michigan and Georgia (see Elesh 1990).

Poor families constantly must choose between paying the rent or the heating or electric bill, between buying food or replacing children's worn-out shoes, between keeping up with doctors' bills or fixing the car that is needed to go to and from work (Johnson et al. 1991:13). Even the

Heritage Foundation admits that the percentage of poor households saying they were uncomfortably cold in a recent winter is double the rate for the general population (Rector et al. 1990). The competing demands make minimally adequate nutrition, clothing, shelter, and medical care an impossibility (Johnson et al. 1991: 13).

Being poor is highly correlated with poor health care, inferior education, inadequate housing, higher crime rates and poorer access to justice, and a dysfunctional family life (Chalfant 1985: xiv). The poor get sick more than anyone else (Harrington 1962: 15): some of the reasons for this are that they may live in slums, jammed together under unhygienic conditions; they have inadequate diets and poorer medical care. With a major illness, they may move to a lower level of living and begin the cycle toward even more suffering.

Poor children are less likely to receive adequate nutrition, decent medical care, and access to early childhood programs. They are more likely to fall behind in school, become dropouts, and engage in self-destructive activities. They face major roadblocks to individual accomplishment and economic self-sufficiency (Johnson et al. 1991: 16).

That the poor have less of good health means less nutritious food, less heat in the winter, less fresh air in the summer, less distance from other sick people, less knowledge about illness or medicine, fewer doctor and dental visits, less preventive health care, and less first-quality medical attention when one is seriously ill. Poverty robs them of their days while they are alive and then kills them before their time (Reiman 1979: 83).

Many poor face cutbacks in wages and/or benefits that carry serious threats to health, development, and well-being of their children. Poor children are more than three times as likely to die in childhood. They have higher risk of disease-related deaths. The Maine Health Bureau estimated that 10,000 children die from poverty in the United States each year (Johnson et al. 1991: 15–16).

In a recent study, Zick and Smith (1991) reported that recent spells of poverty significantly increased the hazard of dying for both men and women, especially women. Employment status, they showed, has a consistently negative effect on mortality. Poverty kills because of such things as hazardous physical environment and inferior medical care (Reiman 1979: 84–86).

A recurring theme of conservatives on this issue is that America's poor are far better off than the poor in other countries. Hennholtz says, "when compared with living conditions throughout the world there may be no poverty at all in the U.S. . . . [Here] even the least productive members of society live in relative abundance when compared with their counterparts abroad" (Hennholtz 1985). Hazlitt argues that the economic position of blacks is incomparably higher than in Haiti or the all-black countries of Africa (Hazlitt 1973: 64).

A report by the Heritage Foundation (Rector et al. 1990) points out that in Mexico or India more persons occupy each room than among America's poor. The American poor own 344 cars per 1,000 persons, roughly the same ratio as the United Kingdom, and more than the average Japanese. Nearly all poor homes have running hot and cold water, indoor flush toilets, and indoor baths. It might be noted, however, that these amenities are generally required by law, and frequently the plumbing does not work properly.

But the major problem with such comparisons is that in many ways it is harder to be poor in America, partly because low-income people in this country are forced to consume items they cannot afford and partly because the fixed cash costs are so much higher in this country than in other nations (see Beeghley 1983: 27). American poor are not somehow less poor because incomes in some other countries are even lower. The poor in this country compare their levels of living with those they see around them, not with levels in Latin America or Africa.

Actually, one comparison found that poor children in Mississippi were not much different from children in Biafra and Pakistan, two underdeveloped countries. Severe medical, nutritional, and psychological deprivation of the poor in that state was documented (Brown 1977).

A related point is the number of "luxuries" that are supposedly owned by America's poor. It is claimed, for example, that 38 percent of the alleged poor own their own homes, 62 percent of poor households own a car, 56 percent washing machines, 17 percent dishwashers, 99 percent refrigerators, nearly half of all "poor" households have air-conditioning, and 81.3 percent have a telephone. Those arriving at these figures contend that since no American households owned a refrigerator or washing machine in 1900, the poor are really better off than the well-to-do in 1900 (Rector et al. 1990; see also Banfield 1970: 118–119; Hazlitt 1973: 51).

As an attempt to minimize poverty in the United States, this point seems an extremely weak one. Owning a home (which may well be old and deteriorating) is hardly a measure of affluence, and it is admitted that 62 percent of poor families do not own one. The possession of a car is just about essential if people are to work (or even look for work), shop, or seek medical care. The grocery store and social services are far away from many poor. Some poor families have one or even two old cars that may have been bought inexpensively from relatives. If the car breaks down there is no transportation. A refrigerator is a necessity to keep many kinds of food fresh, including milk for children. A telephone is often needed for learning about job training and other opportunities, making medical appointments, and the like. Many of the poor live in the South, where some kind of air-conditioning (often simply a window unit) is just about a necessity.

As Tobin (1967) says, plumbing, electricity, cars, television, telephones, plastics—have brightened the lives of almost all Americans, poorer as well as richer. But the society's commitment to them has made them virtual necessities. They are almost compulsory improvements in the quality of life; poor or rich, we have little choice but to accept them and pay for them.

That there have been major problems with large numbers of urban poor is generally conceded: Wilson concludes that the number of ghetto poor has increased, and the severity of economic deprivation among the ghetto poor has risen as well (Wilson 1991a). Even Murray (1988) concedes many problems of the urban poor. (Great attention has been given to this following the Los Angeles riots of 1992.)

But insufficient attention has been given to the severe problems of the rural poor. As described by Duncan and Tickamyer (1988), poverty in the rural areas of the United States is widespread and persistent. While rural areas contain only one-fifth of the population, they contain one-third of the poor. The percentage of poverty in nonmetropolitan areas (18.1) is about the same as in the inner city. (Also see Duncan 1992.)

Hidden in the hollows of Appalachia, in makeshift villages along the Rio Grande, in shriveled industrial towns in Pennsylvania, on the back roads of Maine, and at the edge of cotton fields in Mississippi, the world of rural poverty endures (Smith 1990a), not to mention migrant workers, sharecroppers, and Native Americans on reservations. For most Americans, rural poverty is more remote and invisible.

More than half the people of Tunica, Mississippi, live below the poverty line, two-thirds in substandard housing. Some dwellings have no running water. The pay for picking cotton is $4.50 an hour with no fringe benefits, and there is not enough of even this work (Smith 1990a). Smith adds that it is doubtful that rural poverty is preferable to the urban kind. Food is sometimes more expensive in the country, and the rural poor are more likely to suffer from chronic diseases and disabilities.

Rural areas contain all of the twenty-eight most severely impoverished counties in the nation. In each of these counties, more than half of all children are poor. Their poverty is compounded by lack of access to health care, government aid programs, and other services (Johnson et al. 1991: 2).

Lichter (1989) wrote of rural blacks, who are more spatially dispersed than urban blacks, less visible, and apparently easier to ignore. The unemployed, he says, represent only a minority share of overall hardship. "Hidden unemployment," such as worker discouragement and part-time employment, contributed over one-half of the total labor market hardship experienced by nonmetropolitan blacks.

Two reports on poverty in the United States document the extent of the problem: one, the Physician Task Force on Hunger in America (1985), sponsored by the Harvard School of Public Health, and a study on child poverty in America by the Children's Defense Fund (Johnson et al. 1991).

The physicians found that the problem of hunger in America had grown significantly in the 1980s, and estimated that there are up to 20 million Americans who suffer from hunger (Physician Task Force 1985: xix-xx). While improvement had been registered by 1977, hunger had returned as a serious problem across the nation by 1985. While not as bad as it was two decades ago, the situation had deteriorated. There was no city and no state where they did not find extensive hunger.

According to Brown (1988), a total of seventy-seven studies in the 1980s documented widespread, serious hunger in America. The U.S. Department of Agriculture found a sharp increase in the need for food to feed Americans on an emergency basis, and hunger was "increasing at a frenetic pace." The Center on Budget and Policy Priorities reported that many agencies experienced major increases in the number of hungry people coming for help (Physician Task Force 1985: 14).

The Food Research and Action Center (in 1983) found hunger to be "a large and growing problem once again." The food stamp program was not providing adequate assistance to the needy, and it fails to reach many who are hungry (Physician Task Force 1985: 15). In a more recent study, the Community Childhood Hunger Identification Project projected that 5.5 million American children younger than twelve are hungry, and an additional 6 million are at risk of hunger. More children are hungry in the United States than there are total children in such countries as Angola, Somalia, Haiti, or Cambodia (Johnson 1991: 2, 15).

The Children's Defense Fund claims that one in five American children (over 12 million) are poor, and 5 million children live on family incomes of less than half the official poverty line. The number increased by more than 2.2 million from 1979 to 1989, despite economic growth after 1982 through 1989. The bulk of growth in child poverty during the 1980s was among children younger than six (Johnson et al. 1991: 2). Duncan and Rodgers (1988) report that nearly half of the children in the United States found themselves in a vulnerable economic position at least once during their childhood.

Perhaps surprisingly, there are more poor American children living outside central cities than inside them. The child poverty rate is higher in rural areas than in the rest of the nation. And most poor families with children are working families (Johnson et al. 1991: 2). The 14.9 million children living in rural America are poorer than children in metropolitan areas, are less likely to receive adequate health care, and get shortchanged when it comes to education, says the Children's Defense Fund (Norman 1991).

The major factor contributing to the increase of poor children has been a large decline in wages, especially for young workers. By 1989 nearly half of all hourly workers younger than twenty-five were paid wages too low to lift a family of three out of poverty. Millions of young families of all races have become almost wholly detached from the economic mainstream. More than one in three children living in young families is poor (Johnson et al. 1991: 2–3, 19).

Declining effectiveness of government cash programs in lifting such families out of poverty is the second factor contributing to the problem. The growing proportion of children living in single-parent families is the relatively smallest major force driving child poverty rates upward (Johnson et al. 1991: 3).

Though one writer (Eberstadt 1988) claims that the United States actually has an unusually low rate of infant mortality, the figures show that we are nineteenth in combatting infant mortality, and twenty-eighth in avoiding low-birthweight babies (Johnson et al. 1991: 4).

Child poverty rates for single-parent families in the United States are far higher than in other countries studied: Germany, Great Britain, Norway, Sweden, Switzerland, and Canada. Even if demographic structures were uniform (if the percentage of single-parent families were identical), U.S. child poverty rates still would be one-and-a-half to three times higher than those in Western Europe and Canada (Johnson et al. 1991: 20).

The average poverty rate in five other industrialized countries was five points lower than ours. The United States has the worst rate of children in poverty. "The poverty rate in this affluent society seems exceptionally high, and young people are especially at risk" (Peterson 1991: 8).

Sheldon Danziger shows that more than one-fifth of all American children in 1985 were poor and received either no government assistance or assistance insufficient for them to escape poverty. From the late 1960s through the early 1980s, almost one-third of all black children were persistently poor, and as many as one-quarter of all black children were persistently dependent on welfare (see Hughes 1990).

Poor children have been found to have 23 percent more hearing impairment, they do not grow as tall, are more likely to have hemoglobin problems and several other illnesses, are more often victims of lead-paint poisoning and insect and rodent bites (Schiller 1984: 85).

Although the emphasis on child poverty is a valid one, a word might be added about poverty among the elderly. It is widely believed that poverty among the elderly has been largely conquered. While it is true that the percentage of older Americans who are poor is slightly lower than in the rest of the population, major problems remain. A sizable group of elderly people have been excluded from the gains that have been made (Haveman 1988: 160). The size of the aging population is increasing, and savings are typically inadequate (Schiller 1984: 74–77).

Recent census figures show that though the poverty rate for the elderly was lower than that for children and young adults, it was higher than or not significantly different from that for other adult age groups. Furthermore a higher proportion of elderly than nonelderly were concentrated just over their respective poverty threshold. Consequently, 18.2 percent of the nation's 11.3 million "near poor" persons was elderly, compared with 10.9 percent of persons below the official poverty level (U.S. Bureau of the Census 1991: 2–3).

Lack of employment and age discrimination are special problems for older people. An estimated 2 million elderly Americans are living alone and poor; a disproportionate number of them are women and minorities. There are also 1.6 million elderly living alone who are classified as "near poor," whose income is just slightly above the poverty line. Only about half of those eligible for supplemental security income receive it (Haveman 1988: 83).

Problems of the elderly poor in Virginia are chronicled in one report. The elderly sacrifice food to heat one room of a freezing house, and struggle to pay for medications. In this state, only half of those eligible receive supplemental security income, and two of every five older women are poor or near poor (Booker 1991).

According to a major recent survey, more than one-third of Philadelphia's 252,000 elderly live below the federal poverty line, and as a result, many of them cannot afford the health care they need. This is especially true for elderly women and blacks in the city, almost half of whom say they live in poverty. "A substantial number of elderly residents are vulnerable because of poor health, low income, minimal health insurance coverage, and inadequate social supports" (Kaufman 1991).

A husband's pension income often stops at his death. Some 40 percent of men do not enroll in company joint survivorship programs to cover widowed spouses. Some 4 million women and 1.7 million older males are hurt by this (Booker 1991). The process of applying for public assistance is psychologically damaging for many proud older people.

In a study of the poor (Rosenman 1988), a high incidence of poor people who were "disabled, impaired, or seriously ill" was found—about twice the usual estimates. Rosenman adds that unless certain trends are reversed, the number in poverty will grow comparatively poorer and their numbers will swell with others dropping from the middle classes.

Finally, a perusal of recent newspapers provides indication of continuing and widespread poverty in the nation. As of 1990, welfare caseloads are up in every state except Wisconsin, and they are up 10 percent or more in sixteen states (Randall 1991). Nationally, AFDC caseloads were the highest ever in 1991, and more increases are expected, according to the American Public Welfare Association (Porter 1991).

In New Jersey there are reports of women forced into poverty by domestic violence, car crashes, or men who deserted them and don't pay child support. A food stamp recipient receives fifty-eight cents a meal. A mother and two children get $424 a month plus $277 in food stamps, while the state puts minimum survival at $985. The going rate for a two-bedroom apartment is $700. "There is an enormous gap between what is minimally necessary to sustain an adequate life and what our state provides to those who must rely on public assistance for support," says a social worker (Leusner 1991).

A report on the homeless in Vermont finds an alarming increase in rural families with children. Most have no reserves and no one to fall back on. Fully 60 percent of the shelter residents are two-parent families, often with at least one parent working. The rest are women with children (Matthews 1991).

Thirty-one states are said to lack the funds in their budget for an "exploding demand for health or welfare assistance to the poor." Projected shortfalls in these states collectively totaled $11.6 billion in 1991. Officials said the fiscal squeeze is as severe as the one caused by the 1981–1982 recession. Medicaid exploded by 22–25 percent during the year (West 1991).

A recent estimate of California's poor revealed an ominous increase in both the number and incidence of poverty for the state's overall population during the late 1970s and throughout the 1980s. Sharp increases of poverty were found in the Hispanic minority and among the elderly (Mogull 1991).

A California social service agency can't process needy people fast enough. Women waited two months before receiving aid. In the spring of 1991, there were 10,197 recipients of general assistance, up from 5,780 only two years before, although the staff did not increase in size. An average of 150 to 175 new applicants appeared every day (Rhoads 1991).

According to an Iowa State University study, welfare benefit levels are too low. There are "not sufficient benefits to keep kids properly housed, sheltered, and fed," claims a professor. A family of three receives $426 a month in Iowa. An Iowa family that relies on AFDC today has 37 percent less income than a similar Iowa family did twenty years ago (Rubiner and Fowler 1991).

The Center for Budget and Policy Priorities claims that state budget cuts aimed at the poorest of the poor were so extensive in 1991 and loom so large in 1992 that states seem to be "competing to make themselves unattractive places for the poor to live," according to Steven Gold. Michigan cut general assistance, homeless housing, and aid to low-income families. Cuts have been unparalleled in recent years at the state or federal level (Clements 1991).

In Ohio, cuts in public assistance are detailed, and it is reported that an average family's food stamps and welfare fall $246 a month short of subsistence standard. Families are reported to be choosing between groceries and rent (Petrie 1991). The governor proposed ending the General Assistance welfare program, and other welfare department programs are scheduled for cuts. One official says, "We find more people out of work and in need of assistance" (Holthaus 1991).

The weak economy is forcing a record number of North Carolina residents onto the welfare rolls, straining both the state Medicaid budget and county social service agencies, officials say. The number of North Carolinians qualifying for AFDC rose 22 percent between July 1989 and November 1990. The average state increase was 11.1 percent for the same period. Social service officials say their waiting rooms are full and their staffs are overwhelmed (Ready 1991).

In Alaska, more Anchorage residents than ever are receiving public assistance as "economic refugees" from the Lower 48 flood welfare offices. The number of Anchorage residents who receive aid from at least one public assistance program increased by more than 20 percent from February 1990 to February 1991 (Lipka 1991).

As of late 1991, 5,000 more Colorado families are receiving welfare payments than in 1989. An average of 37,600 families each month received the payments under AFDC, totaling $130 million in 1991—a 14 percent increase over 1989. The number of households receiving food stamps rose from 77,000 in 1989 to 91,000 in 1991 (Foster 1991).

There is no evidence that the situation improved by early 1992. For example, a report from Texas reveals that more residents of that state are turning to the government to help them survive. In the past year [1991] the number of people receiving food stamps, Medicaid, and AFDC surged by more than 15 percent (Eig 1992).

Every day participation in aid programs increases. In suburban Denton county, food stamp rolls swelled 31 percent from 1990 to 1991; in Rockwell county, the number of families on AFDC jumped 46 percent.

Even with the new jobs and new offices, the welfare system cannot keep up. Many previously middle-class people are showing up in the welfare offices. The caseload keeps going up while the budget keeps shrinking. In big cities (e.g., Texas), soup kitchens, homeless shelters, and medical clinics are packed. In the suburbs, food pantries and church groups report they are swamped with requests for help (Eig 1992).

Many similar stories could be told from across the country, including Utah and Oregon, which are not usually thought of as poor states. When these data are added to the reports of reliable surveys and articles by social scientists, the conclusion that poverty in this country in the early 1990s is extensive indeed seems overwhelming.

2

The Culture of Poverty

Of the many theories or perspectives on poverty, perhaps none has elicited more controversy than what has been called "the culture of poverty." While all versions of this approach stress the value characteristics of at least some of the poor that go beyond the lack of money, different writers give quite different connotations to the concept.

The term has been confused with a more recent term, the "underclass." At least one writer (Morris 1989) thinks that the terms are practically synonymous. While recognizing that there is a good deal of overlap, we will concentrate on the value characteristics of the poor (or a subset of the poor), emphasizing their attitudes toward work in this chapter. In the following chapter on the underclass, we will concentrate on the poor in the inner-city and stress the racial component of poverty. This is a somewhat arbitrary yet plausible distinction.

Although Michael Harrington spoke about a culture of poverty (Harrington 1962: 16–17), the term appears to have originated with anthropologist Oscar Lewis, who studied the poor in Mexico and Puerto Rico. He held that patterns of life come to make up a unique lifestyle for the poor that contributes to the perpetuation of their poverty from generation to generation (Lewis 1965: xliv).

> The culture of poverty is both an adaptation and a reaction of the poor to their marginal position in a class-stratified, highly individuated, capitalistic society. It represents an effort to cope with feelings of hopelessness and

despair which develop from the realization of the improbability of achieving success in terms of the values and goals of the larger society. (Lewis 1965: xliv)

Those trapped in poverty may manifest patterns of behavior and values that are characteristically different from those of the dominant society and culture (Waxman 1983: 1). Once people find themselves in poverty, their behavior and attitudes come to form a "deviant subculture" that is self-perpetuating. (This might more accurately be termed a "subculture of poverty," but we follow the conventional use.)

People in poverty are said to have a weak family structure, ineffective interpersonal relations, present time orientation, and unrestrained spending patterns. They develop a "design for living" or a set of solutions to their problems that is passed down from generation to generation. The culture of the poor has its own distinctive social and psychological consequences for its members, affecting the nature of kinship ties, spending patterns, value systems, and sense of community (Lewis 1959: 16).

These values include helplessness, dependence, a sense of inferiority, resignation, and fatalism. The poor are less interested in education and assign little value to work, sacrifice, or self-improvement. Other values include a low future orientation, inability to plan ahead, and a weak sense of personal efficacy; they are ambivalent toward authority but supportive of illegal activities (Corcoran et al. 1985). Exteme present-orientedness may be the principal element in this cultural configuration.

The cultural approach stresses attitudinal and motivational implications of poverty, particularly those traits that inhibit people's ability to identify and react to changing opportunities. The long-term poor may become passive, not actively seeking channels for personal action (Kane 1987). They may have a lack of spirit, of hope for a better life (Schiller 1984: 10).

This theory is saying that adaptive responses to economic deprivation and social marginality take on lives of their own. Lee Rainwater's analysis of lower-class men who assign a low priority to work stability (cited in Farber 1989) may be used to illustrate this.

For the poor, according to Rainwater, the basic barrier to well-being is the lack of resources or goods and services needed to carry out permissible, meaningful, and instrumental activities. A key argument is that when a group is so removed from command over resources that it cannot participate in society, it adapts to its position by developing a lower class culture (cited in Segalman and Basu 1981: 6–7).

Rainwater finds a clear relationship between social class and number of children in the family. He says that a lack of effective contraception "is embedded in particular personalities, world views, and ways of life which have consistency and stability and which do not readily admit such foreign elements as conscious planning and emotion-laden contraceptive practices" (cited in Waxman 1983: 22).

The granting of status to males who engage in early sexual encounters produces more premarital pregnancies and earlier marriages among the lower class than among the middle class. Lower class marriages can be characterized by a high degree of separateness between the marital partners, a rigid division of family responsibility, a matrifocal structure of the family, and the machismo pattern of male counteractivity: these factors disrupt family life among the poor (Segalman and Basu 1981: 6).

Wilson (1987: 26) found that of the 25,000 families with children living in low-income projects in Chicago, only 8 percent were married-couple families, and 80 percent of the family households received AFDC. The serious consequences of teenage births are underscored by Schorr (1988: 12–14). She also notes that the United States birthrates for whites alone are higher than those of teenagers in any other Western country.

Some recent observers point out that half of all households headed by women are poor. Children from these families have lower cognitive abilities and fewer years of schooling. They have less desirable jobs and lower incomes and are more likely to be poor as adults. Daughters from such households are more likely to form female-headed households themselves (Mare and Winship 1991). While Mare and Winship acknowledge the importance of economic trends, they state that the climate of expectations may contribute to further decreases in marriage rates.

A teenage girl may be so downtrodden and isolated from the wider society and its values that she may feel she is doing well by becoming pregnant and receiving welfare. A large part of her identity is provided by the baby, the symbolic passage to adulthood. Girls who have become single parents before her are often her role models (Berry et al. 1991).

An important idea in the cultural view is that deeply ingrained habits prevent low-income people from taking advantage of improved circumstances; that is, people remain poor because they feel no obligation to contribute to society (Rosenbaum and Popkin 1991). While the culture of poverty position implies the difficulty of changing the way of life of these people, it does not say that such change is impossible.

It is often claimed (Chalfant 1985: xv; Schiller 1984: 99) that those who favor a culture of poverty are attributing poverty itself to the value structure of the poor people, what liberals would call "blaming the victim." While this is an interpretation that seems consistent with the general framework of a cultural perspective, it is not clear that the theory itself calls for this:

Lewis (1967), for example, denied blaming the poor themselves. But it is undeniable that many conservatives have used the theory for this purpose.

The conservative interpretation of the cultural view sees poverty as the product of individual characteristics and failings: being poor is a just consequence of one's personal inadequacies. Such approaches make sharp distinctions between the deserving poor and the deviant (see Levitan 1985: 17). Conservatives will not blame the "system" for what they see as moral failures of individuals (Hyde 1990). Such interpretations fit well with a widely held and deeply ingrained public image about why the poor are poor. The implication is that if we can change the poor some way—making them different and better—we will have done all we can do about poverty.

Jencks (1991) uses the term "undeserving poor," and indicates that their poverty is "somehow attributable to their behavior." He adds, "A growing fraction of the population is poor because they have violated rules that most Americans regard as reasonable" (Jencks 1991: 39). He does not, however, appear to endorse the conservative interpretation of cultural views entirely.

A recent report employs the cultural approach when it speaks of "behavioral poverty," a vicious cycle of illegitimacy, destroyed families, an absent work ethic, crime, drug addiction, and welfare dependency (Rector et al. 1990), although this seems to exaggerate the pathological elements. And welfare dependency was seldom or never mentioned by the earlier culture of poverty writers (Morris 1989).

The culture of poverty came to be seen as insulting and demeaning to the poor. Banfield (1970: 125) suggests that their impulsiveness and radical improvidence are explanations for their condition. Another writer speaks of people who won't climb the ladder of opportunity even when the economy or the government dangles it in front of their noses (Kaus 1986).

An explicit attack on the value systems of the poor is made by Hazlitt. (While Hazlitt would not be accorded much respect by contemporary social scientists, his views are probably widespread among the general public.) Following Banfield, he speaks of a lower class that lives from moment to moment, is fatalistic, acting on impulse. Their taste for "action" takes precedence over everything else (Hazlitt 1973: 182–183). He is emphatic in claiming that the poor could make it by trying harder.

For Hazlitt, poverty is ultimately individual, and individual poverty can no more be "abolished" than disease or death can be abolished. Each individual—or at least each family—must solve its own problems of poverty (Hazlitt 1973: 229–230).

Likewise, Gilder believes that the poor are different, many are black, their I.Q.s are genetically lower, and they are markedly prone to violence, crime, and slovenly living (Gilder 1981: 64). Murray speaks of poor people who avoid work and are amoral, and adds that they should be held responsible for their actions (Murray 1984: 146). He finds little to praise in their culture and believes that "welfare children should be indoctrinated with middle-class values" (Murray 1984: 220–224).

Mead refers to an element of the poor composed of street hustlers, welfare families, drug addicts, and former mental patients who will not take jobs, and adds that "in general, low income and serious behavior problems go together" (Mead 1986: 22). According to a reviewer, he portrays the mentally ill on disability as those who simply want to shirk work (Sosin 1986a). In fairness, Mead does say that much of poverty and dependency results from the difficulties the poor have in coping with daily challenges such as work and family life (Mead 1987).

THE DEFENSE OF THE POOR

Not surprisingly, many writers consider such views as attacks on the poor and have argued vigorously against them. Wilson says that this approach erroneously attributes the problems to the social values of the poor, but he claims that liberals have lacked a convincing rebuttal to this argument (Wilson 1987: 139).

Valentine, in a strong argument against such views, contends that traits of the poor are really a way of life that arises simply because the poor have insufficient money. Their lifestyle is based, he says, not on values but on attempts to cope with lack of education, deteriorated housing, and the like (cited in Chalfant 1985: xvi).

In an interesting study of what he calls "shiftlessness," or a lack of ability, ambition, or purpose, Davidson (1976) argues that no more than 10 to 20 percent of the poor are to be found among this group. He found no statistically significant differences between the poor and the nonpoor in any ethnic category.

Tienda and Stier (1991) also studied shiftlessness, which they define as lacking in resourcefulness, incentive, and ambition. In their study in Chicago, they found that less than 1 percent of inner-city parents qualify as shiftless, though there was a potential for 6 percent. Even though the rates of joblessness were high, there was little evidence that shiftlessness was pervasive in the inner city.

Jones (1984) finds insufficient evidence that the poor are different from the nonpoor. While public opinion views the poor as unemployed able-bodied blacks, the evidence does not support this. He quotes Goodwin, "Even if a distinct culture had been empirically associated with poverty, additional traits appear to be only weakly related to the behavior the culture of poverty supposedly impedes—work."

Garfinkel and Haveman (1977) show statistically that poverty is not the result of incompetence on the part of the poor. Their poverty is the result of characteristics of the labor market rather than the inadequacy of the poor. Moynihan wrote about large families who were in every respect normal and respectable persons, with their one deficiency being a lack of education. Poverty was simply not having enough income (Moynihan 1968: xiii).

Several studies of the attitudes and aspirations of lower-class youth generally do not support the interpretation of the culture of poverty outlined above. Gruber (1972) found that youths tended to *overestimate* what they might be able to achieve. It was not limited horizons that kept them from advancing. Gruber believes the culture of poverty is an ideological tool of privileged groups whereby they are able to ignore their own advantages and the inequities of the system as a whole.

Actually, the popular culture of poverty bears little resemblance to the original concepts formulated by Lewis. When left out of a cash economy, and when they see no avenue for breaking into it and no institutional resources outside of the extended family to provide means, some poor people may adopt a culture of poverty as a way of coping. This looks like laziness to others (Duncan and Tickamyer 1988).

Beeghley is typical of many liberals in saying that the issue for many poor is their vulnerability and limited choices. Frustration is pervasive in every facet of poor people's lives and they adopt a variety of analgesic behaviors to blunt awareness of their situation and avoid pain. Over the long run, such behavior becomes rewarding, because what poor people learn is that the problems they have cannot be solved (Beeghley 1983: 13).

Nonpoor persons frequently assume that impoverished persons have the same options they do, and the same ability to solve problems—if they would just try hard enough. This is an inaccurate guide to reality. Many of the poor have learned their chances of success in this world are not very great. Most continue to try. Others give up. They do not protest very often or rebel against the system in which they are locked. Their behavioral and psychological characteristics are developed as a means of coping with stress (Beeghley 1983: 78).

Poor people's deviant behavior usually does not reflect deviant cultural values, says Beeghley, because poor people must choose among severely restricted options, many of which are not effective problem-solving strategies. The world of the poor is utterly unlike the middle-class world. To have hope and be unable to realize hope is to suffer much pain. Poverty is inherently frustrating, and attitudes and actions displayed attempt to cope with the resulting distress (Beeghley 1983: 117, 125).

There have been many case histories of poor people, and they effectively challenge the notion that social problems can be explained in terms of a self-perpetuating culture of poverty apart from specific patterns of economic deprivation (Sullivan 1987). Many of the poor are individuals whose strong endorsement of mainstream values has not relieved their poverty.

One study raises a serious challenge to the view that the attitudes and motivations of the poor are the causes of their poverty. The researchers find little evidence that distinctive psychological characteristics inhibit advancement among the poor or play a role in the transmission of poverty and dependency from parents to children. Changes in economic circumstances lead to changes in psychological attitudes. In short, the economic status of the poor does not appear to have been caused by psychological disposition (Corcoran et al. 1985).

The results of the study strongly indicate that differences between individuals in the motivational components, particularly in expectancies, were largely the result of past changes in economic status and not the cause of subsequent betterment. Data from National Longitudinal Studies provide strong support for the hypothesis that attitudinal measures are changeable in response to significant labor market events (Corcoran et al. 1985).

The researchers believe, with some justification, that their findings undercut the proposition that the primary causes of persistent poverty are the types of motivational and personal qualities that supposedly characterize the culture of poverty. There is virtually no consistent evidence that the motivational and psychological characteristics measured by the study affect subsequent achievement (Corcoran et al. 1985).

In an important recent study, Farber (1989) found that twenty-four of twenty-eight unmarried teen-age mothers hope to achieve some kind of postsecondary education, ranging from training in cosmetology to graduate school. All teenagers say they want to complete high school. These women desire education and respectable work, although they do have deficits in crucial areas of knowledge and skills.

These young mothers recognize the value of education as a means for fulfilling familial and personal expectations and as preparation for working to support themselves and their children. They are well aware of mainstream values about individual responsibility for productive activity. All these young women hope that they will achieve self-support and self-respect through working (Farber 1989).

All of these teen-age mothers hold ideal aspirations that are minimally congruent with societal expectations of functioning citizens. "Young women do not aspire to being welfare mothers; they have internalized the dreams that conventionally define success in our society" (Farber 1989).

Farber believes this to be a powerful argument against the view that the poor live in such a separate world that mainstream values and aspirations cannot fully penetrate the boundaries that define the lower-class response to poverty.

A major follow-up study of adolescent mothers found that a large majority eventually managed to escape from public assistance, and relatively few ended up with large families (Furstenberg 1987: 46).

It is probable that the values of the poor—at least many of them—may be the same as those of the larger culture, but they are capable of only incomplete expression within a poverty environment. For many of the poor, attitudes of hostility and low levels of aspiration may seem consistent with objective facts.

Even if some cultural differences be granted, they are not so profound that they would prohibit the poor from getting out of poverty. They seek from work not only a decent income but the status of worker. Thus the poor's "culture" is not a major cause of their poverty (Riemer 1988: xiii). The poor, concludes Riemer, are not poor primarily because of their own deficiencies. Poverty results primarily from an imbalance between the jobs the poor seek or hold and the jobs made available by the U.S. economy (Riemer 1988: 115).

Much research indicates that when poor (or welfare) families are compared to nonpoor families of the same ethnic background, no significant cultural differences appear (Schiller 1984: 104). The poor have demonstrated a marked ability to move out of poverty when economic opportunies have improved.

One of the key elements in the cultural view is that poverty is transmitted across generations, but there is very limited support for this claim. The respected Michigan Panel Study of Income Dynamics found that only three of every ten young adults reared in poverty homes, compared to one in ten reared in nonpoverty homes, went on to set up poverty households of their own (reported by Wilson 1987: 175).

Using the same data, Hill and Ponza found "a great deal of income mobility from one generation to the next, even among the poorest households" (reported by Wilson 1987: 175). They found a very limited form of intragenerational transmission of long-term welfare dependency among whites and none among blacks.

"A consistently smaller proportion of Americans in poverty are persistently poor, year in and year out, than the poverty statistics imply" (Wilson 1987: 175). Only one percent of the population was found to be poor throughout the nine-year time span. Perhaps surprisingly, the proportion of persistently poor residing in large cities is substantially smaller than the proportion of the poor living in rural areas or small towns (Wilson 1987: 176).

It seems reasonable to infer that the differences found in the poor stem not so much from their culture as from their deprived background. As Wilson says, cultural values emerge from specific circumstances and life chances and reflect one's position in the racial-class structure. It is their restricted opportunities and unpleasant experiences that shape the behavior of the poor (Wilson 1987: 158).

Many observers have noted that much behavior of the poor is designed to cope with specific situations they face. Beeghley shows that much of their behavior does not reflect deviant values, but is merely situational adaptations necessary for survival in poor circumstances. Poor people must choose among severely restricted options, many of which are not effective problem-solving strategies (Beeghley 1983: 117).

People who live poorly do not learn they can overcome obstacles. Rather, they learn that most obstacles are insurmountable. They have very limited options, none of which can solve the problems they face (Beeghley 1983: 128).

Liebow and Stack, authors of well-known ethnographic studies of the poor, found that lack of opportunities led to cultural adaptations which exerted an influence on future life chances. For example, a strong kinship network among poor black families was an adaptation to the problems of poverty, but that reduced their chances to escape from poverty (reported in Rank 1988).

Arguing against a culture of poverty, Liebow says that streetcorner men try to achieve many goals and values of the larger society, and failing to do this, conceal their failure from others and from themselves as best they can. The son independently experiences the same failures as his father (cited in Kane 1987).

That culture and values are different in black and white populations is challenged by empirical evidence. Variation in family behavior is a function of situational and resource differences rather than attitude differences. Most black women prefer to live in traditional two-parent families (Nichols-Casebolt 1988).

A primary challenge to the conservative interpretation of the cultural perspective is that the poor are poor primarily because of a lack of opportunities. Rank's study suggests that opportunity is the underlying cause of most socioeconomic/demographic differences, and hence of any difference in the length of welfare use. Actual and perceived differences in opportunities may lead to cultural differences, which in turn create socioeconomic differences. If poor black women realistically feel that their opportunities for finding a well-paying stable job are dismal, their desire to find such a job may be reduced (Rank 1988).

The importance of expectation is mentioned by several observers. Kane (1988) believes that opportunities are crucial, but changing them will produce behavioral changes only when expectancies are revised.

In response to cultural views that emphasize poverty as a result of deeply ingrained habits, Wilson stresses social isolation, the social and institutional mechanisms that enhance patterns of social dislocations originally caused by racial subjugation but that have been strengthened in more recent years by such developments as changes in the urban economy (Wilson 1987: 137).

Cultural values, Wilson shows, emerge from specific circumstances and life chances and reflect an individual's position in the class structure. They therefore do not ultimately determine behavior. If the urban poor have limited aspirations they are the result of restricted opportunities and feelings of resignation originating from bitter personal experiences and a bleak future. "Social dislocations . . . should be analyzed not as cultural aberrations but as symptoms of racial-class inequality. . . . Changes in the economic and social situations of the ghetto underclass will lead to changes in cultural norms and behavioral patterns" (Wilson 1987: 159).

Feelings of despair and hopelessness invariably accompany poor people's realization of the overwhelming odds against their achieving success in terms of the values and goals of mainstream society. To emphasize the attitudes and behavior of the poor conceals the social causes of poverty, the need for decent jobs and other resources. People's behavior and attitude change when opportunities and situations available to them change (Wilson 1987: 182–183).

One form of explaining poverty by the characteristics of the poor would point to the aged, broken families, large families, and ill people. Schiller's comment on this is instructive: "For the most part the aged poor were poor before they were aged, broken poor families were poor before they split up, large poor families were poor when they were smaller, and sick poor families were poor even when they were well" (Schiller 1984: 231). What has happened is that association has been confused with causality.

Gans believes that because the poor have fewer options, and because they lack the economic resources to fulfill their aspirations, they are forced to develop behavioral norms that diverge from the mainstream, even though they still retain many of the aspirations and values of the affluent society. There is no evidence their behavior would remain the same under different conditions (cited in Wilson 1987: 183–184).

Given the structural barriers to the poor, it is easy to see how discouragement can develop and affect their behavior. Farber (1989) found that while adolescent mothers had high aspirations, they also had profound doubts that they could muster the wherewithal to master their lives. They seemed to believe the future would probably resemble the present despite their best efforts to the contrary.

Lewis commented on the efforts of the poor to cope with feelings of despair and hopelessness that invariably accompany their realization of the overwhelming odds against their achieving success in terms of the values and goals of mainstream society. This in turn could lead to the resignation, passivity, present-time orientation, etcetera, that may characterize some of the poor (cited in Wilson 1987: 181–182).

Popkin (1990) describes the hopelessness and feeling of being trapped of many of the welfare poor. They find few attractive alternatives to receiving public assistance. Even those who believe they would be able to find some type of work are not optimistic about prospects for being able to support themselves adequately. She adds that the longer they receive benefits, the less efficacious they become.

One of the major implications in one version of the cultural view, that the condition of the poor is caused by the attitudes of the people themselves, has been challenged by many writers. Corcoran et al. (1985) show the difficulty of separating the role of personality as a cause of poverty from personality changes as a consequence of poverty. The values, attitudes, and behaviors of poor people are logically grounded in social relations associated with a marginal economic position.

Kane (1987) points out that we do not have to concede that the poor remain so because they prefer a way of life different from that of the mainstream. Their deficits are not immutable flaws in personal character. "Any motivational deficit observed among the persistently poor should not be thought of as an immutable personal pathology" (Kane 1987). The difficulty of changing well-developed orientations, however, could be granted.

If apathy exists among the poor, it results from insufficient food, a deepening degradation which results from an insufficiency of subsistent funds. Many poor would like a better life but are constantly frustrated by a lack of money for essentials.

Beliefs in hard work, responsibilty, and the like are difficult to maintain in the face of contrary experience (Schorr 1988: 251). If one believes one's efforts to succeed are futile, and no amount of diligent job searching will lead to employment, that in itself may lead to a lack of motivation.

In discussing the limited opportunities of poor black women, Rank (1988) indicates that these people may acquire somewhat different cultural adaptations and attitudes than white people. But such adaptations reflect the actual opportunity structure. If opportunities change, cultural adaptations will also change.

Some have claimed that the high rate of teenage births, especially to black mothers, is attributable to a deviant culture. Reservations may be raised about such an interpretation, particularly in light of the failure of society to provide adequate services for such mothers and their children (see Schorr 1988: 69). Further, Wilson points out that about two-thirds of black mothers were in poverty even before experiencing the transition (Wilson 1987: 105).

Exhortations to the poor to summon higher motivation, stay in school, and "just say no" to the temptations of the streets, are largely futile. Structural barriers, the inherent frustrations of daily life, and other realities of lower-class living render these appeals unrealistic.

One implication of the conservative interpretation of the cultural view is that it is simply up to the poor individual to get the education he or she needs to become successful. Murray says, "If you follow a set of modest requirements, you are almost surely going to avoid poverty" (quoted in Duncan and Hoffman 1991). While research shows close ties between schooling and economic success (Haveman 1988: 33), the situation is more complicated than that.

It should be remembered that schools in lower-income areas are notoriously ill-equipped to transmit interest, enjoyment, or ability. The middle-class school tends to be more enjoyable. And the poor family cannot afford to support education as long (Schiller 1984: 103).

Some critics object that the inferior education of the poor is attributable to the inadequacies of the school system and the negative attitude that entire system has toward lower-class children. They do not learn because they are not being taught effectively. Many teachers do not believe that they can learn and do not act to help them to learn. This represents not cultural but educational deprivation (Waxman 1983: 43).

Beeghley claims that poor children have fewer opportunities to learn. In school, such characteristics as self-discipline, the ability to take direction, intellectually-oriented behavior, etcetera, are just the characteristics poor children are least likely to have. Poor children are likely to learn that their ability and effort do not count for very much; they come to think they cannot learn (Beeghley 1983: 148–149).

Further, Schiller shows convincingly that more education does not guarantee an escape from poverty. If there is only one job and four applicants, no amount of educational improvement will succeed in leaving fewer than three persons unemployed. Education by itself can do very little to alter the number of jobs available at any given moment, and keeping some poor persons in school longer may not effectively raise their incomes (Schiller 1984: 117–122).

In a study of AFDC recipients, AuClaire (1979) found that educational level was not associated with higher levels of family income. Among employed recipients relatively high levels of education do not necessarily translate into higher proportions of total family income derived from earnings.

Moore and Laramore (1990), while granting that education for blacks is crucial, argue that education alone is not likely to improve the economic situation of that population as long as it remains concentrated in central cities with low and declining levels of employment growth.

Sigelman and Karnig (1977) found that higher levels of education for blacks did not improve the representation of blacks in public service. The lack of representation of blacks in public service is due to factors other than education.

This does not deny, of course, that education is important. But given problems in the lower-class school and limited job opportunities in poverty areas, something more important is involved. In the current (1992) recession even middle-class people are losing jobs and many are accepting low-wage work. An economic re-structuring, to be discussed in chapter 8, is more essential than more years of schooling per se.

THE CONTROVERSY OVER WORK

A central argument in the debate about the culture of poverty centers on the question of work. If it is true that the poor lack values that appreciate work, this could be a crucial factor in their overall economic vulnerability.

That the poor do not want to work has been claimed by many conservatives. Friedman and Friedman (1979: 23) suggest that most poor are uninterested in work. Gilder urges the poor to work harder than the classes above them, but complains that the current poor are refusing to work hard (Gilder 1981: 68). Hazlitt (1973: 185) speaks of many people who prefer near-destitution to taking a steady job, and Murray (1984: 146) speaks of how the poor like to avoid work.

More recently, Mead (1989) is puzzled by how little the needy do to help themselves. Work levels among the adult poor, he says, have dropped precipitously in the last thirty years. The main cause seems to be the reluctance of many poor adults to accept available but low-paying jobs, and the defeatism of others about their ability to work. Elsewhere Mead claims that enough jobs exist—a position that is extremely difficult to hold by the 1990s—and that "rigid barriers in the labor market are not apparent" (Mead 1986: 51). The general public believes that most poor people could find jobs "if they wanted to" (Schiller 1984: 193).

Rector et al. (1991) claim that seven times more full-time workers are found in the most affluent 20 percent of United States households than there are in the poorest 20 percent of households. This is probably an unfair comparison, however, because they apparently are counting the disabled, elderly, and mothers of small children among the poor who do not work. Further, only part-time work is available to many poor.

Finally, Jencks (1991) refers to men and women who "should" work regularly but do not, and are poor as a result. He concedes, however, that this group comprises only 6.7 percent of all poor families.

Arguments that the poor do not want to work fare poorly when examined in the light of research evidence. As of 1990, 40.3 percent of poor persons fifteen years of age and older worked, and at least one person worked in 59.6 percent of all poor families (U.S. Bureau of the Census 1991). Two-thirds of poor rural families have at least one worker (Duncan and Tickamyer 1988). "The data show that the poor are strongly connected to the labor force and form a major part of it" (Reimer 1988: 25). A combination of low wages, intermittent employment, and large families keeps them in poverty despite their work effort.

This finding by Riemer is illuminating: "Poverty is to a large degree a product of the job market. Millions of people in the United States, pursuing their own self-interest, work long and hard at the best jobs they can find, yet they end up poor" (Riemer 1988: 39). Extensive work effort and experience are characteristic of the poor. The problem is that the hard-working poor do not command wages high enough to assure economic security for an average-size family. This must be terribly frustrating, and yet many of these families respond with even more work effort (Schiller 1984: 64–65).

In some careful research in inner-city Chicago, Tienda and Stier (1991) report that two-thirds of the men and women in poverty were economically active at the time of the survey: 87 percent of these had a job and 13 percent were actively searching for one. One would be hard pressed to conclude that unemployed parents in poor Chicago neighborhoods do not want to work. In an interesting aside, black males appear most willing and white males least willing to accept low-paying jobs.

One of the best studies on this subject is that of Goodwin (1972), who found considerable work effort on the part of the poor. Even mothers who have been on welfare for a long period of time, as well as their teen-age sons, continue to hold a strong work ethic. The poor identify their self-esteem with work as strongly as do the nonpoor, and have as high aspirations as the nonpoor (Goodwin 1972).

One important study of the poor reports a significantly higher degree of work effort, and employment, among the people than is usually credited to poor people. And of those working, 25 percent held a second or third job (Rosenman 1988). Most of the unemployed working-age poor are simply not employable because of personal handicaps, child care responsibilities, or lack of suitable job opportunities (Levitan 1985: 12).

About 80 percent of men who head poor households with children work. Most would remain poor even if the head worked a full year at his or her current weekly earnings rate (Sherraden 1988). The majority of black single mothers worked at least part-time in 1984 (Nichols-Casebolt 1988). Working black women who have children under five years of age worked more hours (37.3) per week than any other category of female householders (Burghardt and Fabricant 1987: 99).

Davidson (1976) found no appreciable difference, among employed men, in the number of hours worked by the poor and nonpoor. Poverty-status black women put in more hours of housework than other black women (or nonpoor Anglo women).

One problem is that the poor worker has no reasonable expectation that his job will lead to better things. If the probability of finding a job is very low, the incentive to enter the labor force is negligible, and it is misleading to point to nonparticipation as an explanation of poverty. Neither hard work nor perseverance can carry the janitor to a sit-down job in the office building he cleans up (Schiller 1984: 38–39, 66).

Beeghley argues that there is no difference in adherence to the work ethic or any other measure of attitudes toward employment. In general, impoverished people work whenever there is opportunity to do so. All the data suggest that poor persons' lives reflect the salience of dominant values, especially the importance of employment (Beeghley 1983: 11).

Summarizing several findings, especially those of Goodwin, Beeghley concludes: "There are no differences between the poor and nonpoor in their desire to work, the desire to get ahead, the desire to be occupationally successful, or any other measures—direct or indirect—of work values" (Beeghley 1983: 75). And no difference was found between long- and short-term public aid recipients in adherence to the work ethic.

Work is as fundamental to poor people as it is to the rest of us. The vast majority of the poor would rather free themselves from their middle-class caretakers and obtain jobs that allow them to take care of themselves. All the surveys of the poor ever conducted point to this conclusion (Riemer 1988: 107).

In a study of poor young people by Williams and Kornblum, it was found that their desire for work, money, and success was dominant. They were not looking for handouts, but their opportunities for work were limited (Williams and Kornblum 1985: 29–46).

The old idea that workers prefer indolence to a higher standard of living and will work only to the point necessary to stave off starvation is not sound, according to Haveman. The growing numbers of multiple wage earners and widespread desire of employees for overtime work argue against this (Haveman 1988: 58).

There is little evidence to support the notion that the poor are turning down abundant job offers. In Washington, D.C., only 12 percent of job vacancies were those the poor might have a chance to get, and nearly all were filled in a day or two (Schiller 1984: 52–53).

Study after study has shown that most welfare recipients would prefer to work (Haveman 1988: 124). Goodwin found that few men or women preferred welfare to work, finding the former humiliating and burdensome. "Bad attitudes" toward work evolved among men *after* the frustrations associated with not getting a long-term job, losing jobs again and again, or only attaining access to low-wage, dead-end jobs (Goodwin 1985: 81–100). A group of welfare fathers was less willing to stay on welfare when job opportunities arose than were a comparison group of fathers receiving unemployment insurance (Goodwin 1985: 100–103).

Even when a job is turned down, it may not be as clear a choice as it appears to the middle-class person. Rejection of employment opportunities may reflect other circumstances not readily apparent to the nonpoor observer. (The job may offer no economic advancement, for example.) One who leaves the welfare rolls for employment incurs a distinct risk. If the job proves unsatisfactory or temporary, then he and his family are left without any financial support while he awaits a new job or more welfare (Schiller 1984: 101).

Finally, several studies report that AFDC recipients would prefer working to assistance (AuClaire 1979). Even mothers who have been on welfare for a long time continue to hold a strong work ethic. Work is viewed positively although there is a great deal of insecurity about the ability to achieve success in the labor market (Goodwin 1972). The difficulty of AFDC recipients to obtain a reasonable job will be discussed in chapter 7.

"Young women do not aspire to be welfare mothers; they have internalized the dreams that conventionally define success in our society" (Farber 1989). These women aspire to a better life but, like the poor in general, they display only a tenuous connection to critical educational and vocational systems.

Cultural Views: An Evaluation

We may conclude that the conservative interpretation of the culture of poverty, that which attributes the condition of the poor to their deviant cultural characteristics, and which implies that the poor lack a work ethic, may be rejected outright. There is little or no empirical support for such claims.

A major reason for stating this conclusion is that there seems good reason to believe that whatever deviant cultural values some of the poor may hold are a *result* rather than a cause of their condition. Lewis himself said that the culture of poverty "is an indictment not of the poor, but of the social system that produces the way of life" (Lewis 1967).

But it need not follow that cultural views are valueless. If we emphasize that we are speaking of only a relatively small segment of the poor, and that we are not ascribing causation, it may be granted that some cultural differences may exist between this element of the poor and the nonpoor. Some empirical support for this is summarized by Waxman (1983: 62) and Kane (1987). Lewis himself believed that there is relatively little of what he would call the culture of poverty in the United States—about 20 percent of the poor (Lewis 1965: xli).

Waxman even suggests that because of the stigmatization and isolation of the poor, there is a somewhat less than successful internalization of *any* cultural system. The lower-class person is not trying to "make it," he is just "getting by" (Waxman 1983: 98). This may be true for an element of the poor, but it should be noted that Waxman blames any lack of culture not on the poor but on their stigmatization, a term he emphasizes.

In a well-reasoned article, Duncan and Tickamyer (1988) show that the culture of poverty theory accurately reflects aspects of the actual situation of persons in poverty. The model can be reformulated and understood as the cultural manifestation of a particular economic position. While poverty results from exclusion from successful participation in mainstream economic activities, this may be reinforced by adaptive mechanisms (attitudes and values) which can undermine any opportunity to escape poverty in the long run.

Rank (1988) proposes a dynamic interplay between opportunity and culture. Actual and perceived differences in opportunities may lead to cultural differences. These cultural differences then have an effect on creating socioeconomic differences. Even Corcoran and colleagues (1985), who are highly critical of culture of poverty theories, accept that there are cultural components that greatly contribute to the perpetuation of poverty.

Waxman acknowledges a "deviant subculture" of the poor (Waxman 1983: 126), though he believes it to be situational as well. Even Wilson grants that cultural traits exist, but correctly points out that culture is a response to social structural constraints and opportunities (Wilson 1987: 61).

While Peterson (1991) is not happy with a cultural position, he suggests that it warns against expecting rapid change in high-poverty neighborhoods in response to broader economic and political change. Cultural theories are most satisfying, he says, when linked to other, more structural interpretations.

A reasonable position is taken by Gans (1981), who believes we should combine cultural and situational views. He says the solution to poverty lies in learning what restraints poor people are subject to in reacting to new opportunities, and how the poor can be encouraged to adapt to these opportunities.

As a complete explanation of why poverty exists, a culture of poverty theory is woefully deficient. But as a reminder that an element of the poor may have developed attitudinal and behavioral characteristics that will be difficult to change, the theory has some utility. What is most important to keep in mind is the salience of structural causes of poverty (discussed in some detail in chapter 10), even though that poverty may at times manifest itself in a distinct culture.

3

The Underclass

If the culture of poverty was extensively debated in the 1960s and 1970s, it has been the "underclass" that has received major attention in the 1980s and early 1990s. Ken Auletta wrote a book with this title in 1982, in which he quoted a 1980 Manpower Demonstration Research Report:

> The nation faces few problems as formidable as the presence of a group of people, largely concentrated in its principal cities, who live at the margin of society. Whether because of distortions in the economy, lack of training or motivation, or the attitudes of employers, these people have been excluded from the regular labor market and find, at most, sporadic employment. Though relatively few in number, they have become a considerable burden to themselves and the public—as long-term recipients of welfare, and as the source of much violent crime and drug addiction. They are simultaneously the source and victims of urban decay (Auletta 1982: 25)

It should be clear from this description that the underclass is not synonymous with the the poor or the lower class. The "respectable" or hard-working poor, those who have been middle-class and have fallen to lower-class status, those who have experienced temporary difficulties, or people with reasonable hope of escaping their plight, are not members of the underclass, even though the sophisticated Jencks has trouble making this distinction (Jencks 1991: 28).

As Morris shows, the term "underclass" is more narrowly focused than the "culture of poverty." It refers to a particular group of people at the bottom of the stratification system. One can assert that an underclass exists without necessarily believing that the disreputable connotations represent the most powerful explanation of the underclass's problems (Morris 1989).

Douglas Glasgow said that the "underclass" described a new population, the static poor, trapped in their situation by a variety of forces, primarily restricted opportunities and "limited alternatives provided by socialization patterns." Rejection by mainstream institutions, especially schools, has fed the rage and desperation of ghetto youth (cited in Katz 1989: 199).

Kilson (1981) claims that data since 1930 show a continuing presence of a black underclass characterized by low income, lack of male opportunity, and a large proportion of female-headed families. (Any race could be considered underclass.) Children have little opportunity to advance. Actually, there has been an identifiable black underclass for all of this century. DuBois's *The Philadelphia Negro* described it, and a type of it was found in sharecropper cabins of the rural South (Lemann 1986).

Previous writers, many in the "Chicago school," had anticipated the discussion of the underclass. Moynihan spoke about "an increasingly disorganized and disadvantaged lower-class group" (Moynihan 1965: 5–6). Suttles (1968) wrote of the slum residents of Chicago with their high rates of unemployment, unwed mothers, delinquency, and gang membership, although Suttles stressed the social organization of the area. Former attorney general Ramsey Clark, not a social scientist, shows a surprising awareness of the problem in his book on crime (Clark 1970).

There is no reason to limit the underclass to inner-city areas: in fact, Duncan and Tickamyer (1988) suggest that poverty is more persistent in rural areas. Lichter (1989) discusses the high unemployment and hardships of rural blacks in terms that sound somewhat like an underclass. However, most of the discussion has centered on inner-city residents, and this will be the focus of this chapter.

William Julius Wilson's work, *The Truly Disadvantaged* (1987), discusses the underclass in such a way as to propose a theory about its origin and development and to suggest some solutions. His work, which may be the most important book on this subject in recent years, has elicited considerable debate (see especially Jencks and Peterson 1991).

Although most people on welfare are not long-term cases, there is a substantial subpopulation that remains in poverty for a very long time. The average poor black child appears to be in the midst of a poverty spell which will last for almost two decades. Long-term welfare mothers tend to belong to racial minorities, have never been married, and are high school dropouts (Wilson 1987: 10, 176; Levitan 1985: 7).

The unprecedented increase in the proportion of births out of wedlock is a major contributor to the rise of female-headed families in the black community. These births now comprise a far greater proportion of total births than they did in the past, and such families are much more likely to be poor (Wilson 1987: 66–67).

A landmark study of teenage pregnancy in industrialized countries claims that the existence of a large underclass whose opportunities for success are severely limited contributes to the high rates of teen pregnancy in the United States. Not surprisingly, risk factors (low birthweight, neglect, poor health, etc.) occur more frequently among children in families that are poor and especially in concentrated poverty areas (Schorr 1988: 28–29).

Wilson stresses a dynamic interplay between ghetto-specific cultural characteristics and social and economic opportunities. An underclass has been produced not only by changes in the American economic organization but by demographic changes, and changes in the laws and policies of the government as well. He emphasizes the relationship between joblessness and family structure and such things as crime, teen-age pregnancy, and welfare dependency (Wilson 1987: 18).

The proportion of U.S. families in which men are the sole breadwinner has declined from 42 percent to 15 percent since 1960. One reason is the worsening economic position of younger men since the mid-1960s, particularly those handicapped in the labor market by low education and minority status (Wilkie 1991).

These problems, Wilson says, reached catastrophic proportions in the 1970s and 1980s. He says the problems do not simply reflect racial discrimination or a culture of poverty, but must be seen as having complex sociological antecedents that range from demographic changes to problems of economic organization (Wilson 1987: 22).

Though Wilson concentrates on northern ghettos, he points out that there are large urban ghettos in Atlanta and Houston that resemble those in the North. Many large cities of the nation had a disproportionate concentration of low-income blacks who were especially vulnerable to recent structural changes in the economy (Wilson 1987: 34).

A recent observer claims, "Rare in the ghetto today are neighbors whose lives demonstrate that education is meaningful, that steady employment is a viable alternative to welfare and illegal pursuits, and that a stable family is an aspect of normalcy" (Schorr 1988: 20). Norval Morris said in

1987 that except for nuclear war, there is no more urgent problem than Americans "locked in the underclass" (quoted in Schorr 1988: 22).

UNDERCLASS PROBLEMS

Undoubtedly much of the problem is attributable to family background. A recent study showed strong influences of parental income, including especially large disadvantages for males raised in poverty. Even after controlling for parental income, the researchers found substantial disadvantages for blacks and those from more welfare-dependent families or communities. They established sizable background effects on earnings, hourly wages, family income, and welfare program participation. Parental income, race, and welfare use were strongly associated with children's economic outcomes (Corcoran et al. 1990; for an opposing view, see Jencks 1991: 68–69).

It would be possible to emphasize the deviant behavior of the underclass as a primary source of their problems. Although he acknowledges some structural causes, Jencks suggests such an approach when he says (as noted in chapter 2), "A growing fraction of the population is poor because they have violated rules that most Americans regard as reasonable" (Jencks 1991: 39). But most analysts view members of the underclass as victimized by conditions over which they have little or no control.

Lappé claims that these conditions violate the rights of the people in these areas. When children are born into neighborhoods where inadequate medical care leaves babies dying at double the national average, where public schools spend only a fourth for each student what is spent in richer districts, where even substandard housing is out of reach, where drug-pushing and violence rule the streets, citizens' rights have been violated from birth (Lappé 1989: 46).

Duncan and Tickamyer (1988) speak of a "distressing web of social problems" and limited individual and community resources to address them. The people have limited potential for job opportunities, and public programs are weak. Their education and skills lag behind. A rigid social stratification often blocks upward mobility. There is an underclass-like trap that can envelop poor households that are repeatedly locked out of the labor force.

The ghettos of today are bereft of many of the concrete examples of hope and achievement that help instill a value system in the young. They lack many of the institutions that were a source of strength to previous generations (Schorr 1988: 252).

As with the Appalachian poor, the pathology and addiction of the inner city are seen as impossible to solve if the economic context is not altered first. Waxman believes that "unless a serious program of economic reform is introduced, the odds are extremely high that the children in these [ghetto] families will be permanently trapped in the underclass" (Waxman 1983: 46).

The external problems faced by this group of people include racism, few job vacancies, indifferent teachers and counselors, temptations of street life, and the disorganization of the community. In such a context, their very survival is uncertain. They usually pay higher prices for goods (Caplovitz 1967), pay higher rents for equal housing and more for consumer credit, and their general purchasing power is less than that of the middle-class, or even the white poor.

In the course of discussing the large amount of street crime committed by the lowest classes, Reiman shows that these young people have no realistic chance to enter college or amass sufficient capital (legally) to start a business or to get into the high-wage, skilled job markets (Reiman 1979: 28; also see Clark 1970). Beeghley speaks of a "beaten-down" effect, to which they sometimes react by criminal behavior, political unruliness, or some form of deviance (Beeghley 1983: 82).

Robert J. Sampson shows that the structurally disadvantaged position of blacks in U.S. society can be seen as the root cause of black violence, and that the same causal chain results in violence among whites as well (cited in Parker 1989). Parker finds no evidence supporting a black subculture of violence that leads to homicide.

Wilson shows that consignment to inner-city schools helps guarantee the future economic subordinacy of minority students. The inner-city schools train minority youth to feel and appear capable of performing only jobs in the low wage sector. These young people are not encouraged to develop the levels of self-esteem or the styles of presentation which employers perceive as evidence of capacity or ability. In many schools the repressive, arbitrary, chaotic, and authoritarian structures mirror the characteristics of inferior job situations (Wilson 1987: 103).

Trouble with school virtually guarantees bleak prospects for the future, for psychological as well as practical reasons. Disadvantaged young people who have never had the experience of acquiring skills and of mastering a socially valued body of knowledge lack a personal sense of mastery and self-esteem. Lower-class children in school are much less likely than middle-class children to believe in their own power, command a rich language, and be confident of success (Schorr 1988: 61, 183).

The chances are overwhelming that these children will seldom interact on a sustained basis with people who are employed or with families that have a steady breadwinner.

> Joblessness takes on a different social meaning. . . . The development of cognitive, linguistic, and other educational and job-related skills necessary for the world of work in the mainstream economy is thereby adversely affected. . . . Teachers become frustrated and do not teach and children do not learn. A vicious circle is perpetuated through the family, through the community, and through the schools. (Wilson 1987: 57)

The economic deprivation of the underclass is abundantly documented. McLanahan (1985) provides support for the idea that economic deprivation is an important source of the difference between one- and two-parent households and suggests that the disadvantages associated with high school dropouts (lack of employment, persistent poverty) could be significantly reduced if the incomes of single parents were increased and stabilized.

Concentrated in central cities, blacks have experienced a deterioration of their economic position on nearly all the major labor-market indicators. Blacks, especially young males, are dropping out of the labor force in significant numbers. There are severe problems of joblessness for black teenagers and young adults (Wilson 1987: 42). According to Jencks, chronic joblessness probably accounts for an even larger fraction of all unemployment today than in 1974 (Jencks 1991: 41).

During May 1990, the unemployment rate for white males twenty years of age and over was 4.2 percent, while that of black males twenty years and over was 9.1 percent. The unemployment rate among black male teenagers (sixteeen–nineteen) was 31 percent, while that of white male teenagers was 14.2 percent (Binford et al. 1990: 65).

The American economy has undergone a significant transformation from basic industry to services, and there has been a tremendous outflow of high-wage industries to low-wage countries. Most new jobs created in the 1980s cannot raise a family of three or more out of poverty (Appelbaum 1989). Kasarda has spoken of the polarization of the labor market into low-wage and high-wage sectors, technological innovations, and the effect of these changes on urban areas (cited in Wilson 1987: 39).

Later research by Kasarda suggests that "the bottom fell out in urban industrial demand for poorly educated blacks: in Northeastern and Midwestern cities, particularly in the goods-producing industries" (Kasarda 1989).

Each year, two to three million workers lose their jobs because of structural factors, in both urban and rural areas. Since 1981, two million manufacturing jobs have been lost. Two-thirds of those displaced were of prime working age. By 2000, it is estimated that fewer than 5 percent of domestic jobs will be on the assembly line. Between 1978 and 1986, we lost close to 5 million jobs paying $28,000 or more (Rosenman 1988).

There is support for the view that poverty in this country is primarily the result of an inadequate system of social insurance payments, an imbalance between the number of employed jobkeepers and the number of available jobs, and an even greater imbalance between good jobs and the number of such jobs in the nation's economy (Riemer 1988: 7–8). Schiller deems subemployment to be a direct, and perhaps the dominant, cause of poverty (Schiller 1984: 51).

Riemer shows that there is a severe shortage of jobs, and concludes that this is a major reason why some employable poor do not work. The implication is that changing the unemployed poor themselves by motivating them to work, improving their education level or giving them skills, and reducing barriers like inadequate transportation and discrimination would not do much to get them into jobs (Riemer 1988: 32–33).

The economist Lester Thurow agrees that there simply aren't enough jobs, good or bad, to go around. Our economy and institutions will not provide jobs for everyone who wants to work. They have never done so, and as currently structured, they never will. We are consistently the industrial economy with the worst record (Thurow 1980: 203). And the situation has become worse since Thurow wrote.

Structural changes such as the spread of microtechnology, automation, and import competition have cost millions of jobs (Wilson 1987: 181). Another who speaks of a structural employment problem confronting disadvantaged workers is Haveman (1988: 166).

Lichter finds little basis for optimism about the absolute or relative employment status of black men in the central cities of the United States. "Economic underemployment among blacks increased substantially during the 1970–1982 period, especially among young adults and those with little education" (Lichter 1988; also see Wilson 1987: 41). But the unemployment rate is only a crude indicator of labor-market hardship in the nation's cities. Many are working at part-time jobs, and others are not earning enough to escape poverty.

Manufacturing industries, a major source of black employment in this century, have suffered many job losses in recent years. And almost all the growth in entry-level and other low education requisite jobs has occurred in the suburbs and other areas far removed from urban blacks (Wilson

1987: 42–45; Moore and Laramore 1990). A sudden increase in jobless-ness creates a ripple effect resulting in an exponential increase in related forms of social dislocation (Wilson 1987: 57).

Lichter (1988) reports that over 50 percent of central city black males in the 1980s were jobless, working at part-time jobs involuntarily, or earning poverty-level wages. And blacks who work outside the ghetto bring back wages too low to offset the drain of their energies and resources (Katz 1989: 58). Black male joblessness is a major contributor of instabil-ity and economic insecurity (Nichols-Casebolt 1988).

In a recent study in Chicago, Kirschenman and Neckerman (1991) noted the subjective importance of the underclass in the discourse of employers. For most, they said, the term "inner-city" immediately connoted black, poor, uneducated, unskilled, lacking in values, involved in crime, gangs, drugs, and unstable families. The authors add that employers' expectations may become self-fulfilling prophecies.

The conservative Hazlitt deems unemployment to be mainly the result of necessary and desirable economic adjustments that ordinarily take time, and adds that unemployment is usually of short duration (Hazlitt 1973: 106), a curious and unsubstantiated position. Even the conservative Gilder admits, "There is no point in denying that the job market has failed to work well for some groups of blacks" (Gilder 1981: 149). He also concedes that bad jobs make bad work habits, weak families, and low incomes (Gilder 1981: 142).

A frequently heard complaint by some conservatives is that the immi-grant groups who migrated to the cities worked hard and eventually made it out of poverty (or their children did), so they should be an example to today's inner-city poor (Friedman and Friedman 1979: 36; Gilder 1981: 64–65; Murray 1988; Mead 1989; Peterson 1991: 13). There are a number of problems with this somewhat simplistic formula.

First, those immigrants came at a time when the economy was under-going a tremendous expansion and there was a dramatic shortage of workers. Many blacks came to Northern cities at a time of high unemploy-ment. The unskilled and semiskilled jobs for immigrants have decreased in number and importance.

Secondly, prejudice and discrimination against European immigrants were not as virulent or as pervasive as in the case of blacks. Many industries that provided employment for millions of immigrants excluded blacks altogether. Blacks were hurt more than others by deindustrialization because of their heavy concentration in the automobile, rubber, and steel industries.

Further, immigrants had political opportunities (such as urban machines) that never existed for blacks. Blacks rarely controlled even their own communities.

Finally, immigrants were poor at a time when the standard of living was generally low, and they could look forward to a brighter future. Today, ghetto blacks are surrounded by affluence, and their prospects are bleak. There are severe strains on the family and community and the mood is often one of resignation and despair (National Advisory Commission on Civil Disorders 1968: 278–282; also see Wilson 1987: 33–34, and Schorr 1988: 249–250).

PHYSICAL AND SOCIAL ISOLATION

One of the key concepts used by Wilson is the geographic and social isolation of the ghetto underclass. There are three elements to this: concentration effects, a spatial mismatch, and social isolation.

Concentration effects are a disproportionate concentration of the most disadvantaged segments of the urban black population, creating a social milieu significantly different from the environment that existed in these communities several decades ago (Wilson 1987: 58). Blacks living in cities were more concentrated in poverty areas in 1990 than whites or persons of Hispanic origin (U.S. Bureau of the Census 1991: 6). Poverty within the inner city is debilitating when it is intensely concentrated (Peterson 1991: 21).

The number of poor persons living in poverty areas in the fifty largest cities increased more rapidly than the number of poor persons in these cities or in the United States (Danziger and Gottschalk 1987). This analysis supports Wilson's claim of an increased concentration of urban poverty.

Mass highways and housing projects have helped to complete the physical isolation of the underclass. Spatial segregation and racial tensions have caused the black population to be concentrated and isolated from employment opportunities (Moore and Laramore 1990). Less educated central-city blacks receive lower wages than less educated suburban blacks (Wilson 1991: 5).

One study of the ghetto poor in the 1970–1980 period verifies that the poorer the neighborhood, the greater the proportion of residents who are members of a minority group (Jargowsky and Bane 1991: 245–246). In a similar study, Farley found little increase in the residential segregation of social classes among either blacks or whites. But the average proportion of the impoverished population in the census tract of the typical poor black increased between 1970 and 1980 (Farley 1991: 274–275).

Darden, who documents the high unemployment of urban blacks, concludes that "the evidence from census reports suggests that black inequality has persisted and is perpetuated and reinforced by high levels of residential segregation in American metropolitan areas and by low levels of suburbanization resulting from discrimination in housing" (Darden 1989). This forces more blacks to live in central cities where jobs and other opportunities are moving to the suburbs.

Poor blacks in Chicago lived in proportionately more impoverished neighborhoods in 1980 than in 1970. But Farley finds that the reason for this is not higher levels of residential segregation by social class or a new outmigration of prosperous blacks, but overall increases in black poverty (Farley 1991: 293).

According to Crane (1991a), neighborhood effects on dropping out of school and teenage childbearing among both blacks and whites were extremely large in very bad neighborhoods, particularly in urban ghettos. (The findings are for 1970.) Elsewhere, the effects were much smaller, though not trivial. The influence of inner-city residence on dropping out was very great for black male teenagers but not for black females. Overall effects of neighborhood on pregnancy are large. "Neighborhood effects are much larger at the bottom of the neighborhood distribution than elsewhere" (Crane 1991a: 318). Wilson feels this supports his theory (Wilson 1991: 473).

Elsewhere, Crane develops what he calls an "epidemic theory" of the ghetto (Crane 1991b). This implies that there are very strong neighborhood effects at at least one point near the bottom of the distribution of neighborhood quality. Adults in the neighborhood serve as role models and sources of social control.

Crane finds an enormous increase in established dropout probabilities for black males in ghettos, and evidence of epidemics of teenage childbearing as well. Neighborhood effects on both dropping out and teenage childbearing were much larger in urban ghettos than anywhere else (Crane 1991b).

Anderson (1991) claims that many adolescents, simply by growing up in an underclass neighborhood, are at special risk. A sense of limited future and ignorance mixed with indifference about reproductive and sexual activity bring on pregnancies and babies. This is reinforced by limited employment prospects.

The meaning of an illegitimate child in the ghetto is not an ultimate disgrace. In lower-class families, the girl loses only some of her already limited options: she is not going to make a better marriage or improve her economic and social status either way. For the boy, the path to higher status seems closed to him in any case (Wilson 1987: 74).

The spatial concentration of the poor increased in the 1970s and 1980s. The huge loss of industrial jobs led to a serious mismatch between the skills of inner city blacks and opportunities available to them. This is one reason why black unemployment rates have not responded well to economic recovery in many northern cities (Wilson 1987: 102; Wilson 1991).

The spatial mismatch hypothesis is that the urban core has been hard hit by industrial transformation, leaving the urban underclass isolated in the inner city with little chance of finding suitable employment. Spatial mismatch provides a plausible explanation for growing differences in joblessness and employment marginality between the races (Lichter 1988).

In an interesting test of Wilson's theory of spatial mismatch, two researchers studied the employment gains of low-income blacks who moved to the suburbs. After moving, suburban residents were 13 percent more likely to have had jobs than city movers. Of those who were never employed before their move, 46 percent found work after moving to the suburbs; for the city the figure was only 30 percent. The results appear to support Wilson's contentions about the importance of role models and social norms (Rosenbaum and Popkin 1991: 348–355).

Social isolation describes the social and institutional mechanisms that enhance patterns of social dislocations originally caused by racial subjugation but strengthened in more recent years by such developments as class transformation of the inner city and changes in the urban economy. The moving out of middle-class families made it difficult to sustain the basic institutions in these neighborhoods in the face of increased joblessness caused by frequent recessions (Wilson 1987: 137–138).

This process is discussed by Anderson (1991): as economic conditions deteriorate, the street culture grows, and more residents adopt its standards of behavior. More of these who are better off leave. The more desperate people are left behind, increasingly isolated from the conventional families and the successful role models they provide. Even a prominent conservative speaks of the isolation of the community from the mainstream (Murray 1984: 188).

Social isolation results from a lack of contact with different groups, which enhances the effects of living in a highly concentrated poverty area (Wilson 1987: 61). In important respects, blacks in ghettos are more socially and economically isolated than before the civil rights victories, particularly in terms of high joblessness, poverty, family instability, and welfare dependency (Wilson 1987: 110).

When black professionals and stable working-class blacks moved away, some stability was lost. It became harder to sustain the basic institutions in the inner city in the face of prolonged joblessness. Social organization declines (the sense of community, positive neighborhood identification, norms against aberrant behavior) and economic and educational resources are weakened (Wilson 1987: 144).

Jargowsky and Bane, who studied ghetto and nonghetto neighborhoods, found a significant geographical spreading of ghetto neighborhoods between 1970 and 1980. Their findings appear to support the hypothesis that a major factor in the increase of ghetto poverty since 1970 has been the outmigration of nonpoor from mixed income areas (Jargowsky and Bane 1990).

According to Schorr, there is no longer the critical mass of stable, achievement-oriented families that once provided neighborhood cohesion and support for churches and other basic community institutions. Missing are the essential practical connections to mainstream society, and informal ties to work (Schorr 1988: 19).

When they studied attitudes of employers in Chicago, Kirschenman and Neckerman (1991) found support for the hypothesis that the increase in ghetto poverty was caused by movements of nonpoor people out of the 1970 mixed-income areas, leaving the poor behind. This appears to support Wilson's theory.

The concept of social isolation implies that if good jobs, good role models, and richer networks of contacts were available, the conditions of the underclass could change. This is precisely what was studied by Osterman, who examined the effects of full employment in Boston in the 1980–1987 period. He documented a sharp drop in the incidence of poverty, including that of minority groups in Boston (Osterman 1991: 130).

THE RACIAL COMPONENT

No discussion of the underclass can disregard the racial element, for although not all members of the underclass belong to a minority group, a very large percentage does, especially in the inner city. Of the 2.4 million ghetto poor in the United States, 65 percent are black and 22 percent are Hispanic (Wilson 1991a).

Discrimination still exists in American schools, though it is less pervasive or blatant than it was. By age seventeen black students are over 30 percent behind white students in measured performance, and their dropout rate is higher (Schiller 1984: 133).

Peterson shows how changes in the United States economy are affecting the economic well-being of young black men. Annual earnings of young men twenty-five to twenty-nine declined by 20 percent between 1973 and 1986. Among blacks the decline was 28 percent. Among those without a high school education the decline was 36 percent (Peterson 1991: 17).

Minority workers are hired less often, for fewer hours, for less desirable jobs, and at lower wages. They are also offered less training on the job (Schiller 1984: 151).

Much market discrimination is unintended. Even persons free of prejudice or animosity may engage in discriminatory patterns of behavior. The process of networking—using friends or relatives to help one get a job—tends to exclude minorities (Schiller 1984: 154–155).

A slack economy has led to a growing polarization in the income distribution of black men (Wilson 1987: 45). In family income, blacks have gained little relative to whites in the last twenty-five years (Lerman 1988; Kilson 1981). From 1939 to 1979, there was an increase in the number of blacks with zero annual earnings (Danziger and Gottschalk 1987).

Following some careful research, Tienda and Stier demonstrate the relative importance of race and residence in producing persistent poverty, chronic welfare dependence, and alienation from the labor market. Black males participated less in the labor force than their white counterparts in all poor neighborhoods, but the differential was greatest in neighborhoods where 30–35 percent of all families were poor (Tienda and Stier 1991: 146).

Charles Hirshman shows that black males have always experienced higher unemployment than their white counterparts, but in recent years the difference has widened. The situation is even worse than indicated by unemployment rates since those rates reflect only the experience of those actively seeking work. Labor force participation has been falling, particularly among black males (cited in Cuciti 1990). The labor force participation rate for black men dropped more than 10 percent from 1960 to 1982 (Sokoloff 1988; Thurow 1980: 185).

Fully one-third of inner-city blacks are jobless, unable to find full-time jobs, or unable to earn enough money to raise themselves significantly above the poverty threshold (Lichter 1988). Lichter believes that race had more bearing on the likelihood of being underemployed in 1982 than it did in 1970. The proportion of black men in stable economic situations is even lower than that conveyed in unemployment and labor-force figures (Wilson 1987: 83).

The gap in unemployment rates persists, even when blacks have the same level of education as whites. Blacks with one to three years of college have a higher rate of unemployment (12.5 percent) than whites with only four years of high school (6.8 percent), and this has changed little since 1977 (Darden 1989).

Race is an important factor in hiring decisions. According to one study, Chicago employers view black males as unstable, uncooperative, dishonest, and uneducated. This suggests that racial discrimination deserves an important place in an analysis of the underclass. In the minds of these employers, "black" and "inner-city" were inextricably linked, and both were linked with "lower-class" (Kischenman and Neckerman 1991: 230).

Hispanics came into the labor market at a time when opportunities for the uneducated and unskilled were shrinking. Over 40 percent of Hispanic adults have only an elementary school education. They face many of the same bleak economic prospects as blacks (Schorr 1988: 251).

Young men who cannot earn a decent living are less likely to marry and create stable families. Between 1973 and 1984, the ability of young men (of any race) to support a family plummeted. Sixty percent were able to earn enough to keep a family out of poverty in 1973, but only 42 percent were in 1984. The number of female-headed families doubled (Schorr 1988: 18).

Black women are confronting a shrinking pool of economically stable or "marriagable" men. Thus black female-headed families are directly related to the increase in black male joblessness. Wilson says, "the weight of existing evidence suggests that the problems of male joblessness could be the single most important factor underlying the rise in unwed mothers among poor black women" (Wilson 1987: 73). Others agreeing with the view that unemployment is related to marital instability are Furstenberg (1987: 152) and Nichols-Casebolt (1988).

Women (especially in the inner city) consider marriage only if a prospective husband earns more than some minimum threshold (Duncan and Hoffman 1991: 163). Mark Testa found that black males in inner city Chicago who have stable work are twice as likely to marry as black males who are jobless and are not in school or in the military (cited in Wilson 1991). Further, the high black mortality and incarceration rates reduce the number of marriageable black males.

The average black child in this country can expect to spend more than five years in poverty; a white child, about nine months. Differences in expected poverty were also very large between black and white children living with household heads with comparable levels of education. Clearly the severe poverty experiences of black children cannot be thought of as a simple "family structure" or "education" problem (Duncan and Rodgers 1988).

It is reasonable to associate this country's high rates of infant mortality, especially for black infants, with socio-environmental conditions. The percentage living below the poverty level has a substantial positive relationship to both black and white infant mortality. Neither the black nor white unwed birth rate has been found to substantially affect infant mortality (LaVeist 1989).

Ignoring such evidence as we have summarized, Gilder denies that racism still prevails in American society, and argues that any gaps in income between truly comparable blacks and whites have nearly closed (Gilder 1981: 93, 128). But when he says, "There is much evidence that without discrimination, present and past, blacks would achieve earnings comparable to whites" (Gilder 1981: 132), he seems to be admitting that racism does still prevail, or that gaps in income between comparable blacks and whites have not closed.

While acknowledging the impact of discrimination, Wilson stresses that the disadvantaged minority group members tend to lack the resources to compete effectively in a free and open market. There are many blacks for whom hardly anything would change if racism magically disappeared from America (Wilson 1987: 113). Riemer appears to agree, arguing that if discrimination were done away with, poverty would not be ended but would just be more fairly spread around (Riemer 1988: 98).

Wilson believes that antidiscrimination legislation and affirmative action laws had more to do with the progress of the black middle-class than the underclass (Wilson 1987: 30). He concedes that discrimination has contributed to or aggravated the social and economic problems of the ghetto underclass. But he thinks that concentrating on this obscures the impact of the more important economic and demographic changes.

Race-specific policies, he believes, do little for the truly disadvantaged. Programs based solely on the principle of equality of individual opportunity are inadequate to address the complex problems of group inequality in America. The point is that their environments effectively inhibit the development of their talents or aspirations (Wilson 1987: 111–113, 117).

Centuries or even decades of racial subjugation can result in a system of racial inequality that may linger on for indefinite periods of time after racial barriers are eliminated, because the most disadvantaged members of minority groups are those who have been most denied the resources to compete effectively in a free and open market (Wilson 1987: 113, 146). Feagin (1988) claims that the institutionalized structure of current discrimination perpetuates the effects of past discrimination.

Wilson's theory appears to be a solid, realistic perspective on the underclass and its problems, emphasizing as it does economic and structural barriers, without ignoring social-psychological variables. Wilson has been criticized for minimizing the role of discrimination, and it may be that he might give this aspect somewhat more attention. But nowhere does Wilson suggest that race is unimportant; he simply stresses that the problems of the underclass are so extensive that programs to improve their life chances must be those to which all races and classes can positively relate.

It is important not to stereotype the underclass. The poor of America, even in inner-city areas, are highly heterogeneous. Wilson himself cautions that the term should not be used to discredit the urban minority poor, and even says we might consider dropping the term (Wilson 1991b: 475–476). But he cautions that any crusade to abandon the concept could result in premature closure of ideas (Wilson 1991a).

Many of the ideas in this chapter have an obvious relevance to the Los Angeles riots in the spring of 1992. In particular, the severely limited job opportunties for the blacks of the disadvantaged segments of the urban black population, all relate to underlying problems that helped spawn the riots (see Wilson 1987: 42, 58).

South Central Los Angeles has long been one of the poorest sections of the city. Average income is just $10,000 a year per adult. About 30 percent of the area's families are below the poverty line ("This Land is My Land" 1992).

Waxman (1983: 46) warned that unless the economic context was altered young people would be permanently trapped. Most striking is the comment by Sampson that the structurally disadvantaged positon of blacks can be seen as the root cause of black violence (quoted in Parker 1989).

These observations do not fully account for, or justify, the events in the spring of 1992. Considerations concerning racial unrest and particularly police violence need to be voiced, as do concerns about illegal drugs and criminal gangs. But the overall deprivation of a large segment of the population must be stressed as a major underlying cause of the turmoil.

It is also crucial to realize that the problems of the underclass are not intractable. Writing about full employment in the Boston area, Osterman makes it clear that the poor did respond to economic opportunity when it was offered. The sharp drop in the incidence of poverty and the high percentage of the poor who began working undercuts the idea that an active government social policy is debilitating (Osterman 1991: 130). Freeman provides further evidence that a strong job market does improve the employment and earnings of the disadvantaged (Freeman 1991: 119).

Schorr supplies hard evidence that systematic intervention and support from outside the family early in the life cycle can improve the lifetime prospects of children growing up at risk. Help from outside is possible for children growing up in persistent and concentrated poverty (Schorr 1988: xx, xxii). Crane (1991b) also provides support for the view that investment in at-risk neighborhoods should be effective in preventing "epidemics" of social problems.

Riemer, after summarizing the problems of job shortages and an abundance of low-wage jobs, states that these problems are not ineluctable. They can be eliminated by building on potentially more powerful features of American culture, economy, and government. Vision and leadership are the key (Riemer 1988: xiii).

4

The Homeless

The media and the public first discovered America's homeless in the early 1980s. We have been made acutely aware of the destitution and suffering of tens of thousands living in cars or abandoned buildings, sleeping on grates, in cardboard boxes, or on benches under blankets of newspapers, or other makeshift shelters. Few of our contemporary social problems rival this subject in the public attention received in this decade.

Homelessness exists when an individual lacks a regular nighttime residence, or the available residence is temporary shelter (Foster et al. 1989). Homelessness is the loss of personal residence, often precipitated by external circumstances beyond one's control: job loss, eviction, separation or divorce, illness, and the like. Most share three characteristics—extreme poverty, poor physical and mental health, and high levels of social isolation. Homelessness finally occurs when family, friends, and community resources are unavailable, unused, or depleted (Baumann and Grigsby 1988).

There are critics who believe that a major homeless problem does not exist, or that it has been exaggerated by the media. Wooster (1988) claims that nobody even knows how much—or even whether—the number of homeless is increasing. He suggests that the increase in the number of people using shelters in New York City is attributable to people's leaving temporary housing for free beds and food.

Some argue that there has been ample housing for American families, though government programs have been a failure. "Housing is better and

more widely distributed in the United States today than when the public
housing program was started," but this has come through private development (Friedman and Friedman 1979: 110). There is good reason to
question this assertion.

Most cities are reporting annual increases in the number of known
homeless of from 15 to 50 percent, and there are a growing number of
families (Foster et al. 1989). Kozol reports that in Washington, D.C., the
numbers of homeless went up 500 percent in one year (1987) and 12,000
people were on a waiting list for public housing. He writes that in Phoenix
and Los Angeles shelters overflowed and people slept in huge encamp-
ments on the edges of the seamy areas of town (Kozol 1988: 8). As one
indication, the Salvation Army in Austin, Texas provided lodging and
meals for 16,863 in 1980, and 156,451 in 1985 (Snow et al. 1989).

The National Alliance to End Homelessness claims on any given night,
as many as 735,000 people in the United States are homeless, and between
1.3 million and 2 million were homeless for at least one night in 1988
(Foster et al. 1989: 3). Wright (1989a) puts the annual homeless population
at 1.5 million, but he adds that the majority are episodically, rather than
chronically, homeless. He believes that the current rate of homelessness
exceeds anything witnessed in this country in the last half-century. Rossi
(1989) says these people suffer a more severe form of housing deprivation
than did the homeless of twenty or thirty years past.

It is generally agreed that the census figures do not begin to record the
actual number of homeless. The 1990 census, which did make an effort to
count their number, undoubtedly missed many. No counting at all was
attempted in many areas of the country. Only 7,706 homeless persons were
found in Los Angeles, while estimates in that city start at 50,000. In
Houston, they found 1,931, whereas a 1989 study estimated 10,000 (Chriss
1991).

CHARACTERISTICS OF THE HOMELESS

There appears to be a controversy as to the types of persons who find
themselves homeless. One view, popular in conservative quarters, is that
most of the homeless are male adults, many of them transients looking for
welfare, who have failed in their major roles; most of them are alcoholics,
drug addicts, or mentally ill. This view holds that a large percentage of the
homeless actually prefer the street or the shelters to a disciplined life of
work. If only they had more motivation, they could get jobs and establish
respectability. (Much of this section will critique this simplistic view.)

The diversity of the homeless population is well established (First and Toomey 1989; Wright 1989a). One may find people of every age, race, and health status. Their composition often varies among different communities. The U.S. Conference of Mayors reports that two-parent homeless families are more likely to be found in the West and Southwest than in large eastern cities, where female-headed families are predominant.

According to Hoch and Slayton, authors of a recent book on the homeless, characterizations of the "old" Skid Row homeless are inaccurate. There is little demographic difference between the old homeless in Chicago and the new. What separates the two groups is their accessibility to cheap, decent housing. The new homeless have been "shelterized," warehoused in environments that promote dependence rather than autonomy (LaGory 1990).

It is possible the homeless in Chicago are not typical, for other reports indicate a major change in the make-up of these people. Middle-aged men are a decreasing proportion of homeless people and families with small children have become the fastest-growing segment. No longer are the homeless confined to the back alleys of inner cities, but their growing numbers and their changing composition have thrust them into public awareness of communities and neighborhoods that not long ago would not have known of their existence (Foster et al. 1989: 2).

Most cities report that homeless males tend to be long-term residents of their city. Almost two-thirds were born into the counties in which they were interviewed or lived there longer than a year (First and Toomey 1989). Transients are generally attracted to a new town because of its potential for employment, not because of any public benefits it might offer (Foster et al. 1989: 5).

First and Toomey (1989) report that 65 percent of the homeless are white, 31 percent black, and 5 percent Hispanic or other. But the percentage of minorities among the homeless is growing, and some studies report they are a majority (Burt and Cohen 1989). Minorities are significantly overrepresented among the homeless in larger cities, reflecting the higher proportion of minorities who live below the poverty level (Foster et al. 1989).

The U.S. Conference of Mayors reports that 56 percent of the homeless population were individual males and 25 percent were individual women; families with children comprised 33 percent (*Christianity Today* 1988). Burt and Cohen (1989) report about 20 percent women. (In 1963, families comprised only 3 percent of homeless.) Men and women averaged between thirty-four and thirty-seven years of age, with the women slightly younger than the men. Homeless men were less likely never to have been married than homeless women. Homeless adults who have never married are usually not members of households and therefore often lack the ties that are helpful in finding shelter (First and Toomey 1989).

In a report from Rhode Island, 60 percent of shelter residents are two-parent families, often with at least one parent working. The rest are women with children. A shelter worker says, "Most who come to us aren't on welfare and don't even know how to apply for aid" (Matthews 1991).

Only 3 percent of homeless people who sought care at health projects were elderly (Foster et al. 1989: 7); Wright (1989a) gives the same percentage. Few studies report more than 10 percent elderly except in Chicago, where the figure approaches 20 percent.

The percentage of homeless with high school diplomas has increased over the past twenty-five years: in 1963, only 19 percent of the homeless in Chicago were high school graduates; in 1985, 55 percent were (Foster et al. 1989: 4). A slightly different report says that 53 percent have not finished high school (First and Toomey 1989). Educational attainment is highest among homeless single women, but only 43 percent of homeless women with children hold a high school diploma.

Vietnam veterans make up a significant proportion of the male homeless. Homeless veterans tend to be older than nonveterans, better educated, and more likely to have been married. This group is more likely to report substance abuse as being largely responsible for their living conditions (Foster et al. 1989: 5).

One observer says that "today's homeless bear little resemblance to the stereotypical skid-row bum. Instead, they are beginning to look a lot like our next-door neighbors" (Spring 1989). Shelters and missions say there are fewer hitchhikers, vagrants, and transients, but more hometown people. The U.S. Conference of Mayors estimated 22 percent of the homeless held full or part-time jobs in 1987. Several studies have found that 5 to 10 percent of homeless adults are employed full-time, and between 10 and 20 percent work half-time or when they can find work (Foster et al. 1989: 5).

In New York City in a recent year, 50 percent of individuals served at city shelters said they were there for the first time (Kozol 1988: 4); the same percentage may hold throughout the nation. Many new homeless are children or females; they include the working poor or the recently unemployed. They have a surprisingly high level of education, and many come from middle-class backgrounds. The majority of new homeless do not have any especially debilitating physical or mental condition (Swanstrom 1988).

"This is a new population," says a homeless advocate in Massachusetts. "Many are people who were working all their lives. When they lose their jobs they lose their homes" (Kozol 1988: 4). Stephen Burger, who runs a mission in Seattle, says, "We are seeing more and more people who are close to the line economically. . . . Even people living out in the suburbs are often one or two paychecks away from disaster" (quoted in Spring 1988).

Many families across the nation live from paycheck to paycheck. Salaries at $150 a week will not pay for apartments that start at $450 a month in Dallas. Many live on disability checks of $468 a month in New York or San Francisco where the average monthly rent for a small apartment is well over $500 (Spring 1989). Many are cancelling their hospitalization and other insurance because they simply cannot afford it.

Several sources speak of increasing numbers of women among the homeless (Foster et al. 1989: 5; van Vliet 1989; Burt and Cohen 1989; Johnson and Kreuger 1989). Wright (1989a) says that women and children make up from one-third to two-fifths of the homeless. The number of sheltered homeless families more than quadrupled from 1984 to 1988. In their study of 240 homeless women in St. Louis, Johnson and Kreuger found that 77 percent were black, and 73 percent had dependent children. Those without children were much more likely to need psychosocial services and alcohol treatment than those with children.

The rise in the presence of homeless families is primarily a phenomenon of women's poverty, since a large majority of these families are female-headed single-parent households (Burt and Cohen 1989). Families with only the mother as the present parent were more likely to be in urban areas, while two-parent families were more common in rural areas (Foster et al 1989: 5). Homeless mothers were likely to be single or divorced, have had some high school education; they were in their late twenties and drawing AFDC. Their racial and ethnic makeup reflected that of the area, with a large proportion of blacks and Hispanics in cities, whites in rural and suburban areas.

Illness, wife battering, divorce, job loss, eviction, and foreclosures are among the reasons for homelessness among women (van Vliet 1989). They may double up with friends or relatives under conditions of severe overcrowding, or live in cars, abandoned housing, transportation terminals, shelters, welfare hotels, or the streets.

Women with children have the shortest current episodes of homelessness, with two of five homeless for three months or less (Burt and Cohen 1989). More single women have been homeless for several years. Homeless women with children rely less on working and more on welfare. The homeless woman with two children is, on the average, getting $360 a month in cash and about $100 in food stamps. The single homeless are much more likely than women with children to obtain cash with handouts.

The National Academy of Sciences (1988) estimated that 100,000 children under the age of eight, not counting those forced to leave their homes, were homeless on a given night. One account says that small children have become the fastest-growing segment of the homeless (Kozol 1988: 4). There were a reported 28,000 homeless children in emergency shelters in New York City, and 40,000 citywide in all. In Massachusetts, three-fourths of all homeless people are now children and their parents. Children, the majority under five, and their parents now make up one third of the homeless in twenty-six U.S. cities, and the majority of those seeking emergency food are families, according to the U. S. Conference of Mayors (Rome 1989).

Women, especially those with children, are much more likely than men to be consistent users of shelters. This picture would have been much different at the beginning of the 1980s, when virtually none of the shelter beds in the country were appropriate for families. Shelter accommodations have almost tripled from 1983 to 1988. The image of children on the streets mobilizes resources faster than that of a mentally ill or alcoholic single person (Burt and Cohen 1989).

A recent report from the Children's Defense Fund says that many homeless children grow up surrounded by diseases no longer seen in most developed nations. Whooping cough and tuberculosis, once regarded as archaic illnesses, are now familiar in the shelters. Shocking numbers of these children have not been inoculated and therefore cannot go to school (*Outside the Dream* 1991).

Unaccompanied youths include homeless runaways and those whom some experts have called "throwaway youths" (evicted by their parents), often victims of abuse. They may have run away many times, stayed away for good, and wound up on the streets. In twenty-five cities, 4 percent of the homeless population were unaccompanied youth (Foster et al. 1989: 5).

An estimated one million youths ages ten to seventeen are runaways, most without a place to stay. Runaway and homelesss youth sought services from the centers for a wide range of problems, most family-related such as poor communication, parental strictness, and emotional neglect. Two-thirds cited problems with parents as the major reason for their being there. Close to half of youth served at centers were identified as having poor self-images (Foster et al. 1989: 6).

While almost all attention to the homeless has been devoted to large cities, a surprising number (perhaps 20 percent) may be found in rural areas (Ropers 1991: 78–80). Some rural people never go to shelters, but according to one social worker, "they're definitely out there, though" (*Providence Bulletin* 1991).

In categorizing types of the homeless, First and Toomey (1989) identified three groups of homeless men. One type, consisting of 43 percent of the total, were those who had faced a crisis in housing, family composition, or employment. They had the fewest serious disabilities and the most positive work histories. They believe that almost half of the homeless men could return to independence following short-term interventions and policy initiatives leading to job creation (First and Toomey 1989).

A similar group is described by Baumann and Grigsby (1988). These have lost a job, been evicted from an apartment, and although they are still employable, most work is too short-term to allow them to save for rental and utility deposits. Many of these men probably can be in the labor force; they can be employed and helped to return to independent living. Most in this group maintain some contact with friends and/or family.

It is very likely that many homeless do not have access to information about community resources. Some may be newcomers to a city. Many are unlikely to rely on newspapers for information. Television and radio are often unavailable. Entrenchment is thus perpetuated and their problems worsen (Baumann and Grigsby 1988).

A second group would require longer rehabilitation, but have a reasonable chance to return to conventional living. A final group would be the long-term needs group, those with serious mental illness or alcoholism or serious personal limitations. These walking wounded, isolated and disoriented, have been in their situation for years. Many will need consistent, long-term support (First and Toomey 1989; Baumann and Grigsby 1988).

PROBLEMS OF THE HOMELESS

Homelessness is at base a function of poverty (Burt and Cohen 1989). Poor people living in objectively inadequate housing because they lack the means to do otherwise number in the tens of millions (Wright 1989a). Poor renter households are being required to pay an increasing amount of their income for rent. In the 1980s women with children experienced the largest increase of any household type in the proportion of households in poverty.

One recent survey of homeless people found that their most important self-identified need was employment or employment training. This might mean literacy and job training, or referral to employers and/or a retraining program (Swanstrom 1988).

The difficulty of a homeless person's getting a job and returning to conventional society has not been recognized as much as it might. When someone is looking for work, gaps in the work record may represent time spent in an institution or on the streets. Good references will be hard to come by. Without an address or telephone, it is difficult to fill out an application or expect a contact. A driver's license may have been lost, or one cannot afford a car.

Although her work centered on male Skid Row alcholics, much of what Jacqueline Wiseman said about their attempts to get a job and return to conventional society applies to the homeless, or even to much of the underclass. Most nonpoor tend to apply middle-class standards to these people, making certain assumptions about an "intact" family, a steady job, a room, clean house, and an emphasis on sobriety and responsibility that may be unrealistic for lower-class individuals.

One may have to get a menial job like dishwashing and stick to it for at least six months, and get a room, some decent clothes, and abstain from liquor. Personal credit must be reestablished; he or she must try to save money, start a small bank account, and get an address in a respectable neighborhood. One must patiently work his or her way toward the goal of reintegration.

Someone from the underclass or the homeless population is probably not *returning* to (conventional) society, but trying to break in for the first time, and usually an must do so without the support of friends and relatives. He or she is usually an individual of inadequate skills and education. Learning to feel like part of middle-class society may be extremely difficult.

With a low-paying job, finding even a modest room may be difficult. If the room is in a slum area, the problems and temptations of the street will not be far away. He or she is torn between his or her fear of failure and anger at what he or she perceives to be exploitation (adapted from Wiseman 1970: 216–238).

A recent writer on the homeless points out that it is unrealistic to expect that jobs can be pursued, obtained, and competently filled so long as homelessness remains a sword above the heads of these people. Prolonged anxiety renders their return to work, no matter how appealing, very hard. A permanent home need not always be the preconditon to employment (Kozol 1988: 198).

Without work histories, these people lack the references they need to convince potential employers of their reliability; the longer they lack work, the harder it is for them to find a job; tainted in employers' perception by discrimination, a reputation for low skills, and poor work haibts, they remain at the end of the line for hiring; when they are hired, they usually work only a short time (Katz 1989: 214).

Kozol visited over fifty cities in almost every region of the nation. Everywhere he found the loss of work and loss of homes, rising rents, and declining federal benefits (Kozol 1988: 6). The actual purchasing power of today's welfare dollar is roughly half what it was twenty years ago (Wright 1989b). The average income of today's homeless is barely a third of the income of the homeless in 1958; and interestingly, only about half of the homeless receive any form of social welfare assistance (Wright 1989a).

In Oklahoma, Arkansas, and Texas, Kozol met heads of families who had been owners of farms, employees of petroleum firms, shopkeepers, who had lost their farms, their jobs, their stores (Kozol 1988: 7). Some could get a minimum-wage job, but that might pay $450 a month, insufficient to cover essentials, let alone catastrophes like a major illness.

In a study of twelve cities, the number of poor people increased 36 percent from 1979 to 1989, while the number of rental units they could afford decreased 30 percent (Swanstrom 1988). More than half the homeless in San Antonio are employed but still can't find housing (Rome 1989).

Many counties (126) that got aid for the homeless in 1989 were dropped for 1990. They include twenty double-digit with unemployment and one with a poverty rate of 42.7 percent (*Dallas Times-Herald* 1990). In 1991, eleven states cut emergency payments intended to avert homelessness, and nine cut programs to help the homeless (Clements 1991).

In Sacramento, an estimated 10,000 families who rely on the state's homeless assistance programs may be cut. Local officials call the situation "disastrous" and "horrendous." Denver's largest shelter for homeless families and mentally and physically ill closed its doors to new residents in March of 1991, leaving a gaping hole in the region's safety net (Gottlieb 1991).

In a sense, food is more important than shelter. One survey found that 41 percent of single homeless men and a substantial percentage of women say they sometimes or often do not get enough to eat. Forty percent of single men and almost 20 percent of the women reported going without food for at least one day out of the last seven (Burt and Cohen 1989).

Homelessness causes a great deal of physical illness and mental distress. Forty-four percent of single women, 40 percent of women with children, and 33 percent of single men saw their health as fair or poor. Homelessness aggravates any unhealthy condition, and increases the risk of infection, injuries, and parasitical diseases (Burt and Cohen 1989). Many suffer from dental disease, cardiovascular disorders, and poor nutrition.

The percentage of the homeless who are mentally ill has been the matter of some controversy. Rossi (1989) found almost one-half had symptoms of depression indicative of the need for clinical attention, compared to less than one-fourth in the general population. Snow et al. (1986) would disagree, claiming only 10 to 15 percent are mentally ill. Baumann and Grigsby (1989) estimate about 33 percent are mentally ill, about the same percentage found by Wright (1989a), and this estimate may be the most reasonable.

Among the homeless, both single women and single men are more likely to have histories of mental hospitalization and attempted suicide than are women with children. But only one-fourth of single women and one-fifth of single men report such histories (Burt and Cohen 1989).

One review suggests 20 to 40 percent of the homeless have alcohol problems, compared with 7 to 10 percent of the general population (Baumann and Grigsby 1989). Wright estimates that less than 40 percent of all homeless abuse alcohol, though about half of the men do (Wright 1989a).

Women with children have the lowest experiences with alcoholism; single women have more than double the rate of women with children; and single men double the rate of single women. Less than half the single men and a majority of all subgroups have not experienced either mental hospitalization or inpatient treatment for chemical dependency (Burt and Cohen 1989).

There are obvious problems with homeless school-age children in America. More than one-quarter do not make it to classes regularly. They may not be in one place long enough; they may not be able to afford transportation; they may not have school records or a permanent address; they have difficulty in doing homework, and struggle academically, socially, and emotionally (*Dallas Times Herald* 1990). Dr. Ellen Bassuk says, "We're beginning to raise a generation of kids in the streets. That has dire consequences for the future" (quoted in *Newsweek* 1987).

Burt and Cohen (1989) found that two-thirds of the men have served jail or prison time and 29 percent have served time in a state or federal prison. But more than three-fourths of all single women and 85 percent of women with children have never served time.

An interesting claim is that while the homeless have a higher overall arrest rate, the majority of offenses for which they are arrested are public intoxication, followed by theft/shoplifting, violation of city ordinances, and burglary. This challenges the depiction of homeless men as serious predatory criminals (Snow et al. 1989).

Most of the crimes committed by homeless men occur because their daily routines and idiosyncratic appearance and behavior bring them to the attention of the police. Stigmatized in the eyes of the police, they are subject to closer scrutiny. Actually, they pose little direct threat to the personal safety of other citizens, and only a modest threat to their property.

SOME CAUSES

Much of the material contained in this chapter implies that attributing the major causes of the homeless problem to the personal traits of the people caught in this situation is most inadequate. (For a cogent statement about structural causes of homelessness, see Elliott and Krivo 1991.)

In a study of public beliefs about the causes of homelessness (in Nashville, Tennessee), Lee and colleagues found that almost three-fifths of their informants attributed homelessness to structural forces, but less than two-fifths thought the condition was due to personal choice. Bad luck was cited as a cause more often than aversion to work, and much more often than it had been in previous research. Respondents also gave healthy support to a wide range of ameliorative measures for the problem (Lee et al. 1990).

Some of the most frequently mentioned causes are structural changes in the economy; unemployment; heavy concentrations of minorities and female-headed families; a shortage of low-income housing; more restrictive eligibility requirements for welfare and disability benefits; job and housing discrimination; alcohol and drug dependency; the deinstitutionalization of the mentally ill with inadequate provision for community support systems; and the absence of social services to help people get a new start (Baumann and Grigsby 1988; Elliott and Krivo 1991; Ropers 1991: 78).

Current shifts in the economy are producing a growing number of poor people who cannot pay enough in rents or mortgages to make low-income investment probable. The result is a supply-and-affordability crisis that is pushing those least able to cope onto the streets (Appelbaum 1989).

When poverty increases, more people must choose between paying for housing and meeting other needs such as food, clothing, and medical care. A notable portion of homeless people work in unstable jobs of short duration (Elliott and Krivo 1991).

The transfer from smokestack industries to service and high-tech jobs has left thousands of laborers without jobs (Spring 1989). Further, poor jobs often do not raise one out of poverty. Between one-half and two-thirds of all jobs created in the last decade paid poverty-level wages. Low-rent, multifamily units are being torn down or converted to luxury condominiums—and not being replaced. Rent allowances covered by welfare were frozen for ten years at their 1975 levels, whereas rents in New York City for example, nearly doubled.

Median monthly rents in the nation rose by 192 percent between 1970 and 1983 while monthly income of renters increased by only 97 percent. By 1983, 22 percent of renters paid 50 percent or more of their income towards rent (Elliott and Krivo 1991; Appelbaum 1989).

The stock of low-cost housing in the United States fell by two million units from 1974 to 1983, according to the National Association of Home Builders (Nasar 1986). A prominent economist says, "The inadequate provision of housing at modest cost in contrast with that of, say, automobiles or cosmetics, can be considered the single greatest default of modern capitalism" (Galbraith 1987: 290).

Areas with more blacks, Hispanics, and female-headed families have significantly higher homeless rates. The homeless rate is negatively correlated with the amount of low-rent housing and with measures of mental health expenditures (Elliott and Krivo 1991).

Some 75,000 units of public housing are lost annually to demolition. A large amount of assisted housing is threatened as well (Applebaum 1989). Between 1970 and 1982 more than 110,000 single room occupancy (SRO) units, representing 87 percent of the total supply, were lost in New York City alone. Nationally, 1.2 million or 47 percent of the total supply of SROs have disappeared (Burghardt and Fabricant 1987: 24). More than half a million low- and moderate-income families may lose federally subsidized apartments by the year 2000 (Kozol 1988: 202).

This country has never had a coherent long-term federal commitment to housing (Appelbaum 1991). Only one out of every four persons in poverty is able to find subsidized housing. In 1989, the administration was proposing 100,000 additional subsidy vouchers for the entire nation, when New York City alone could use more than 500,000.

The Reagan cutbacks severely impacted public housing. Allocated funds went from $32 billion in 1981 to $6 billion in 1989. The federal government spent $7 on defense for every $1 in housing in 1980; when Reagan left office in 1989, the ratio was 46 to 1 (Appelbaum 1989). The number of subsidized units a year fell from 187,000 in the late 1970s to 17,000 in the late 1980s (Swanstrom 1988).

A minor controversy has emerged on whether rent control is a major cause of homelessness. William Tucker has claimed as much on several occasions. Quigley finds the claim "just plain silly," and shows that by adding a variable measuring low income, price, and vacancy rate, the statistical significance of rent control vanishes. The existence of rent control is irrelevant to the extent of homelessness in the cities studied, and its repeal would not affect the level of homelessness in any meaningful way (Quigley 1990; also see Ropers 1991: 84–88).

The supply of low-income housing, income maintenance, support services, and access to health care for the poor and insured (about 37 million Americans are without any form of public or private health insurance) are causes of homelessness mentioned by several. Surely decent, affordable housing is every American's right. Lissner believes we should take the steps that would end the quasi-monopoly of land and make homesites available to all who need them (Lissner 1985).

Hope and Young include as causes inadequate services for the mentally disabled, unemployment, and inadequate social benefits. The problem is primarily a problem of insufficient supply of low-income housing, but not of this alone. Recessions and the reductions in public assistance benefits are also important. They suggest strengthening universal, federally financed programs that will help us all (Keigher 1988).

This problem will continue to escalate alarmingly and overwhelm private efforts providing help, unless a thorough commitment on the federal as well as the local level is made to end this national disgrace. Chapter 8, which proposes solutions for the problem of poverty in general, will include many steps that should reduce the extent of homelessness.

5

Welfare

If there is one word in the entire area of poverty that arouses controversy, it is the word "welfare." "Welfare policy is the slate on which our most trenchant social anxieties are written. What the powerful reveal in discussions of welfare, they wouldn't dare express elsewhere" (Kornbluh 1991). Ellwood believes that welfare, by its very nature, creates conflict and frustration and tension (Ellwood 1988: x).

This chapter discusses the controversy surrounding the War on Poverty beginning in the 1960s and moves on to a discussion of the relative advantages and disadvantages of welfare, by which is meant public programs that give cash and noncash income to persons unable to adequately provide for themselves and their families (Binford et al. 1990: 2). The argument that AFDC may increase the birth rate, and the issue of fraud, will also be considered. The question of welfare dependency has aroused so much discussion that the following chapter will be devoted to it.

The role of the government in assuring some minimal standard of living for its citizens was largely set in the Depression of the 1930s. Galbraith reviews the controversy and concludes that the ample and effusive rhetoric in opposition to welfare did not translate into action; the welfare state has become firmly a part of modern capitalism and modern economic life (Galbraith 1987: 219). Even Gilder concedes that modes of welfare and cooperation have been integral to private enterprise systems at every phase of development (Gilder 1981: 107).

But the War on Poverty, officially declared by Lyndon Johnson in 1964, has been extremely controversial. It has been the object of attack not only by conservatives but not infrequently by liberals as well. Most of these criticisms are well summarized by Schwarz, who reviews the charges that the programs failed to eliminate poverty, sometimes actually making things worse, retarded economic growth, and that incompetence and even fraud were rampant (Schwarz 1983: 19–33).

Social security, unemployment compensation, and direct relief were all expanded to cover new groups, and Medicare, Medicaid, food stamps, and numerous other programs were added. Public housing and urban renewal programs were enlarged. Two economists believe that while the objectives have all been noble, the results have been disappointing. Many expenditures soared out of sight, and the welfare program became a "mess" saturated with fraud and corruption (Friedman and Friedman 1979: 96, 107). They feel it was a bad means to achieve good objectives.

In a similar manner, Gilder claims that welfare recipients in most states kept up with inflation or improved their position through the tripling of food stamps and other in-kind supports (Gilder 1981: 19). When the government offers these kinds of benefits it often deters productive work, and when it raises taxes on profitable enterprises to pay for them, demand declines (Gilder 1981: 45).

The best-known proponent of the view that public assistance in the Great Society era made things worse is Charles Murray, who claims that beyond a certain point increased spending on public assistance has become counterproductive. By the 1970s, he argues, welfare benefits had soared so high that they made living in poverty a meaningful option for the poor. "The number of people living in poverty stopped declining just as the public assistance program budgets and the rate of increase in those budgets were highest" (Murray 1984: 58). Thus the programs have done more to cause poverty than to alleviate it. As of 1980, "the many overlapping cash and in-kind benefit programs made it possible for almost anyone to place themselves (*sic*) above the official poverty level" (Murray 1984: 57; for a concurring view, see Eberstadt 1988). The Great Society reforms, he claims, exacerbated many of the conditions they sought to alleviate.

Nathan Glazer says that the Great Society programs, social insurance programs, and public assistance programs consumed an increasing share of GNP over time, with disappointing results. "The programs grew, in number and scale; the problems remained" (Glazer 1984). He does concede that the social insurance programs were effective.

Criticisms of the War on Poverty are not limited to conservatives who distrust almost any government program. Moynihan said the War on

Poverty was too hastily conceived. The enthusiasm, idealism, and zeal contributed to "maximum feasible misunderstanding" (cited in Waxman 1983: ix) Fierce competition for project funding led to bitter conflicts. Wilson believes that the War on Poverty failed to relate the problems of the poor to broader processes of American economic organization (Wilson 1987: 132).

One liberal writes that it is "axiomatic that programs for poor people tend to be poor programs—inadequately funded, intrusively administered, and widely resented" (Lekachman 1982: 11). A recent writer says that while the War on Poverty helped many, it failed to reduce poverty rates among the nonelderly much (Skocpal 1991). While praising many of the programs, Gifford thinks the war ignored the American distribution system, failing to change the economic and social system (Gifford 1986: 63–64).

The first element of an answer to the critics is that the War on Poverty was a limited program that was never funded to the extent its critics assume (Chalfant 1985: xix). At least two writers have termed it a "skirmish" rather than a war (Harrington 1984: 3; Whitman 1991). The first-year budget for the Economic Opportunity Act was $1 billion, amounting to about $28.50 per year for each person in poverty (Carouthers 1966: 72). Even at its height, the federal war on poverty never cost as much as one percent of the federal budget and was scuttled before completing the start-up time needed to test any nationwide program (Lappé 1989: 42). It failed to commit the resources necessary for a sustained drive to eliminate poverty (Levitan 1985: 137).

The image held by some of massive transfers of money to the poor is unjustified. The programs aimed at reforming poor people so they could enjoy the benefit of the free market (Weier 1987); the emphasis was mainly on the environments of the poor (Wilson 1987: 131). Many of the programs were to help people obtain education and skills and (except for Volunteers in Service to America and Head Start) are now defunct (Beeghley 1983: 40).

Some programs were insuring people against medical catastrophe, disability, for example—insuring against events that are largely beyond the control of the individual. Ellwood shows that the great social planners did not get the policy they really wanted for their War on Poverty, and only modest reforms were enacted (Ellwood 1988: 35–37).

The Economic Opportunity Act of 1964 was not as lavish as its image. Sargent Shriver never tired of telling audiences it was "not a hand-out program." Title 1 established a job corps, authorized it to enroll 100,000 young people to do conservation work while improving their basic education. Another 200,000 youth were to be given "work-training" of various types, and a "work-study" program offered fifteen hours of work a week for 140,000 college students from low-income families (Walch 1973: 214).

Peterson feels that the War on Poverty was little more than a call for citizen participation combined with a hodgepodge of educational, job training, and neighborhood service programs that had little internal coherence and only limited financial backing (Peterson 1991). He adds that the war did not fail in any absolute sense; the poverty rate no longer continued to decline, but it remained fairly stable.

What many observers miss, however, are the numerous positive results of the War on Poverty. The enhanced federal role spurred action on problems long ignored by state and local officials (Levitan 1985: 19). Levitan claims that the legacy of the Great Society includes major strides toward the elimination of poverty in America that the media have failed to publicize. "A close examination of programs in aid of the poor—ranging from cash and in-kind assistance to services for the working poor and the young—yields evidence of the Great Society's impact and promising prospects for future gains" (Levitan 1985: 23). It may be that Levitan endorses these programs too uncritically, but pointing out their positive impact is a needed emphasis.

"The development of the nation's welfare system, shaped and greatly accelerated under the Great Society, has improved the lives of millions of Americans by expanding opportunity and reducing deprivation throughout the life cycle" (Levitan and Johnson 1986: 74). Again, this may exaggerate somewhat, but it is worthwhile to note the contributions of these programs.

The official rate of poverty went from 22.4 percent in 1959 to 17.3 percent in 1965 to 11 or 12 percent throughout the 1970s. Schram finds evidence of a decrease in poverty when spending grew in the late 1960s and an increase in poverty when welfare payments decreased in the late 1970s and early 1980s (Schram 1991). In a mere ten years the real buying power of productive workers went up by more than 15 percent (Harrington 1984: 232).

The argument by Skocpal that the War on Poverty did not reduce poverty among the nonelderly very much can be answered. Several areas of aid, including food stamps, Medicaid, and Section 8 housing assistance, are not counted in measuring the official poverty rate, and the Supplemental Security Income (SSI) program affects only the elderly and disabled poor. It would therefore be unrealistic to expect the War on Poverty to have affected poverty rates among the nonelderly very much. But dramatic improvement in infant mortality and in nutrition occurred after 1968 (Greenstein 1991).

While the programs did not eliminate impoverishment, they alleviated some of its worst aspects by expanding the system of public assistance (Beeghley 1983: 1).

Schram and Wilken show that poverty declined in the 1960s while expenditures rose, and climbed in the late 1970s and 1980s when expenditures initially leveled off and subsequently declined (Schram and Wilken 1989). From 1959 to 1973, the adjusted poverty rate fell by one-half, some gaps between blacks and whites and rich and poor narrowed, and housing, health, and nutrition indicators rose (Haveman 1988: 22).

Of course not all aspects of the War on Poverty were equally successful: there were real problems, for example, in the Comprehensive Employment and Training Act (CETA) and in some urban renewal programs (Katz 1989: 136). While the positive impact of federal training programs has been questioned, others claim that "though limited, the effectiveness of federal training programs has been well documented" (Levitan and Johnson 1986: 82).

The strongest defense of the War on Poverty is offered by Schwarz. He points out that by the second half of the 1970s only 4 to 8 percent of the American public remained beneath the poverty level compared with about 18 percent in 1960. These figures take into account the income Americans received from every source. Thus poverty had been reduced by about 60 percent, and Schwarz shows that most of this gain was accomplished through the government's programs (Schwarz 1983: 32–33).

> The government's programs were vital in fighting poverty precisely because the private sector was itself incapable of making more than a marginal dent in poverty among the many millions of Americans who remained trapped within the weaker economic groups, either too old to get work or channeled into dead-end jobs that often paid little more than half-time wages for full-time work. (Schwarz 1983: 39)

While these points partially refute Murray's contention, further examination of his claims is in order. He said that food stamps and AFDC payments had a negative effect on poor black family formation and work incentives. But the real value of these two combined programs increased only from 1960 to 1972; after that time, their real value declined sharply, yet "there were no reversals in the trends of either family composition or work effort" (Wilson 1987: 17).

Murray contends that despite increased spending on social programs, from 1968 to 1980 the poverty rate failed to drop, indicating these programs were not successful. But the unemployment rate in 1980 was twice that of 1968. When unemployment goes up, poverty also rises. Many people slipped into poverty because of an economic downturn, and were lifted out by the broadening of benefits (Wilson 1987: 17).

The economy did grow in the 1970s, but the growth was insufficient to handle the unusually large numbers of women and young people who were entering the job market, resulting in an increase in unemployment. And real wages stopped growing in the 1970s. Thus the economy was the major cause of the failure of poverty to decline in the 1970s (Wilson 1987: 18).

Poverty climbed in the late 1970s and early 1980s when welfare expenditures leveled off and then declined. The adverse demographic changes in the 1970s, such as the rise in the number of female-headed families, were the primary factors behind the reduced proportion of the poor lifted out of poverty (Schram and Wilkin 1989).

Murray gives inadequate attention to trends in the relative advantages of welfare vs. work after 1970. Real benefit levels have fallen dramatically since the early 1970s. "No other group in American society experienced such a sharp decline in real income since 1970 as did AFDC mothers and their children" (Greenstein 1989: 16).

The failure of poverty to decrease after 1973 (and its increase after 1978) was related to such factors as general income stagnation, the erosion of wages for nonsupervisory jobs, and a large decrease in real benefit levels provided by the states under the AFDC program (Greenstein 1991).

A writer for *Fortune* magazine claims that the evidence does not prove that past antipoverty programs did more harm than good (Nasar 1986). Finding less starvation in the country in the late 1980s, Smith gives much of the credit to food stamps and to the WIC (Women, Infants, and Children's) programs (Smith 1990a).

A study of four major health programs, Medicaid, Medicare, maternal and child health, and neighborhood health clinics, found that access to health care had been improved for the poor and those families involved with catastrophic illnesses. Further, infant mortality was cut in half from 1968 to 1980, when Medicaid and other health programs were instituted and expanded (Greenstein 1991).

Lester Thurow observes: "While the social welfare expenditures of the late 1960s and early 1970s are often described as a failure, they were, in fact, extremely successful" (Thurow 1980: 159). He adds that this was particularly true among the elderly (also see Harrington 1984: 3; Haveman 1988: 57; Katz 1989: 113).

Treas shows that the growth of public transfers has had a major impact on reducing income disparities for female-headed families and unrelated men and women. This effect has not been found for husband-wife families and men living away from relatives (Treas 1983).

One aspect of the War on Poverty not always remembered is that it inspired volunteers to work with the poor, who themselves may have been changed by the experience. As Schorr points out, gifted and committed people responded to articulated human need (Schorr 1988: 274).

Danziger and Weinberg examined the effects of different antipoverty programs and concluded that even though income-transfer programs were not the major component of the Great Society initiatives, their growth has accounted for the greatest portion of the rise in social spending and is responsible for much of the observed decline in poverty. They concede that they have not promoted greater self-sufficiency among those able to work (Gronbjerg 1987).

A reasonable conclusion is offered by Danziger and Weinberg, namely that antipoverty programs have been reasonably effective in reducing poverty (perhaps "alleviating suffering" would be a better phrase), but have given insufficient attention to problems of structural unemployment, to providing opportunities for the able-bodied poor to earn their way out of poverty (Gronbjerg 1987). They reject the view that antipoverty programs have eroded work incentives as inconsistent with the data (and see chapter 6).

THE ATTACK ON WELFARE

Numerous attacks have been made on public assistance programs (for a summary of these, see Champagne and Harpham 1984; Joe and Rogers 1985). We summarize some of the most frequently heard attacks, leaving the question of welfare dependency to the following chapter.

Several conservatives have suggested that welfare is part of the problem of poverty, rather than part of its solution. The sociologist William Graham Sumner argued that the welfare state was destructive of the family virtues of thrift, self-help, and the will to win (cited in Galbraith 1987: 166). Nathan Glazer lists some deleterious effects of welfare on the behavior of poor families, including out-of-wedlock births, female-headed families, and less labor-market participation (cited in Schram 1991).

Many imply that some welfare might be acceptable, but its expenses have skyrocketed and have gotten "out of hand" (e.g., Hazlitt 1973: 71). Murray speaks of "huge increases" in expenditures (Murray 1984: 63).

Some conservative writers claim that adjusted for inflation, welfare spending at the state, local, and federal levels rose consistently through the 1980s (Rector et al. 1990): this claim is in error, but it reflects widespread public opinion.

Even the liberal Haveman worries that redistributional policies grew from about a quarter to nearly half of federal activities (Haveman 1988: 109). This is misleading, however, in that much of this "redistribution" was in the form of social security, veterans' programs, health services, education, and the like, which are not usually considered a part of "welfare."

It is argued that some families who manage to receive assistance from numerous programs end up with an income higher than the average income for the country (Friedman and Friedman 1979: 108). Gilder claims that the average welfare family of four received close to $18,000 worth of subsidies in 1979, whereas the median income of Americans that year was only $16,500 (Gilder 1981: 111–112). (These claims are incorrect, but they are typical of complaints by conservatives.)

A common argument is that some types of welfare lead people to have more children. Hazlitt speaks of those who have children to go on relief (Hazlitt 1973: 102, 196). Gilder suggests that AFDC offers a guaranteed income to any teenage girl over sixteen who is willing to bear an [out-of wedlock] child (Gilder 1981: 123). Murray suggests that AFDC recipients have children to receive their grant (Murray 1984: 18).

Predictably, one objection heard to welfare is not so much its excessive cost but the power it gives to the government and the resulting bureaucracy. Some argue that social engineering leans too far toward centralized planning (see Atherton 1989). "A vast bureaucracy is largely devoted to shuffling papers rather than to serving people" (Friedman and Friedman 1979: 107). The role of the government in antipoverty legislation will be discussed in chapter 9.

More liberal writers are often critical of welfare as well, though for somewhat different reasons. Ellwood says that welfare requires stepping into an administrative apparatus that seems designed to frustrate, antagonize, and discourage those who are seeking help. Its recipients may have to deal with several different workers, may have long waits, go to different offices, provide documentation, make several trips, etcetera. (Ellwood 1988: 139–140).

Single parents, he says, are often supported by a welfare system that humiliates, stigmatizes, and isolates them (Ellwood 1988: 128). Our welfare system sometimes seems to be the worst of all worlds. It antagonizes, stigmatizes, isolates, and humiliates. It discourages work rather than reinforcing and supporting it (Ellwood 1988: 137). (It should be noted that Ellwood has some thoughtful proposals for replacing welfare.)

THE DEFENSE OF WELFARE

The image promulgated by many conservatives, that our country has a massive welfare state with billions of dollars flowing to indigent people, most of whom refuse to work, does not square with the facts. Most of the expensive items are either entitlement programs or programs about which there is general consensus; they hardly qualify as "welfare" in the usual sense.

The bulk of expenditures flows to veterans and the elderly, not the families on welfare and food stamps (Lekachman 1982: 80). The lion's share of the money goes to social security, employment-related benefits, and medical protection, and most of these people are elderly or disabled (Ellwood 1988: 40–41).

Kuttner argues cogently that ours isn't a "welfare state"; it's a "social security state" or a "military state." Here we haven't achieved even the basic protections to health and to child welfare, nor help for job seekers, that most Westerners call a "welfare state" (cited in Lappé 1989: 60). "Government intervention in the economy does not a welfare state make" (Gans 1981).

Actually, the United States could be called a "welfare laggard." In the postwar era, the United States consistently devoted a lower proportion of its GNP to social welfare spending than other capitalist democracies. By international standards U.S. levels of public assistance and incidence of coverage are quite low (Devine and Canak 1986; Morris and Williamson 1987). Beeghley goes so far as to say that public assistance does not cost very much money when it is compared to the total federal budget, to outlays for social insurance, and to expenditures for other income maintenance programs, nearly all of which go to benefit the nonpoor (Beeghley 1983: 11).

Expenditures for public aid are less than 9 percent of the federal budget. The poor do not receive any of the money spent on Medicaid, the most expensive program by far (the funds go to the medical industry). It is a similar picture with housing subsidies (Beeghley 1983: 42).

Ellwood himself defends the concept of something like welfare. He notes that helping is motivated by a sense of compassion and a desire for fairness. People sense that our economy does not always provide for everyone who is willing to participate and that accidents of birth and nature leave some people in a weak position to compete (Ellwood 1988: 15).

He also shows that our current welfare system gives virtually nothing to poor single individuals and childless couples. It provides only slightly more to poor two-parent families, and offers more (though still far less than enough to avoid poverty) to single-parent families. Surely a system that allows children and their mothers to escape an unhappy, destructive, or even dangerous family environment can be beneficial to the individuals and to society (Ellwood 1988: 21–22).

Most defenses of welfare have underscored the good the programs have done. Relief and welfare programs do relieve pain caused by economic deprivation; they do not bring people out of poverty, because the causes are social. Transfer payments have played a critical role in softening the blow of recent economic recessions (Smith 1987). And as Katz points out, "Without the minimal safety net that exists, hunger, homelessness, infant mortality, and disease would be catastrophes unimaginable to most Americans" (Katz 1989: 4).

Social consumption expenditures (education, housing, essential services) arguably enhance human capital via increasing education, better and more affordable housing, improved sanitation, health care, and the like (Devine and Canak 1986).

Galbraith describes the welfare state as having a modest stabilizing effect. Unemployment compensation acted as a compensatory force against economic contraction and unemployment. Other welfare expenditures cushioned and secured the flow of purchasing power (Galbraith 1987: 257).

Peter Edelman correctly shows that the poor would be still worse off without such programs as social security, AFDC, Medicaid, and food stamps. "The government's specific efforts to alleviate poverty have not been counterproductive, only gravely insufficient" (quoted in Schorr 1988: xxv).

Food stamps have been described as a program that has worked: hunger is a much rarer phenomenon because of it, even though the maximum benefit is low (Lekachman 1982). Even its critics admit the program has helped feed tens of millions of Americans. It has contributed to a dramatic improvement in nutrition (Greenstein 1991). The program has been described as one of the most flexible and efficient means of helping the poor, and it would work a definite hardship on the most needy if cut (Amidei 1981).

In defending AFDC, Dear points out that it directs benefits to families with the highest risk of poverty and for whom there is no visible income alternative. It provides money to millions of needy people, removing a sizable amount of its families from poverty. Its recipients often qualify for other benefits such as medical care, surplus food, and housing allowances. It has high target efficiency, allows children to remain in their own homes, and recipients can spend the cash benefits as they wish (Dear 1989).

The argument that AFDC leads women to have children has been examined by many investigators and largely dismissed. An important recent study in Wisconsin found that women on welfare have a substantially *lower* fertility rate than women in the general population. The longer a woman remains on welfare, the less likely she is to give birth. "The economic, social, and psychological situation that women on welfare find themselves in is simply not conducive to desiring more children" (Rank 1989). Ellwood and Bane conclude that high benefits have no effect on the decision to have a baby. Welfare certainly couldn't have caused the black family patterns that W.E.B. DuBois noted in Philadelphia in 1899 (Kaus 1986; Nasar 1986).

The growth in benefits and the growth in recipients stopped in 1972. There is no doubt that the disposable income available to welfare mothers fell consistently between 1972 and 1984. Yet the number of children on AFDC actually fell by over a half million in this period (Elwood 1988: 59).

There is a suggestion of a link between welfare and child-bearing reported by Plotnick. He says that welfare policy appears to have been related to out-of-wedlock childbearing by black and white adolescents during the early 1980s. (There was no relation for Hispanics.) He correctly points out that other recent and empirical work has not uncovered evidence of a link, and adds that the evidence is not strong enough to make this conclusion fully compelling (Plotnick 1990).

Another study does concede that women living in states with higher AFDC benefits are more likely to have had children out of wedlock, though this falls short of .10 significance (and see contrary views below). The researchers add that although economic incentives do matter, they appear to have had a relatively small effect on the choices made by black women who were teenagers in the 1970s (Duncan and Hoffman 1991).

State-by-state comparisons show no evidence that AFDC influences childbearing decisions. Sex and childbearing among teenagers do not seem to be a product of careful economic analysis. We now know that the availability of income support through AFDC can be ruled out as a determinant of unmarried and teenage childbearing (Schorr 1988: xxv, 61). Even Gilder—in a footnote—cites a study that revealed no consistent causal link between welfare and family breakdown (Gilder 1981: 278).

The purchasing power of AFDC plus food stamps did rise between 1964 and 1976, but out-of-wedlock births hardly increased at all. The number of out-of-wedlock births did rise after 1975, but by then real AFDC benefits were falling. Nor do unmarried women in high-benefit states have appreciably more babies than those in low-benefit states (Jencks 1991: 90; Kaus 1986; Duncan and Hoffman 1991).

Keefe found that increases in welfare benefits in California did not produce increases in fertility, even when the benefits for additional children rose. The amount of extra benefits given to a welfare family if it has one more child does not affect the probability that such a child will be born to a woman in the AFDC program (Keefe 1983). A family-assistance program in Canada did not raise the birthrate, and in fact it came down (Gans 1971).

The least appealing way to discourage the formation of single-parent families is to make life worse for single parents. Such a policy is of questionable effectiveness and may harm some of the neediest families and children (Ellwood 1988: 78).

One study found that a reduction in welfare benefits would result in only a small reduction in the proportion of female-headed families (Danziger et al. 1982). An earlier study found that women who were receiving public assistance were not more likely to have early births. There is no difference in fertility behavior and reception of welfare aid. Generally, public assistance is seen as the result of early fertility rather than the cause (Presser and Salsberg 1975).

Nichols-Casebolt (1988) claims that neither welfare nor changing family structure adequately explains the rise in the numbers of black single-parent families and their impoverishment. A literature review by Garfinkel and McLanahan of empirical studies of the impact of welfare found that increasing welfare benefits account for only one-tenth to one-seventh of the total growth in mother-headed families (Nichols-Casebolt 1988). (Economic and structural trends reviewed in chapter 3 go further toward explaining this phenomenon.)

Countries with far more generous social welfare programs than the United States—Germany, Denmark, France, Sweden, and Great Britain—all have sharply lower rates of teenage births and teenage crime (Schorr 1988: xxv).

The evidence is clear that increases in female-headed families, especially among blacks, cannot be adequately explained by the effects of income-assistance programs, but result from structural unemployment (Danziger and Weinberg, cited in Gronbjerg 1987).

A Reagan administration report on the family acknowledged that "statistical evidence does not confirm those suppositions" that welfare is responsible for the high illegitimacy rates in some minority groups (Ellwood 1988: 4). There is a wealth of statistical evidence that the receipt of welfare does not have much of an impact on the structure of families. No highly regarded scholar has indicated that welfare has played more than a minor role in the changing patterns of families overall (Ellwood 1988: 23, 57).

Wilson cites three studies that show very little or no difference between illegitimacy rates and benefit levels (Wilson 1987: 78). One study that found that when women were on welfare they were less likely to desire an additional pregnancy, and less likely to become pregnant. Other studies report that women on public assistance desire fewer children than women not on assistance, and were less likely to have planned their first birth (Wilson 1987: 78–79).

Haveman believes that welfare benefits have played a trivial role in causing intact families to split or never-married women to have children. He shows that the impact of the welfare system is far weaker than some have asserted. There are a number of more basic causes of these troubling changes in family patterns than welfare programs and benefits: such things as women having children at a very young age, independent women, jobless black males, and changing attitudes about marriage and parenthood (Haveman 1988: 77, 136).

Wilson's conclusion would appear to be well grounded in empirical data: "Contrary to popular opinion, there is little evidence to provide a strong case for welfare as the primary cause of family breakups, female-headed households, and out-of-wedlock births" (Wilson 1987: 90).

Another program about which comments have been favorable is Women, Infants, and Children's formula (WIC), which has proven to be cost-effective (Beeghley 1983: 63). This provides milk, infant formula, cheese, eggs, juice, cereal, beans, and other protein to low-income women and children under age five. More than twice as many met the requirements to participate as can be served with the funds appropriated. A comprehensive evaluation of WIC over a five-year period found unequivocally that WIC had made impressive contributions to women's and children's health (Schorr 1988: 128–129).

In addition to WIC, Schorr itemizes three federal programs that stand out as successes in improving maternal and child health over the last two decades: Medicaid, Early and Periodic Screening, Diagnosis and Treatment program, and federal support of neighborhood health centers and maternal and child health clinics (Schorr 198: 124).

Head Start, the program for disadvantaged children, has won praises from almost all quarters. It has helped poor children and their families to overcome physical, intellectual, and social impediments to a successful start at school (Schorr 1988: 184). The long-term effects of Head Start and other preschool programs on participating children and their families are today better documented than any of the other interventions discussed by Schorr (1988: 191). "Study after study demonstrates that Head Start by and large does what it was designed to do," though it serves only 10 percent of today's eligible children (Henkoff 1990).

What is often overlooked is the extent to which many of these programs have been cut over the years. (For a good review of the cuts in the Reagan administration, see Joe and Rogers 1985). And in addition to actual cuts, welfare expenditures have not kept pace with the needs of the poor; that is, they have declined relative to need (Schram 1991).

Reagan's social program cuts fell most heavily on the poor. Programs affecting them declined by 9.3 percent a year from 1981 to 1983 (Abramovitz 1983). Cuts in human resources programs reduced federal expenditures over the 1982–1986 period by over $100 billion, or about 5 percent a year, falling primarily on those who had least (Haveman 1988: 21). The attempt to shift responsibility for certain welfare programs back to state and local governments largely failed (Levitan 1985: 20).

Assuming that even low-wage employment by itself is sufficient to raise even large families out of poverty, the Reagan administration returned to sharp distinctions between the "truly needy" who cannot work and the "undeserving" poor who are presumably employable and capable of self-support. Financial incentives for welfare recipients to work were sharply reduced and in some cases eliminated, and assistance to the working poor with some earnings was cut dramatically. Thus low-income Americans were forced to make no-win choices between employment and dependency, a situation that contributed to the travails of the working poor (Levitan 1985: 19).

Cuts in AFDC have already been mentioned. An estimated 370,000 to 507,000 families were removed, most of whom were the working poor (Burghardt and Fabricant 1987: 94). Estimated average disposable income of working AFDC families (including earnings, benefits, and food stamps) for the nation declined from 101 percent of the poverty line to 81 percent (Joe, cited in Wilson 1987: 106).

Inflation-adjusted median AFDC benefit level for a family of three fell by 39 percent between 1970 and 1990. Reductions in food stamp benefits, housing assistance, and other in-kind assistance further hurt poor families with children (Johnson 1991: 21–22; Haveman 1988: 77). In 1973, 80 percent of children living in poverty were covered by AFDC; by 1988, this fell to 58 percent (Rubiner and Fowler 1991).

A study by the Government Accounting Office estimated that between 400,000 and 500,000 families were eliminated from the AFDC rolls due to the 1981 program changes. This represented a substantial loss of income that they did not make up by increased earnings or other means. The average monthly income loss for working single-parent families who lost AFDC eligibility was $186 in Memphis, $229 in Dallas, $180 in Milwaukee.

In the 1980s, over $12 billion was cut from school meals and food stamps alone (Brown 1988). From 1981 to 1984, it was estimated that overall, cash welfare benefits declined by 17 percent. These cuts eliminated one million people from food-stamp coverage. SSDI cuts affected 450,000 recipients (Burghardt and Fabricant 1987: 17; Howell 1988: 38). And in the 1990s, many state budget cuts have been aimed at the poorest of the poor (Taylor 1991).

It will be recalled from chapter 1 that the idea that all poor people receive practically every available benefit is unwarranted. There are many reasons needy individuals and families may not know of aid, may not qualify, or may have too much pride to seek it.

Stringent property limitations have been established for those who seek public assistance. A welfare family may possess no more than $1,000 in personal property exclusive of a home and car. And there are wide variations in the amount of aid from state to state. Those who do receive aid are maintained below the levels society otherwise deems minimally adequate (Schiller 1984: 167–168).

Social consumption expenditures (education, housing, essential services) arguably enhance human capital via increased education, better and more affordable housing, improved sanitation and health care, and the like. It is true that direct income more likely accrues to provider groups rather than the poor (Kluegal 1987).

Economist Nicholas Barr has given what has been called a rational, well-thought-out analysis of public assistance. He says that welfare-state programs are needed to correct for inequities and inefficiencies inherent in market economics. The welfare state, he argues, can achieve both social justice and efficiency (DeViney 1988).

A final controversy involves fraud and misuse. Welfare programs have been called a "mess" saturated with fraud and corruption (Friedman and Friedman 1979: 96, 107). Substantial cheating by welfare recipients, for example failure to report income from other sources, has been charged (Hazlitt 1973: 100).

Some chiseling is unavoidable under any tax or transfer system. There is some evidence that the concern may be misplaced. In New York City, in an experiment undertaken at thirty-seven Welfare Centers, applicants made declarations of need and were not subject to investigation. A 10 percent sample was then given the traditional investigation. A year's experience showed that 2.7 percent of new cases were found to be ineligible according to Bruno Stein (cited in Walch 1973: 44).

Back in 1966, the state of Arizona appropriated as much money to ferret out the alleged chiselers on the welfare rolls as it had appropriated for all the staff and services in Maricopa County where 50 percent of the poor people live. They discovered that only 2 percent of the total number on the welfare rolls were in any way guilty of anything that could be called chiseling (Walch 1973: 38).

In 1971, Senator Abraham Ribicoff reported that cheaters constituted less than 1 percent and loafers less than 5 percent of the public assistance rolls. This concern, he argued, ignores the real and legitimate needs of at least 95 percent on welfare through no fault or failing of their own (Walch 1973: 388). A recent estimate puts food stamp fraud at 1.5 percent (Spolar 1991).

Nearly all the fraud in these programs is white-collar crime committed by relatively affluent people who have the skills and opportunity to engage in it. Paupers (Beeghley's term for welfare recipients) generally have neither of these traits. With their low education, they are rarely capable of committing fraud on a large scale. In any year, less than one percent of all AFDC cases will involve suspected fraud and a much smaller proportion will be proven guilty (Beeghley 1983: 8, 70).

Indigent people cannot embezzle money, construct unsafe automobiles, fix prices, or use computers to abscond with bank deposits. (Nor, we might add, are they responsible for savings and loan disasters.) Crimes caused by white-collar people are more dangerous and more costly than street crimes (Beeghley 1983: 100, 105). Underpaying income taxes is often considered a challenge, not welfare fraud, although the dollar amounts lost to the government must be considerably higher (Abramovitz 1983).

Of course some people have manipulated the food stamp system, for example, to their advantage; this will occur in any public or private activity. Undoubtedly some fraud has gone on with respect to church and other charitable relief efforts, but few would suggest that this nullifies the good they are doing.

Finally, the extent to which welfare assistance helps the nonpoor should not be overlooked. We have just noted that the providers of such things as housing and health care receive much of "welfare" money. Social security payments to the well-to-do exceed the total volume of welfare expenditures to the poor (Haveman 1988: 160). The notion that the poor get something for nothing while other segments of the population do not is inaccurate (Beeghley 1983: 45). The beneficiaries of the welfare state are primarily the lower middle class and working class (Atherton 1989).

There is a history of government policies that moves income and wealth toward the "haves" of society—depletion allowances, water subsidies, trade and tariff restrictions, and the like (Haveman 1988: 104). While social welfare programs are popularly regarded as serving only the poor, they not only assist the nonpoor, but, with respect to dollars spent, benefit levels, and survival of programs, upper-income groups fare best with social welfare programs (Abramovitz 1983).

The government aids private homeowners through deductions for property taxes, mortgage interest, and special tax rates on capital gains for sales of homes. Scholarship income, tax exemptions for parents of college students, and tax deductions for child care for working parents are examples (Abramovitz 1983).

Those opposed to government income transfers, says Thurow, have little reason to complain since the distribution of income has not been made more unequal. The rich are as rich as ever (Thurow 1980: 156). Thurow goes on to predict (accurately, so far) a more unequal distribution of family income in the 1980s and 1990s. Some of the ways that antipoverty efforts are valuable to the society as a whole will be discussed in chapter 10.

CONCLUSION

This defense of public assistance should not imply that this is the best system to deal with poverty in this country. In fact, some of the criticisms, especially from liberal quarters, have some point. Many of the programs provide bare subsistence, without offering the opportunity to get out of poverty. What we can conclude is that further cuts in the already stingy welfare benefits would do far more harm than good, unless the programs are replaced with something more comprehensive and humane. In chapter 8 we consider proposed solutions to the problem of poverty in this country, including those that would replace welfare altogether.

6

Welfare Dependency

The classic argument against welfare is that it stifles incentive and leads
to dependency, a complaint heard so frequently that we devote an entire
chapter to it. The claim is that people who receive public assistance have
an incentive to remain on relief in order to retain their aid and they have
worked less as a result (see Beeghley 1983: 7).

It is argued that welfare programs reduce the incentive to hold on to an
old job or to find a new one (Hazlitt 1973: 90–91). "Those on relief have
little incentive to earn income," and their incentive to save and innovate
is reduced (Friedman and Friedman 1979: 107, 127). Gilder claims the
programs have a dramatic negative impact on motivation and self-reliance
(Gilder 1981: 112). Some say that welfare spending seriously diminishes
work effort and earned income, and makes families more dependent on
welfare (Rector et al. 1990).

Hyde (1990) claimed that the government has encouraged poverty in
our cities by rewarding poverty more than work. Kaus (1992) argues that
"without welfare, those left behind in the ghetto would have had to move
to where the jobs were."

Conservatives worry that permanent dependence will undermine incentives for self-support. This is likely to happen, it is claimed, whenever we
offer an able-bodied adult in charity or relief more than or even as much
as he could earn by working. A relief program that tries to provide more
than subsistence will in the end do more harm than good to the whole
community (Hazlitt 1973: 39).

In a well-known study on spells of poverty, Bane and Ellwood (1986) found that most of the people helped by programs to aid the economically disadvantaged use them only briefly. But the bulk of resources almost certainly go to a much smaller group of people who have very long stays in poverty. More than one-half of all persons observed to be poor at any given point are in the midst of spells that last eight years or more (Corcoran et al. 1985; Kane 1987; Wilson 1987: 10).

Wilson points out that the average poor black child appears to be in the midst of a poverty spell which will last for almost two decades (Wilson 1987: 10). Note that these observations do not necessarily establish dependency in the sense conservatives stress, but they do indicate that there is a sizable number of long-term poor, many of whom receive welfare.

Mead writes, "Policy-makers have not really solved poverty, only exchanged it for the problem of large-scale dependency" (Mead 1986). He believes economic independence is of paramount importance. The reason government has refused to give more to the current poor, says Mead, is because few people now believe that doing so would help them, not because no one cares (Mead 1989). Murray speaks of "forces (welfare) that encourage them to remain poor and dependent" (Murray 1984: 233).

A work by Richard E. Wagner argues that the present form of the welfare state fosters dependence and servility. We should either abandon the welfare state or privatize welfare (Wagner 1989: 196). Murray proposes that we scrap the entire federal welfare and income-support structure for working-age persons. This would leave no recourse except the job market, family, and private services (Murray 1984: 227–228). He claims that relief from the state would undermine incentives to industry, frugality, and self-support. It also undermines the incentives of the working population through the taxes it levies (Hazlitt 1973: 83–84).

People's capacity for independence, for making their own decisions, atrophies through disuse. In the absence of welfare programs, many of those now dependent on them would have become self-reliant individuals instead of wards of the state. "Once people get on relief, it is hard to get off" (Friedman and Friedman 1979: 107, 119).

The government dole, according to this line of reasoning, blights most of the people who come to depend on it. It leads to a plague of family dissolution (Gilder 1981: 12). The poor choose leisure not because of moral weakness, but because they are paid to do so (Gilder 1981: 68). In a striking sentence, Gilder argues, "in order to succeed, the poor need most of all the spur of their poverty" (Gilder 1981: 118).

One writer speaks of the "corrosive effect of the social-democratic welfare state, whose very benefits, when 'delivered' to atomized individuals, obviate the need for family, church, trade union, community" (Katz 1990). He suggests that the poor can consume and watch television while the welfare state takes care of everything and everybody. Herbert Gans's response to Katz will be summarized later in this chapter.

Segalman and Basu (1981) take the position that AFDC creates dependency and disincentives. Murray (1984: 18–19) suggests that changing incentives through AFDC has encouraged dependency. AFDC makes more families dependent and fatherless (Gilder 1981: 111). Another suggesting that AFDC creates dependency is Bernstein (1986: 41–42).

Gilder is impressed with AFDC reforms instituted in the state of California. In a determined effort to enforce work and child support rules, Governor Reagan's measures were hailed a success by many. Over a period of two years costs were controlled and the rolls were reduced by 400,000 below previous levels. But reformers "set the whole new structure on fire" by agreeing to index the benefits to the rate of inflation and raising grants for families certified to be truly needy by 43 percent (Gilder 1981: 119–121).

Some support for dependency is provided by Gottschalk (1990), who found that the probability of having a child and receiving assistance is substantially higher if the parent did participate in AFDC. (Gottschalk does not argue for cutting AFDC.) Bould (1977), though not fully supporting the dependency argument, did find that women who must depend upon AFDC and other stigmatizing or unstable sources of income feel least able to plan for their lives.

A recent study found that the longer a woman has been on AFDC the lower her score on the efficacy scale (a belief in capabilities to mobilize the motivation, resources, and courses of action to control task demands). About one-third said they believe that AFDC makes it hard for them personally to become self-supporting. The longer they receive benefits, the less efficacious they became (Popkin 1990). However, Popkin appears to favor more benefits rather than less.

Hughes says bluntly, "An out-of-wedlock birth to a young mother is a direct path to long-term poverty and welfare dependency" (Hughes 1990). This is much more true, he says, for never-married than for divorced mothers. Smith, although she does not stress dependency, does say that both women without partners and married women have had to exchange their dependency on men for dependency on the state (Smith 1987).

THE ARGUMENT AGAINST DEPENDENCY

The arguments summarized above have not gone uncontested. The widely cited work by Bane and Ellwood (1986), while it did acknowledge a large number of persons in long-term poverty, also found that most of those who ever become poor will have only a short stay in poverty. Their research suggested that most of those helped by programs to aid the economically disadvantaged use them only briefly.

In the past, most welfare recipients (between 75 percent and 90 percent) have either received assistance for a relatively short time or used public aid as a means of supplementing their low incomes. For most of these people, wages provide the largest share of the income they receive over the long run. Only a small minority have given up (Beeghley 1983: 11). Conover calls welfare dependency a "myth" (Conover 1989).

"A consistently smaller proportion of Americans in poverty are persistently poor, year in and year out, than the poverty statistics imply" (Wilson 1987: 175). Coe found only 1 percent of the population to be poor throughout the time span (nine years), and Hill only 3 percent over ten years (cited in Wilson 1987: 175). Only a small segment of the population remains poor and dependent on welfare for long periods of time. These are frequently the poorly educated, aged, black, female, or residents of an inner city (Levitan 1985: 7).

Hill and Ponza, using a fourteen-year segment of the Michigan Panel Study of Income Dynamics, found "a great deal of income mobility from one generation to the next, even among the poorest households. The data revealed a very limited form of intergenerational transmission of long-term welfare dependency among whites and none among blacks" (Hill and Ponza 1983: 64).

Reporting on the same data, Corcoran and colleagues agreed that the data show generally weak links between the poverty or welfare status of parents and that of their children. They also believe that we can devise public policies for dealing with poverty without undue concern that poverty programs will generate dependency among the majority of those they help (Corcoran et al. 1985).

There was substantial upward mobility among young adults from poor families. Only one in five individuals who were at or near the poverty line as children was at or near the poverty line after leaving home. There was substantial economic mobility even among young adults from the very poorest of the poor families (Corcoran et al. 1985).

One-quarter of the children were raised in families that received welfare at some point, but only 4 percent of those families had received more than half of their income from welfare during the period in which the child lived at home. Thus long-term welfare dependency was a rare experience for children (Corcoran et al. 1985). Interestingly, if there was a slight suggestion of dependency, it was more likely to be among whites than blacks.

Sidel claims that substantial evidence shows that the issue of dependency has been exaggerated. The University of Michigan Institute of Social Research found that in half the cases in which welfare was utilized, it was to dig out following a major crisis. The process generally ends with a new foothold in security. Others are using welfare to supplement income from other sources. Less than 20 percent of welfare recipients seem to be chronically dependent on the system (Sidel 1986: 98). Most adult children from welfare families were not receiving welfare themselves, and most of the adults who were receiving welfare income did not come from welfare households (Joe and Rogers 1985: 24).

Similarly, Kemper reports that all but about 15 percent of the people who endure the social stigma and personal humiliation of applying for welfare benefits do so only as a last resort or a stop-gap measure to tide them over between jobs. Most families, she says, leave the welfare rolls within two years (Kemper 1988).

In arguing against Mead's ideas about dependence, Sosin mentions studies that fail to find correlations between attitudes signifying welfare dependency and later employment and that thus question the importance of alleged dependency in unemployment (Sosin 1987a).

Schram finds an inverse relationship between welfare spending and "dependent" poverty in recent years, the antithesis of what dependency theorists have argued. When expenditures in this period declined, especially relative to need, the "pre-welfare" (dependent) poverty rate increased markedly. "Dependent" poverty increased when expenditures fell relative to need, not when they grew. "Our analysis suggests that the trend data no longer, if ever, supported the dependency argument" (Schram 1991).

Several measures fail to indicate a significant relationship between spending and poverty, especially not with "dependent" poverty. A statistical analysis indicates that welfare spending and benefits can not be singled out as primary factors in creating more welfare dependency and thereby more poverty (Schram and Wilkin 1989).

In response to Katz's complaint that the welfare state has such negative consequences, Gans replies that he has never seen any reliable evidence of these effects. There is a good deal of historical and other evidence that poverty is responsible for the kinds of effects Katz blames on the welfare state, for when people are involved in a battle for survival, it loosens their "sense of responsibility for and to each other," and also "breeds individual narcissism and callousness." Families are breaking down because of poverty, not welfare (Gans 1990).

There may be some support for welfare dependency if this means that some poor people perceive themselves as helpless. Careful studies suggest that it is likely that the descriptions of dependency really indicate depression and low self-esteem. Descriptions by experts note these problems strike the unemployed, those living doubled up with relatives, those who neither work nor obtain government benefits (such as the homeless), and some of the poor elderly as well as AFDC recipients. Such psychological problems can hardly be traced to welfare (Sosin 1987a).

Though it has been suggested that work efforts are reduced when unemployment benefits are higher, there is no solid support for this. Unemployment is not higher where benefits are higher. Several countries with benefits much higher than in the United States have had lower unemployment. In Austria, laid-off workers get 80 percent of their previous pay for at least a year, but the jobless rate there has been half of ours for many years (Lappé 1989: 51).

A study by Fred Black found no evidence that welfare benefits have discouraged work. Labor force participation grew rapidly during the same period that social welfare benefits expanded. By increasing purchasing power and human capital, investments in social welfare will increase more wealth than they consume (cited in Katz 1989: 174).

A reviewer of Mead's work concedes his claim that individuals work less when welfare is more readily available. But the difference in work effort is relatively small and indicates a problem, not a crisis that explains unemployment. The bulk of existing evidence suggests that only a minority of individuals even temporarily rely on unemployment compensation when other jobs are available and that this group includes higher earners more often than lower, as well as those bringing in a second income more than primary earners (Sosin 1987a).

Kaus's claim that "without welfare, those left behind in the ghetto would have had to move to where the jobs were" (Kaus 1992) seems most simplistic. It implies that subsisting on the minimal benefits provided by welfare, in a deteriorating environment, is a fully satisfactory situation for these people. How easy is it for a poor person in the ghetto to move to a more advantaged area? Would not that person face discrimination as a poor person and often as a member of a minority? And could that person compete with the established middle-class for a reducing number of jobs?

The real value of most welfare benefits has fallen significantly in the last twenty years or so (Duncan and Hoffman 1991; Schram 1991;

Greenstone 1991). (Chapter 5 summarized the cuts made in welfare payments.) This is in sharp contrast to the conservative view that the absolute reward for such behavior has increased.

As Schiller says, very few welfare families are even tolerably comfortable, much less riding high. (Their situation has become even worse since Schiller wrote.) It would be a strange individual who forsook any but the poorest paying and most loathsome job for such a "free ride" (Schiller 1984: 167).

Thought should be given to the likely consequences of further cuts in assistance programs. "Depriving poor people of needed income does much to retard their ability to acquire needed resources and impede their efforts to create the conditions under which they might be able to put their lives on a better footing and begin the process of lifting themselves out of poverty" (Schram 1991). Less, not more, welfare creates dependency. Sarri and Russell describe a considerable health and financial burden on families who were victims of welfare termination in Michigan and Georgia (Elesh 1990).

Countless studies conclude that the antipoverty impact of government transfer programs is significantly greater than the antipoverty impact of dependency-reduction programs. There is no strong empirical evidence demonstrating that transfer programs have a long-term impact on self-sufficiency (Morris and Williamson 1987).

Social spending has been more effective than economic growth in reducing poverty, and the positive antipoverty effects of social spending have far outweighed its relatively modest negative work and family effects. These researchers stress the need for more economic growth, indicate economic growth itself is not enough to eradicate poverty, and that cutbacks in income transfers focused on the poor will only increase poverty (Schram et al. 1988). Further conclusions from this work include: Poverty rates are more tied to unemployment than to benefit levels; reductions in work effort attributable to increases in benefits are insufficient to account for work declines among the poor; and stable poverty levels over the last decade or so are largely a product of a stagnant economy (Schram et al. 1988).

Maximum benefits have been found to be significantly but negatively related to child poverty. High benefit states tend to have a relatively lower proportion of their children in poverty than low-benefit states. By using median income instead of per capita income (which these researchers consider more appropriate), they find no relationship between benefits and poverty (Schram et al. 1988).

There has been considerable research on the alleged dependency impact of AFDC. A consensus seems to have emerged that such effects are slight. Only about 10 percent of all AFDC recipients are long-term recipients; most use the assistance for less than three years, and most eventually become self-supporting (Beeghley 1983: 82). The longer a woman remains on welfare, the more likely that employment will lead to exiting from public assistance (Rank 1988).

In an excellent, longitudinal study of adolescent mothers, Furstenberg and colleagues (1987) found that most teenage mothers do not become chronic welfare recipients, and no more than a fourth of women who receive public assistance become welfare dependent. No direct path from welfare as a child to welfare at the seventeen-year follow-up was found. This challenges the notion that once on the rolls, even as a child, one develops a predilection to dependency that is not shaken by periods of economic independence (Furstenberg et al. 1987: 40, 61).

A study of child poverty found that the poverty rate for children grew between 1969 and 1983 but the real value of AFDC benefits fell by one-third; they declined in real value in all states but Maine (Schram et al. 1988).

Jimy Sanders reviewed the literature on whether AFDC promotes the growth of poverty and reduces the incentive to work. Using data for states from 1959 to 1980, she finds no negative consequences for AFDC during the 1960s and statistically significant but substantially insignificant effects during the 1970s (see Elesh 1990).

Working black women who have children under five years of age worked more hours per week (37.3) than any other category of female householders, according to one report. So the welfare allotment does not seem to create dependency. Women have a long, hard struggle for daily survival that is neither caused nor intensified by welfare dependency (Burghardt and Fabricant 1987: 99).

As Schorr explains, it is almost impossible to help poor children without helping their families, yet we worry that support to young families will rob them of their incentive to work and sap their motivation. But careful research has shown that public assistance has not had this effect, and many kinds of support have just the opposite effect (Schorr 1988: xxvi).

Most studies show little, if any, effect of welfare assistance on willingness to work. The income loss to a young woman who has a child out of wedlock or does not finish high school has actually increased in recent years (Peterson 1991). Welfare dependency has not increased since the early 1970s, and illiteracy, teenage motherhood, and violence have declined somewhat (Jencks 1991: 96).

One study suggests that a dollar of AFDC income is valued far less than a dollar of a woman's own earnings or the earnings of her spouse (Duncan and Hoffman 1991). Having a job is still a measure of status in America for the non-student, non-retired person.

Beeghley reports how from 1965 to 1980 recipients were able to combine low-wage work and assistance. Reducing aid on a graduated scale depending on income, child care needs, job expenses, and the like often avoided forcing households to choose between assistance and employment when they had a chance to increase their wages. Then in the early 1980s the size of the pauper population was restricted by eliminating various deductions from gross income. The result is that low-wage workers are now often forced to choose between public aid and employment: nearly all have chosen the latter (Beeghley 1983: 7).

Breaking the cycle of dependency by making it more difficult for mothers to receive aid will not solve the child's problem. In fact, if lack of income is the cause of the intergenerational correlation in welfare participation, then higher benefits or additional programs to raise the earnings capacity of the children may lower the correlation (Gottschalk 1990).

Raising AFDC payments will increase resources available for human capital development, which may lessen the need for assistance in the next generation. Raising family income through the tax system, or other alternatives to welfare, will make more resources available to the family without inducing future participation by the child (Gottschalk 1990).

Proposed solutions to child poverty, such as a family allowance and other proposals that would eliminate AFDC, will be discussed in chapter 8.

CONCLUSION

We are not arguing that in no cases does some dependency occur among some welfare recipients. But the weight of evidence seems to say that such dependency occurs in only a minority of cases and is much less significant than is usually claimed. In fact, the argument that a decrease in assistance leads to more dependent poverty (made by Schram and others) seems strong.

In discussing the culture of poverty, we granted that something like that might exist for a minority of the poor, but argued that it was a result and not a cause of their plight. In a similar way, while there may be a relatively small number who have become dependent on public assistance, their situation is a consequence of their overall deprived condition, not simply a result of assistance per se.

The thinking behind many dependency arguments seems to go like this: there are many people who live in an area where self-support is highly feasible, either in terms of available, well-paid jobs or an overall climate that encourages financial enterprise in some form. Positive role models are readily available; schools provide positive encouragement; some capital (if needed) is available in the form of grants or loans; and overall conditions are conducive to self-support. But because welfare is also available as an easier alternative, many choose this route and soon find that their "incentive" has been destroyed and they have become "dependent" on welfare. If assistance would be eliminated, such people would quickly move into independent positions.

But the assumptions in the preceding paragraph are rarely if ever borne out in reality. And in the cases where dependency may be a fact, the circumstances in these people's lives are very nearly the opposite of those suggested above. Those who have become dependent on welfare, apparently a small percentage of all those receiving it, are likely to lead lives of desperation and futility. Cutting or eliminating their benefits would have only a negative effect on their situation.

Ellwood appears to grant a type of dependency when he says, "When you give people money, food, or housing, you reduce the pressure on them to work and care for themselves" (Ellwood 1988: 19). The question seems to be whether this is a major element of the system which constitutes a fatal flaw, as many conservatives argue, or an unavoidable by-product that does not negate the overall benefits. The evidence strongly supports the latter conclusion.

Further, why is dependency on public assistance more debilitating than other types of dependency? All children are dependent, but do they necessarily learn lifetime dependency from the experience? If a young man is supported by a wealthy parent and never seeks employment, is he not "dependent" on his parent's income? Is not a fifty-five-year old retired businessman "dependent" on his pension fund?

Historian Arthur M. Schlesinger has an interesting comment on Gilder's assertion that the poor need most of all the spur of their own poverty. He writes:

The argument that economic security saps initiative is one the well-off apply to the poor rather more than to themselves. If the rich really believed in the salubrious effects of economic insecurity, they would favor a 100 percent inheritance tax so that their own children would not be denied this great moral benefit. Instead, the Reagan tax law cut federal inheritance taxes in half. By the Reaganite creed, the poor need the spur of poverty in order to succeed, and the rich the spur of wealth. (Schlesinger 1986: 248)

7

Workfare

The popular image of welfare "loafers" has led to a strong movement for requiring work of all employable persons who receive assistance. Since relatively few able-bodied males receive much assistance, emphasis has been placed on "welfare mothers," that is, female recipients of AFDC. Would it help if such people were encouraged or even required to accept paying jobs outside the home? This chapter discusses this sometimes emotional controversy, beginning with a brief history of AFDC.

Designers of the Social Security Act recognized that insurance benefits earned through prior work could not meet all economic and social needs, so they created Aid to Dependent Children (ADC, now AFDC), federal funds for cash payments to children. The basic AFDC is limited to families in which a child is deprived of parental care or support because of the death, disability, or continued absence from the home of a parent (Binford et al. 1990: 26). As of 1981, the program was permitted to apply to families with unemployed fathers.

In 1975 the Earned Income Tax Credit sought to assist low-wage workers. Those with children and receiving less than a specified amount (in 1988, the limit was $19,340 a year) got a tax credit (in 1989, the maximum credit was $910) (Binford et al. 1990: 16–17). In 1977 the Carter administration proposed a jobs-creation program, but it was defeated by Congress.

Since the mid-1970s, the AFDC grant has been rapidly devalued. It is the only federal cash-assistance program not indexed to keep pace with inflation. Eligibility and benefit levels vary greatly among the states, and are very low in several (in Texas, for example, the grant is $184 for a woman with two children). Even when combined with food stamps, the combined value remains below the poverty level in all states but Alaska (Joe and Rogers 1985: 20ff.; Kemper 1988; Caputo 1989).

The reductions in social programs under the Reagan administration were reviewed in chapter 5. Some families were removed from AFDC rolls and benefits were reduced for others (Joe and Rogers 1985: 33; Sidel 1986: 86). Fewer people were eligible for benefits and many would receive reduced benefits. The amount of earned income that could be disregarded in determining AFDC benefits was reduced. Mothers would be able to keep less of their earned income before their benefits were cut or eliminated altogether.

AFDC recipients are automatically eligible for Medicaid. Losing AFDC eligibility means losing Medicaid coverage in twenty-one states. (Medicaid is of vital concern to AFDC families.) AFDC recipients can also apply for training under the Job Training Partnership Act (Binford et al. 1990: 41–42).

In a study of AFDC recipients in Georgia, Wodarski and colleagues (1986) describe the hardships of living under the program. Over one-third of their sample had bills over two months overdue, and 80 percent had run out of money at one time or another. A significant proportion studied by Donovan and colleagues (1987) said that income was insufficient to cover even the basic expenses of food, clothing, and shelter, and Sidel (1986: 85) claims the payments are not adequate for even a minimum standard of living.

"To date, no federal policy has satisfactorily provided for adequate assistance to low-income working women and their children" (Wodarski et al. 1986). We are the only industrialized country without a universal children's economic support program (Mason et al. 1985).

THE CASE FOR WORKFARE

There is strong feeling among many that those who are able to work should do so. Alarm has been expressed about creating a permanent underclass with no tradition of self-support or skills to find and keep jobs (Gideonse and Meyers 1988). Some claim the "cycle of dependency" is difficult to break (e.g., Bernstein 1986: 41). Requiring work would ease the burden on the taxpayer, according to this view, and would allow individuals the independence and sense of accomplishment that providing for oneself and one's family brings. It might enhance the psychological well-being of participants, provide a service of value to community organizations, and enhance the image of welfare held by the public (Dickinson 1986).

Monsma (1987) believes that work is an obligation owed to society, and certain social obligations should be enforced on those receiving welfare benefits. Though he concedes that a large number of individuals and families have a very low potential for ever becoming economically self-supporting due to severe physical, emotional, or mental limitations, he thinks work is the way out of poverty.

Bernstein claims that welfare clients responded favorably to the new efforts at work orientation under the Omnibus Budget Reconciliation Act (OBRA) of 1981. (See history of workfare attempts later in this chapter.) Employment programs, she says, must be pursued and expanded. She believes that child care has not been an insuperable obstacle in the employment of welfare mothers: many made their own arrangements with relatives, friends, and neighbors (Bernstein 1986: 41).

Women should be helped to obtain the kind of job available to a high school graduate, though she admits earnings are likely to be modest. "The working mother is an independent figure, a much better model for children than the mother who is a long-term dependent on welfare" (Bernstein 1986: 45).

Mead is one who believes our policies are too permissive and we should use state authority to enforce low-wage work. A display of public competence by the poor will integrate them into the larger national community, and enforced work will lead to true equality for the poor. Workfare, says Mead, sends a valuable message to recipients and non-recipients: one's income is the result of one's labor. The programs probably must be mandatory to succeed (Mead 1986: 69–70; Mead 1989).

Mead would strengthen mandates for work search in the disability and unemployment compensation programs. His most important recommendations are for administrative reforms in work search requirements in AFDC, currently part of Work Incentive Program (WIN). He calls for hiring more staff to insure that welfare recipients look for work and doubling the proportion of the AFDC caseload that must participate in WIN. A work search should be mandated for mothers with children at least two years of age (Mead 1986: 82–85).

Kaus believes that no benefits should be paid to mothers who refuse to work. He thinks that AFDC mothers, of all "underclass" groups, are the most capable of making the transition to the world of work. Workfare should be a long-term program to destroy the culture of poverty. He admits it may not be possible to apply a truly mandatory work requirement to the entire caseload of a large state, and he also admits the wage will be insufficient to support a family (Kaus 1986).

A HISTORY OF ATTEMPTS AT WORKFARE

There have been several earlier attempts to link welfare and work. The Community Work and Training Program (CWTP), passed in 1962, allowed all states, at their discretion, to enroll AFDC adult recipients in workfare programs. They had to be engaged in meaningful public service work that would not displace another worker. The program involved as many as 27,000 participants, but it expired in June of 1968 (Foster et al. 1988: 71; Dickinson 1986). A part of Title V of the Economic Opportunity Act (EOA) of 1964 allowed states to develop work experience demonstration projects using EOA funds for AFDC mothers. Participation peaked at 72,000 persons in 1967, expiring in June of 1969 (Binford et al. 1990: 77).

The WIN program was enacted through the 1967 Social Security Amendments to make AFDC recipients less dependent on welfare through training and work experience with supportive services. The program required registration of "appropriate AFDC recipients," and included counseling, referral, and assistance in obtaining basic education and job skills. By 1971 WIN was deemed unsuccessful in view of the numbers of participants who gained employment (Binford et al. 1990: 78; Gideonse and Meyers 1988), and was continuously thwarted by inadequate funding (Caputo 1989).

Dickinson (1986) claims that WIN did not lead to substantial increases in enrollees' acquisition and retention of jobs. It was not successful in job placement for a significant number of clients. Dickinson goes on to say that social services have had little, if any, impact on the work activity of AFDC mothers. WIN "has not been regarded as a success" (Schiller 1984: 198), and did not materially reduce welfare rolls.

Research on WIN suggests that the program has not improved the rate at which individuals find jobs. Mead's suggestions, as Sosin puts it, would add to the cost with no payoff (Sosin 1987a). Rein claims that there is no evidence that efforts such as WIN have been successful in reaching the stated goals. The ideology of work for the poor has not had a practical outcome. She thinks a type of work program might be preferable (Rein 1982). Beeghley feels that training for minimum wage jobs is not a solution to the AFDC problem (Beeghley 1983: 85–86).

In the 1960s, legislation was designed to get people off the welfare rolls by making them self-sufficient in the labor market. Amendments largely restricted AFDC benefits and made mandatory a work-training program for all persons over sixteen receiving AFDC. A work incentive, "$30 plus one-third disregard," allowed more working parents to remain eligible for partial AFDC grants. The first $30 of earnings and one-third of the remainder were made exempt. It was thought that mothers were more likely to work their way off the welfare rolls (Joe and Rogers 1985: 20ff.; Dickinson 1986). But Dickinson claims that work effort, as measured by those at work while on welfare and cases closed for employment, did not increase.

When Ronald Reagan was governor of California, he initiated a welfare reform project known as the California Community Work Experience Program (CWEP), which ran from July 1972 to July 1975. Participants were assigned to public service jobs to "work off" their benefits, and were required to work up to eighty hours per month. Most evaluations agree the program failed, partly because of disagreements about policy and procedure. A study by Health, Education, and Welfare found that the program had no effect on the work and welfare status of participants. CWEP placed only 4,760 AFDC recipients out of a total of 182,735 in jobs (Binford et al. 1990: 79).

With the passage of OBRA, the $30 plus one-third disregard, which used to be applied indefinitely, could only be used for four consecutive months by each person with earned income in the household which receives assistance. OBRA also provided that a family could no longer be eligible for AFDC if it had total income exceeding 185 percent of the state's need standards (Binford et al. 1990: 30–31; Joe and Rogers 1985: 34).

Following the passage of OBRA, employment among AFDC recipients fell by one-half from 1981 to 1982. By 1986, the proportion of men employed had risen to the pre-OBRA days of 9 percent, but the proportion of employed women has never recovered (Foster et al. 1988: 29).

Instead of fostering independence, the new law put mothers in a position where they either had to stop working or lose benefits; individuals either had to try to deceive the authorities or stop working. The General Accounting Office estimated that more than 400,000 families were dropped from the rolls by 1985 because of the new restrictions. Unfortunately, it was the working poor who suffered (Binford et al. 1990: 31; Joe and Rogers 1985, ch. 2).

The new policy, in addition to other restrictions, required that the Earned Income Tax Credit (EITC) be counted as income in determining AFDC benefits whether or not it was actually received. An AFDC grant might be reduced even though the family had not received the tax credit (Joe and Rogers 1985: 35). Budget cuts in food stamps and Medicaid also hurt AFDC families.

The changes reduced a working family's income almost to the level of a nonworking family's income; in fact, in some states working mothers would end up with a net income loss if they earned more money. This virtually eliminated any financial incentive for AFDC mothers to work (Joe and Rogers 1985: 41). While there was a slight savings per recipient, returnees to welfare cost the government millions more (Wodarski et al. 1986).

In 1987, the Job Training Partnership Act (JTPA) provided about one million disadvantaged participants with job search assistance or other services. About one-fifth of these were AFDC recipients. Two-thirds of the AFDC mothers in JTPA programs had children under age six. Some mothers had access to child care assistance through other supportive services, so they could participate in this program. The majority of AFDC mothers found jobs upon leaving the program, but critics charged that the most employable individuals from the eligible population were selected to participate (Binford et al. 1990: 80–81).

Carolyn L. Marck reported on a five-year study of new work and welfare initiatives in eight states, and found mixed results. It did not appear that participants were coerced into distasteful jobs, but the workfare did not inhibit people from applying for welfare, nor did it significantly improve the skills of the participants (Foster et al. 1988: 77).

Massachusetts experimented with an Employment and Training Choices (ET) program. Even Kaus, who encourages workfare, thinks that claims for ET tend to wilt on close inspection. The program resulted in very few full-time jobs, and the participants might have gotten them anyway (Kaus 1986).

Changes were made with passage of the Family Support Act (FSA) of 1988. Designed to "break the cycle of poverty," its intent is to force welfare mothers into the work force. States are required to try to find employment for able-bodied adults on welfare, with the exception of those who care for children under age three. States were to have enrolled at least 7 percent of their welfare recipients in job training or education programs by 1990, with a minimum 20 percent enrolled in 1995. The bill requires either the father or mother in a two-parent welfare family to perform at least sixteen hours a week of community service beginning in 1994. Welfare parents under age twenty-five without a high school diploma will be allowed to complete their education in lieu of the work requirement (Kemper 1988; Binford et al. 1990: 77).

As FSA goes into effect in the 1990s, state budgets are in even worse shape than they were in the middle 1980s. Services established under Title II (JOBS) will almost certainly be even lighter on meaningful training and heavier on work alone. If provided at all, child care will almost certainly be of minimal quality. Many poor women may be cut off from welfare support for failure to perform menial jobs at minimal wages (Kornbluh 1991).

However, FSA will offer women a buffer against the worst exigencies of the labor market and family system. Even limited state support allows some women to escape exploitive jobs and abusive relationships. Job training and placement provisions will help some women acquire skills, income, and the autonomy that comes with them (Kornbluh 1991).

Experiences with workfare in California, Utah, and Massachusetts showed that skills of workers were not upgraded and the welfare rolls were not reduced. The efforts do not significantly reduce the number of malingerers on the welfare rolls as studies indicate only a small number of such undeserving welfare recipients exist (Goodwin 1981).

Evidence from the work/welfare programs established at the state level prior to FSA is less than encouraging. In New York City, 30 percent of families in mandatory work programs have already been "sanctioned" for failure to comply with requirements. In the 1980s, recipients were offered negligible training, education, or challenging work. One study found that most were offered just "job search activities and unpaid work experience" (Kornbluh 1991).

REMAINING QUESTIONS

Many questions remain about coercive work programs for welfare mothers. It appears that the bill's greatest concern is not to meet the needs of the nation's poor, who are mostly women and children, but to trim the welfare rolls, thereby cutting federal costs, and to provide a source of cheap labor (Kemper 1988; Gideonse and Meyers 1988).

It is unlikely, says Kemper, that such mandatory jobs will lift former welfare recipients out of poverty. Several state workfare programs had a poor record (also see Burghardt and Fabricant 1987: 104–105). Employers in search of a cheap labor force will likely be the bill's primary beneficiaries. Forcing welfare mothers to accept low-paying jobs will likely result in more poor children who do not receive adequate child care, medical care, or nutritional care (Kemper 1988).

"Lawmakers decided to force welfare recipients to go to work without adjusting the minimum wage, without making provisions for long-term affordable child care, without making health insurance more widely available, and without addressing the nation's worsening housing crisis" (Kemper 1988).

Programs aim at the mismatch between workers' characteristics and employers' requirements, rather than at the wage structure of the labor market itself. The women often lack specialized skills and extensive job experience needed for better paying jobs. It is unlikely that the measures have increased significantly the proportions of welfare recipients who would have gone to work without the programs (Gideonse and Meyers 1988).

Critics of the program claim that the most employable from the eligible population are selected, that the ones who receive training are those most likely to succeed anyway (Gideonse and Meyers 1988). The tendency is fostered by the heavy use of performance-based contracts, in which the amount paid to a private trainer of JTPA participants is based on the number of participants placed in jobs (Foster et al. 1988: 75).

Many welfare recipients need considerable educational help before they can even begin employment training programs or get entry-level jobs (Foster et al. 1988: 78). They often lack literacy and computational skills needed to benefit from job training (Gideonse and Meyers 1988). Senator Paul Simon refers to the problems in finding work when one is handicapped or functionally illiterate. Getting a job becomes almost impossible for many of these people (Simon 1987).

State welfare agencies have expressed concern from the start that the administrative costs of creating and handling workfare jobs and overseeing statewide programs are beyond their resources, especially with potential day care costs (Foster et al. 1988: 74). Some administrators might enforce welfare requirements arbitrarily and unjustly (Schiller 1984: 13).

A frequently heard objection to such programs, not without some basis, is that people are punished for being poor. The jobs tend to be meaningless, make-work, distasteful ones, and there is a real possibility that placing a welfare recipient in a "real" job would displace a nonwelfare worker (Foster et al. 1988: 74; Kittlaus 1989; Dickinson 1986).

According to Conover (1989), forced labor is profoundly different from paid employment. Education, training, and employment preparation aspects of the programs that help welfare recipients move from welfare to employment should be voluntary. He raises questions about the quality of education, training, and work preparation programs; the job opportunity structure for those who complete training; the readiness of the recipients to respond; and the perception of the program by those who would be served.

It is unclear how enforcing low-wage work as a condition for receiving welfare, as Mead suggests, will remove the stigma of receiving public aid; it would seem more likely to increase the stigma by reinforcing the idea that poverty is the result of personal failings. It is not clear that enforcing work will lead to community; it may lead to a surly mass of resentful people, requiring ever greater increments of force to discipline. It could be "little more than a cynical acceptance of second-class citizenship for the poor" (Weir 1988).

Workfare programs do not have either the incentives (adequate wages, the potential for upward mobility, skill development) or supports (child care) to affect substantial movements into the job market (Burghardt and Fabricant 1987: 157).

Kane, who studied motivational factors for welfare recipients, believes his work implies that involuntary workfare may be a bad idea, usurping rather than granting control (Kane 1987).

A key issue in the debate is the extent to which welfare mothers are dependent on welfare; proponents of workfare claim such efforts will break this cycle (Bernstein 1986: 41). But the evidence reviewed in chapter 6 raises serious questions about the dependency thesis, and our experience with workfare raises questions about its ability to end dependence.

One writer claims that workfare occupies a person's time but does not prepare him or her for the real world of work. Such activity is meaningless when a person could be in school or in training, preparing for work which will pay more than minimum wage (Kittlaus 1989).

Mead admits that there has been no study that directly evaluates a mandatory workfare program alongside a voluntary one, all else being equal (Mead 1990). Lynn argues that the goal must be to move significant numbers of welfare-dependent people toward self-sufficiency, not just to churn them through bureaucratic routines (Lynn 1990).

And a real question can be raised about the availability of the jobs the welfare mothers would presumably take (Howell 1988; Gideonse and Meyers 1988). As was noted in chapter 3, jobs for unskilled workers in large cities, where many welfare mothers live, have declined precipitously since 1970 (McLanahan and Booth 1988; Sidel 1986: 74). AFDC mothers are needed more to raise children than to look for poverty-wage employment when 7 million Americans are already unemployed and looking for work (Sherraden 1988).

Arguing that no workfare program really got off the ground, Wilson believes that they are not a fundamental shift from the traditional approaches to poverty in America. Their focus is exclusively on individual characteristics. The effectiveness of such programs ultimately depends upon the availability of jobs in a given area. With unemployment high, members of the underclass are going to have a very difficult time competing successfully for the jobs. And they may simply be taking jobs away from others who are nearly as disadvantaged (Wilson 1987: 161–162).

It is a fantasy to believe that, given the present economic structure, a majority of the welfare population would quickly move into jobs. They would join the long queue composed of other unemployed workers competing for a small number of unfilled jobs, plus employed low-wage workers competing for the dramatically smaller number of unfilled high-wage jobs (Riemer 1988: 64).

A study of joblessness in inner-city Chicago revealed not the absence of a work ethic but limited opportunities to secure employment. "If society really expects single mothers with limited skills to work, social policy must specify the income guarantees, child care assistance, and other supports that will be provided so that the work will not aggravate the economic deprivation of their children with social deprivation" (Tienda and Stier 1991).

As Goodwin says, "Training welfare mothers for low-skilled jobs, even under the best of conditions, cannot resolve the welfare problem unless there is a concomitant effort to raise wages and increase the number of these jobs" (Goodwin 1985: 137). "Significant improvements in self-sufficiency cannot occur without dramatic increases in the numbers and favorable locations of available job opportunities for the marginally-prepared worker" (Lynn 1990).

Employers are not likely to employ the hard-to-employ (such as single parents) if they can get better-qualified individuals. Single mothers are hard to employ in the sense that many lack skills requisite to jobs that are economically worthwhile (Caputo 1989).

Further, the assumption that acceptance of a full-time job rescues one from poverty may be questioned. Most jobs available to welfare recipients pay too little to move a family above the poverty line (Gideonse and Meyers 1988). More than 40 percent of all poor people in the United States over age fourteen worked (in 1987), and the number of working poor has increased by 50 percent since 1978. The number of working poor people is more than twice the number of adults on welfare (Kemper 1988). Many find that working makes them ineligible for welfare, but does not provide enough to meet the expenses of basic amenities (Wodarski et al. 1986).

Levitan and Shapiro dispel the basic American myth that work provides a route out of poverty. Two million adults work full-time and yet their families are poor, and 7 million work part-time with the same result. A substantial proportion of heads of households could not keep a family out of poverty even if they worked fifty-two weeks at their current weekly earnings (Caputo 1989).

Minimum wage jobs will not make up for the loss of Medicaid, nor pay the costs of child care. "Reform" that forces single women off welfare into low-paying, dead-end jobs will simply plunge them deeper into poverty. Haveman claims that about two-thirds of all female family heads fail to earn enough to raise their families out of poverty (Haveman 1988: 73).

The problem is more acute for women, who have a higher unemployment rate than men (Donovan et al. 1987), and when they do work, they earn less than men at every level (Sidel 1986: 66). In the past twenty years more than three quarters of a million jobs have been lost in the clothing and textile industry in this country, and the great majority of these workers were women. Earnings of single mothers are far lower than those of single women or married couples (Ferree 1989; Wodarski et al. 1986). Further, women and minorities are most at risk of becoming impoverished when they lose their jobs.

Our society's economic deck is stacked against women more than any other group in our society (Kemper 1986). Even the conservative Gilder admits, "Once a family is headed by a woman, it is almost impossible for it to greatly raise its income" (Gilder 1981: 69). A writer in *Fortune* speaks of stereotyping and preconceptions about women, and "subtle but pernicious forms of discrimination" (Fierman 1990).

Ellwood, who does see some advantages to a mother's working, shows that the employment of women outside the home may introduce a new source of stress. If a single mother is forced to go to work when she has just become the head of a family, work may increase the stress and tension she is feeling during an already difficult period (Elwood 1988: 134.)

Those who work part-time apparently believe that the rewards they now get from working do not compensate for the time they have to spend away from their children and home, for the cost of day care, and for the headaches associated with the full-time jobs they may be able to get. And work is even more difficult for single mothers than for wives. There is no one to help when the child is sick, no one to take the child to the dentist, and no one to help with the day-to-day crises, and problems of day care and economic opportunity are at least as serious for single mothers as for married ones (Ellwood 1988: 134).

Lekachman is blunt: "Workfare is expensive to administer, a nuisance to supervisors, provides little or no useful results, and occasions resentment among public employees on regular payrolls" (Lekachman 1982: 95). He finds no evidence that it prepares conscripts for normal participation in the job market.

Bernstein (1986), cited earlier, does not express sufficient concern with the problem of child care for working mothers (Dickinson 1986; Wodarsky

1986; Schorr 1988: 206). Relying on neighbors and relatives is not a feasible option for most persons in this situation, and competent day care facilities are often prohibitively expensive. Many jobs are night jobs, making it even more difficult to obtain child care. The child care tax credit provides little help to poor parents who have little federal income tax liability (Caputo 1989). Current mechanisms to offset the costs of child care to AFDC mothers are probably inadequate to meet even existing demand (Hughes 1990).

Few writers (though it is mentioned briefly by Dickinson 1986) speak of the problem of transportation. Many potential workers, especially in the inner city or isolated rural areas, lack a reliable automobile to get to and from work, or to take and pick up their children from day care, and public transportation is inadequate in many areas. Further, costs of transportation further reduce the low paycheck.

Because Medicaid eligibility is linked to AFDC, there is a serious disincentive to becoming independent of welfare because most jobs available to women receiving welfare do not usually carry health insurance (McLanahan and Booth 1988).

Welfare mothers are often concentrated in disadvantaged neighborhoods with high crime and poverty, low employment, and poor schools (McLanahan and Booth 1988). Living in socially and economically disadvantaged areas lowers the opportunity for economic mobility and reduces the chances for jobs. Several researchers have found support for this argument, though it may apply more to blacks than to whites.

The greatest growth in black single-mother families has been among young, never-married women (Nichols-Casebolt 1988), women who are the least prepared for assuming family financial responsibility. The unavailability of work may force many black women into working only part-time. More than 43 percent of black women below the poverty line are involuntarily part-time workers who work fewer than forty hours a week.

Paula Roberts of the Center for Law and Social Policy observes that obtaining food stamps and other forms of assistance can be a full-time job itself. People trying to get help generally have to visit several offices located in different parts of town, have numerous interviews with different caseworkers for each program, and give the same information over and over again, filling out applications and providing documentation (Hunger Action Forum 1990).

In addressing this issue, the United Methodist Church has said that rather than adopt "punitive" proposals, "the nation would do far better to concentrate first on providing job opportunities for the millions of unemployed who desire them than to set about requiring work from welfare recipients" (United Methodist Church 1984: 96). The statement continues:

> We strongly reject the demand that mothers of children under sixteen should be required to take jobs outside the home. They, like other American mothers, should be allowed to make their own decision as to where their life efforts are most needed—whether in making a home for their children, or in the commercial job market.

They go on to say that welfare support should not be reduced because of earnings of welfare recipients except at rates which will allow significant improvements in the financial position of recipients because of their earnings. They also specify a number of safeguards to be applied to jobs.

Popkin, who studied the attitudes of AFDC recipients, reports that even those women who believe they could find some type of work are not optimistic about their prospects for supporting themselves adequately. They name several obstacles that prevent them from finding work, most of which have been listed above (Popkin 1990).

Past programs did not noticeably reduce poverty (Gideonse and Meyers 1988), and it is unlikely a major impact on poverty will result from current programs (Morris and Williamson 1987).

According to Levitan, for the vast majority of these poor (female heads of households), jobs alone are not the answer, and in the absence of some income support their chances of escaping deprivation are low (Levitan 1985: 12).

A reasonable conclusion is that current workfare policies do not appear to be a feasible solution to the problem of poverty or welfare. The concept does contain one or two sound ideas: for certain types of the poor, independence and self-sufficiency might be achieved through working. Whether this is feasible given the present structure of the economy is problematic, especially during the current (1992) recession. Suggestions that might move us toward a more comprehensive solution of these problems will be considered in the next chapter.

8

Toward a Solution

Many volumes have been written about finding a solution for poverty. This chapter summarizes some of the most important recent proposals and supplies some perspective on what may be the best direction to go. Political implications and the role of the government will be discussed more fully in chapter 9.

American citizens have a constitutionally guaranteed right to the basic necessities of life: food, housing, clothing, health care, and education; this goes back to John Locke and the Declaration of Independence (Ackley 1978). There are grounds for maintaining that individuals are genuinely free only if they are economically secure (Higgens 1982).

There is a need for both income and services—not one without the other—and non-economic issues should not be ignored. A thorough program will deal with the causes of poverty rather than mitigate its symptoms, which has largely been our approach thus far.

Many Americans have soured on "throwing money" at human problems that seem only to get worse. Though they are compassionate, they feel helpless and convinced that nothing can be done. They are also afraid of doing harm while trying to do good, and the threat of unmanageable costs has paralyzed national policy-making (Schorr 1988: xvii).

But Schorr demonstrates that we now have a critical mass of information that totally transforms the nation's capacity to improve outcomes for vulnerable persons, especially children. There is hard evidence, she says, that systematic intervention and support from outside the family early in the life cycle can improve the lifetime prospects of children growing up at risk (Schorr 1988: xix-xx). A recent book by Nicholas Lemann convincingly rejects the notion that "nothing works" to help the poor (Whitman 1991).

Some thirty years ago, much of the discussion about ending poverty centered on some type of Guaranteed Income or Negative Income Tax. Although attention has shifted elsewhere in more recent years, we summarize some of these proposals briefly.

A Guaranteed Annual Income, such as that proposed by Robert Theobold, would guarantee 100 percent of an income to any individual or family up to the point necessary to give that family a living wage. Theobold feels that society owes to everyone a minimum share of the economic goods that can so easily be produced. Recipients with private income would retain a fraction of such income and would thus be permitted to increase their total incomes above basic economic security and other benefits (Walch 1973: 19).

In the form presented by James Tobin, the basic allowance for each family member would be reduced by one-third of a dollar for each dollar of wages earned. The family would continue to receive government help in lessening amounts up to a point (Walch 1973: 20). This helps answer the argument that such a plan would destroy any incentive to work.

One argument for such a proposal is that payments would be uniform, and a poor family would not suffer because of residence in a poor or unresponsive state or county. Another point is that social workers could concentrate on helping people. Social work could devote itself to a range of new services and programs which presently receive an inadequate part of the resources of social work (Walch 1973: 56).

Recent proposals by Haveman are too extensive to summarize here, but one element of his plan is a unified and universal system integrated with the personal income tax; the government would guarantee a social minimum for every citizen (Haveman 1988: 153–154).

Would such a plan reduce work effort? While this is highly controversial, nearly all observers agree that when income guarantees are set significantly below the poverty line, they produce no decline in hours worked (Beeghley 1983: 89). Excessive concern that a relatively low level of guaranteed income, even around the poverty level, would cause people to drop out of the work force reflects a misunderstanding of the life and work orientation of the poor (Goodwin 1972).

A Negative Income Tax is a similar proposal. To the credit of conservative Milton Friedman, when he voices his concerns with the present welfare system, he at least has a proposal to put in its place. With income below a set allowance, people would receive a subsidy from the government. The plan would fit into the current income tax system and dispense with most of the bureaucracy now used (Friedman and Friedman 1979: 120–123).

Ozawa details the adverse side effects on poor families of current assistance, and recommends a negative income tax as a more effective alternative (Ozawa 1983). In a study of the effects of a negative income tax, findings indicate that the poor receiving such funds do not drop out of the labor market but continue to work to improve their level of income (Wright and Wright 1975).

There are many critics of such proposals, and Waxman may be representative. He argues that there can never be a minimum decent subsistence level. A minimum subsistence level must become indecent and undesirable, and the nonpoor will continue to stigmatize its undesirables (Waxman 1983: 115).

A hotly debated subject is the results of state experiments with something like a guaranteed income. Gilder claims the programs in Denver and Seattle were a catastrophic failure, reducing work effort by between one-third and one-half and increasing marital breakdown by about 60 percent, compared to a control group largely on AFDC. So he concludes that a guaranteed income would be far more destructive in every way than the current welfare system (Gilder 1981: 120).

Some conservative writers claim that the Seattle/Denver income maintenance programs reduced labor and earnings by 80 cents for every dollar given in welfare (Rector et al. 1990). A more cautious Murray says the negative income tax experiments reduced work effort nine percent among husbands and 20 percent among wives. Since it also led to the dissolution of marriages, it made a shambles of expectations (Murray 1984: 150–151).

Recent estimations have qualified the negative assessment of the experiments: work effort declined less, and marriages did not become as unstable as earlier results suggested (Kornbluh 1991). Others claim that evidence from the experiments showed only marginal reductions in work effort among poor families as a result of the negative income tax. In New Jersey, male workers reduced their working hours by less than 5 percent (in Seattle and Denver, about 9 percent). Women reduced their work efforts somewhat more, but that is not necessarily negative (Devine and Wright 1990).

The experiment in New Jersey clearly proved that a broad income-maintenance program can be administered. It cut administrative costs by more than 50 percent below welfare norms. It was termed "virtually self-administering" since 80 percent to 90 percent of the families were able to fill out and file their monthly reporting forms ("Can Handouts Make Better Wage Earners?" 1970).

The results seem to show that sample American low-income families are gripped by the familiar Puritan work ethic. Instead of squandering their modest governmental monthly income additions, the families used it to add to their possessions, primarily furniture (Strout 1970).

There is no evidence that the experiments led to higher fertility: in New Jersey, the experiments indicate no effect. In the Seattle and Denver experiments, white recipients had significantly lower fertility, Mexican Americans had higher fertility, and blacks showed no effect (Wilson 1987: 79).

The experiments did accompany a reduction in the stability or frequency of marriages, but at the highest income level, the payments had no effect on marital stability. In addition, the experimental conditions differed substantially from those under which states actually dispense AFDC payments (Wilson 1987: 95).

Except for a family allowance, which is a type of guaranteed income, attention has shifted away from such proposals. While there is a consensus that fertility is not affected, there is still controversy over effects on family stability and work incentive. Some question whether even a reasonable cash grant alone can provide for the basic needs of many of these families (Levitan 1985: 139). For example, if such a grant replaced Medicaid, many families could be wiped out by a major illness. Exclusive reliance on income transfers as a "solution" to poverty serves to perpetuate the poverty problem (Schiller 1984: 164). And the political feasibility of a guaranteed income is questionable at best.

One possibility is to accept the current structure of public assistance and build on it, emphasizing those programs that have had demonstrable success. In chapter 5 we outlined successes achieved by food stamps, Women, Infants, and Children's formula (WIC), and Head Start. Other programs with favorable evaluations include the National School Lunch program, Child Care Food program, School Breakfast program, Summer Food Service program, Special Milk program, and Temporary Emergency Food Assistance program (Binford et al. 1990: 48–51).

Even the much-maligned AFDC program has many supporters (e.g., Dear 1989). A major improvement on the present system would be to set a national minimum AFDC standard and require it to be indexed to inflation (Nasar 1986). Many states do not allow AFDC payments to two-parent families (Kornbluh 1991). An assured minimum level of support for poor children probably represents the most politically feasible form of targeting (Hughes 1990).

A crucial area that requires more attention is the plight of the working poor. Their plight looms as one of the greatest barriers to the elimination of poverty (Levitan 1985: 140). One obvious way to address this would be with a higher minimum wage. Not surprisingly, such a proposal finds strong opposition.

The standard conservative position is that the minimum wage law condemns to unemployment all the workers incapable of earning that minimum, and some even believe that the law is a main cause of unemployment among black teenagers (Hazlitt 1973: 63, 107). Some economists cite it as an example of (unwarranted) interference by government. It requires employers to discriminate against persons with low skills (Friedman and Friedman 1979: 19, 237). Some claim it is inflationary. Among others to argue against it are Segalman and Basu (1981: 335–342).

But such arguments do not stand up to solid evidence. Despite its inefficiency in reaching the poor, a higher minimum wage would significantly reduce poverty among working families. Disemployment is not a major factor, because its effects fall heavily on teenagers, who make small contributions to family income (Mincy 1990). Mincy adds that economists still favor a higher minimum wage.

Authors of a careful study said that while a minimum wage may decrease the number of available jobs to a slight extent, the overall benefits clearly outweigh the costs (Levitan and Belous 1979; Haveman 1988: 70; Binford 1990: 82). Further, a high minimum wage encourages work over welfare. A low minimum wage itself has work disincentives.

There is persuasive evidence showing that the wages of millions of workers tend to cluster around the statutory minimum wage. It can help reduce the inherent conflicts between transfer programs and work incentives (Levitan 1985: 143). The historical record shows that enforcement of the minimum wage has coincided with great expansion in employment and productivity (Lappé 1989: 59).

Devine and Wright provide a good answer to the charge that the minimum wage is inflationary. Most minimum wage jobs are found in the service industries, and no one has claimed that rising prices of services are a major inflationary pressure. Health, energy, and housing positions have few minimum wage jobs (Devine and Wright 1990).

Real family incomes have been essentially constant in the United States since before 1970, even though the average number of earners per family has increased. In constant dollars, the current minimum wage is where it was in 1956. Its buying power has eroded 40 percent since 1968. Full-time workers at minimum wage have gross earnings equal to 55 percent of a four-person poverty level (Devine and Wright 1990; Ellwood 1988: 110).

The declining real minimum wage has been a particular problem for women.

Ellwood favors an increase in the minimum wage in spite of its possible effects on employment. He would support an increase to the level of the 1970s, adjusted to the rate of inflation or the growth of other wages. The lowest wage we pay workers, particularly those with families, sends an important signal about how valuable and important we think their efforts are (Ellwood 1988: 112).

There is an existing program which has great potential for enhancing the lot of low-wage workers, and that is the Earned Income Tax Credit (EITC), especially if adjusted for family size. The program helps the working poor with dependent children by refunding a sum keyed to their payroll tax, and reducing their marginal income tax rates. It would increase the likelihood that a family with several children could earn enough to remain outside the welfare system (Pechman 1990).

EITC is virtually administration-free, a cost-efficient income subsidy program. Low-income families receive a 14 percent tax credit against their first $6200 in earnings. Credit is reduced by ten cents for each dollar earned over $10,000. (It is now possible for families earning less than $21,245 to get up to a $2020 tax refund, even if they didn't pay any federal taxes.)

Expansion of the EITC would raise the incomes of the working poor at minimal administrative cost and without harmful side effects. Additional costs would not be excessive and would be partially offset by rising income taxes and savings (Devine and Wright 1990).

Since the program is in place, expanding it would be simple (Ellwood 1988: 114). It could be of real help to many rural poor (Duncan and Tickamyer 1988). Others have cogently argued for its expansion (Chernick 1990; Levitan 1985: 140; Riemer 1988: 130–131; Duncan and Huffman 1991; Greenstein 1991).

Riemer favors providing to all low-income workers a carefully constructed wage supplement that elevates them all above the poverty line. He also argues for a mandatory subsidy program, one that requires all low-income persons to obtain insurance coverage and then provides them with income-adjusted subsidies. Thus utilization of health-care services would increase substantially (Riemer 1988: 126, 151).

The conservative Gilder cites, apparently with approval, a recommendation by Nathan Glazer that secondary jobs be made more attractive by surrounding them with government fringes, such as medical care, child allowances, and other benefits (Gilder 1981: 142).

A related issue that could help the working poor is a reduction of taxes. The Tax Reform Act of 1986 did reduce taxes for the poor, but this was not followed at the state and local levels. The Center on Budget and Policy Priorities reports that a recent study on the tax system in two states found that poor families pay ten times as much in state and local income and sales taxes and local property taxes as they pay in federal income and payroll taxes (Binford et al. 1990: 17). Taxes continue to place a substantial burden on the poor, including property and excise taxes (Chernick 1990). Further, twenty-two of the thirty-four states that raised taxes in 1991 did so in a regressive manner (Taylor 1991).

But while expanding worthwhile programs and cutting taxes for the poor would be a big help, there is a real question how far such efforts would go in eliminating root causes of poverty. As Schiller says, maintenance reforms can meet the need for income support, but they cannot eliminate the need itself. If relied on exclusively, public assistance programs would perpetuate poverty and the need for extensive public assistance expenditures (Schiller 1984: 189).

Most of these programs would leave the educational and employment opportunities of the poor unchanged. Wilson believes, with justification, that present programs are insufficient to address the manifold problems gripping the ghettos. We must generate new initiatives if we are indeed to move significant numbers of American citizens out of the underclass (Wilson 1991b: 478).

This nation has failed to develop a universal system to meet the basic needs of the poor and to blend income support with services that expand future opportunity and self-sufficiency. We need an integrated approach to reducing poverty, greater hope for advancement and self-support while focusing federal resources on those areas and groups with the greatest potential or need (Levitan 1985: 138).

One proposal, made by Ellwood, would replace the current welfare system with three types of support. One is supplemental support for the working poor; a second is transitional support (like training and short-term cash support) for those not working because of temporary difficulties; jobs are a last resort (Ellwood 1988: 12). While the political feasibility of Ellwood's proposals could be argued, their strength is that they recognize the very different types of poor in this country.

JOBS

The one subject that has received the most attention as a possible solution to poverty is jobs. The extreme shortage of jobs (at least good-paying ones) was emphasized in chapter 3, but this point should be reinforced. A powerful case for the scarcity of jobs is made by Riemer

(1988: 31–33). One study of a small town found that the ratio of unskilled jobs advertised in the newpapers to the official unemployment rate was 1: 185 (Beeghley 1983: 79).

Work is closely tied in with the social and psychological development of people. Without work a person has little on which to base his or her identity or to identify how he or she fits into the society. "A nation which cannot provide every member with a meaningful job at a decent wage is . . . telling too many of its members that they are superfluous" (Segalman and Basu 1981: 9).

Full employment would, without question, do more to reduce income poverty than any other approach (Sherraden 1988). Harrington favored full employment, and suggested that a labor shortage in the United States would probably do more to eliminate poverty, sexism and racism than all other policies combined (Harrington 1984: 234). Full employment reduces inequality (Shulman 1990).

When people who wish to work sit idle, goods and services are not produced, the nation pays in higher welfare and unemployment benefits, and much individual frustration and suffering are produced. Providing a decent job to every person who wants one would be an important first step toward dealing with family instability, dependent women and children, crime, and retreatist life styles. Every unemployed person costs the government about $25,000 a year in lost revenue and direct outlays (Lappé 1989: 33). If the question is asked if we can afford to provide jobs, the relevant answer is that we cannot afford high unemployment.

Improvement in the life chances of poor people cannot occur unless labor markets offer much more abundant and attractive job prospects— direct routes into the mainstream—to ordinary, unmarketable citizens who are otherwise likely to fall into chronic dependency on welfare and the underground economy (Lynn 1990b). Lynn calls for a tight labor market, worker democracy, universally available social services, and expanded public works programs to create jobs.

High employment in Boston in the mid-1980s demonstrates that full employment does in fact deliver many of the benefits its advocates have promised. It was found that both white and black families experienced considerable improvement in their financial situation. The poverty rates of both groups declined at the same pace. It is clear that the poor did respond to economic opportunity when it was offered. The sharp drop in the incidence of poverty and the high percentage of the poor who were working undercuts the idea that an active government social policy is debilitating (Osterman 1991: 127–130).

Local labor market shortages greatly improve the employment opportunities of disadvantaged young men, substantially raising the percentage
of employed and reducing their unemployment rate. So a strong job market
does improve the employment and earnings of the disadvantaged (Freeman 1991: 119).

Wilson is a strong advocate of policy programs that confront the
fundamental causes of poverty—underemployment and unemployment.
To handle the economic dislocation of low-income blacks, attention must
be given to the changing nature of the national economy (Wilson 1987:
134).

The problem of joblessness, urges Wilson, should be a top priority item
in any public policy discussion focusing on enhancing the status of
families. The country needs a tight labor market that enhances the employment opportunities of both poor men and women (Wilson 1987: 105–106).
"We have done close to nothing to create the job opportunities that are our
most pressing need" (Schiller 1984: 233).

Without full employment it is much more difficult to shift from income-
testing and stigmatized public assistance programs to universal programs
of social welfare (like family allowances) found in Western Europe.
Universal welfare programs depend on full employment so that workers
can combine their income from transfers with income from employment,
maximize tax revenues, and thereby reduce the strain on the welfare budget
(Wilson 1987: 124).

In a review of poverty research as of 1985–1986, Tomaskovic-Devey
concludes: "If the 1980s taught us anything, it was that attention should
focus on industrial structures and on national policies stimulative of the
types of structures that create jobs that pay adequately" (quoted in Elesh
1990).

The same writer observes, "If poverty is not to increase significantly
over the next decade, the United States will require a genuine industrial
policy and large-scale reinvestment in its educational and economic
infrastructure" (Elesh 1990). He notes that the Bush administration dis-
banded its own advisory group on poverty policy without adopting any of
its relatively modest recommendations.

One study of food stamps relates the problem of hunger to the issue of
jobs and income (Devault and Pitts 1984). In a recent discussion of
homelessness, a cogent case is made that "stable well-paid employment
must replace this segment of the economy to reduce the current levels of
homelessness" (Elliott and Krivo 1989).

The ability of private enterprise to save and create jobs has not been
noteworthy (Gans 1981). Corporate decision makers believe that the

business of business is to make a profit, not generate decent jobs (Rosen-man 1988). The work ethic cannot work when there is no work.

If the private sector provided adequate jobs for all who wished to work, most liberals would gladly accept such a situation. But Thurow has a strong point when he says that since private enterprise is incapable of guarantee-ing jobs for everyone who wants to work, the government must institute the necessary programs (Thurow 1980: 204). A conservative thinks there are enough jobs (without providing evidence), but admits that if there were not, government job-creating efforts would become more necessary (Mead 1986: 73). Another conservative grants that real public jobs are often extremely productive, sometimes more valuable than private jobs (Gilder 1981: 160).

Government jobs, of course, have a long history. Some 8 million individuals worked on Works Progress Administration (WPA) projects at some time or other between 1935 and the end of 1940. WPA built 651,000 miles of new roads, built or reconstructed 124,000 bridges and viaducts, built or reconstructed 120,000 public buildings. Most of the thousands of projects were devised locally. Some built streets and sewers, parks, play-grounds, and levees for flood control, schools and libraries. Others taught illiterates to read and write, manned thousands of public health centers and home nursing services, and organized symphony orchestras (Phillips 1971).

One advantage to public jobs is that public services—sanitation, trans-portation, education, protection, recreation services, etc.—are not well provided for in the market context. Public service employment can channel new labor demand to those areas or population groups most in need (Schiller 1984: 200).

The neo-liberal manifesto by Charles Peters wants to bring back the WPA to rebuild the nation's infrastructure, to give people jobs, to give the poor money to spend. The government is viewed as employer of last resort. For the New Deal did not believe in welfare as a solution. It believed in jobs and, when necessary, in public employment (Schlesinger 1986: 251).

With guaranteed jobs, real economic competition would almost cer-tainly increase. If the jobs are to be real jobs, the program must produce some economic outputs (Thurow 1980: 204). Thurow adds that transi-tional aid for retraining, relocating, and getting through a period of unemployment should be generous (Thurow 1980: 210).

Thurow favors the creation of some low-wage jobs and some high-wage jobs, with most jobs in the middle. Abilities and talents will play a role within the distribution of job opportunities, but no one who desires full or part-time work will be denied it (Thurow 1980: 204). This universal feature is calculated to receive more widespread political support.

Haveman recommends direct job creation and employment subsidy programs. The New Jobs Tax Credit (NJTC) was successful in creating jobs for low-skill workers, and at a rather low cost to the treasury. The NJTC provided a tax credit equal to 50 percent of the first $6,000 of wages paid to the fifty workers hired in a firm above 102 percent of the previous year's employment level. Haveman finds this a potent job creation device (Haveman 1988: 166–167).

As Riemer explains, conservatives duck the question about the availability of good-paying jobs, assuming that for the remaining poor to work full-time and year-round is a satisfactory state of affairs. He advocates the creation of community-service jobs and the expansion of the current federal wage-supplement program (Riemer 1988: 4, 7).

While education and training for the poor are worthwhile (Rosenman 1988), Riemer shows conclusively that simply providing them to the unemployed poor would do little to reduce overall poverty (Riemer 1988: 64). There would be more people competing for jobs, but what would probably happen is that there would simply be a slightly different group of poor people. Employment and training programs have succeeded only when coordinated with full-employment macroeconomic policies (Schiller 1984: 203).

Eliminating poverty requires hiring the unemployed poor and raising the income of the working poor (Riemer 1988: 10). We need to address the question of the supply of jobs and the structure of wages, to implement this right through acts of government, and to finance this by expending public funds (Riemer 1988: 93).

In an article supporting workfare, Kaus urges the government to provide a job for every able-bodied person over eighteen at slightly below the minimum wage; the jobs should be rationed to those who need them most (Kaus 1986, 1992). But that the jobs should pay below the minimum wage seems counterproductive, since one such job would not raise even a small family out of poverty.

Riemer's proposal appears better: he says the pay of community service jobs should be above the poverty line, but somewhat less than one could get at an existing job (Riemer 1988: 122). There is an abundance of useful and needed work to be done, such as repairing our rotting bridges, sewers, and roads, cleaning up the air and water; and well-designed programs can do it. This work should not displace existing jobs: there is no purpose to hiring an unemployed person at the price of laying off another (Riemer 1988: 125–126).

In addition to a commitment to jobs, Lappé suggests affordable credit to small businesses, helping match workers to jobs, retrain and relocate workers, and if necessary to subsidize wages. Further, corporations should no longer be allowed to take wealth generated by workers here and use it to transfer jobs overseas (Lappé 1989: 36).

Sweden has made a great public investment in programs to make jobs available for all who wish to work, using both public and private channels. They have consistently less than half the unemployment rate of the United States, and a surprisingly high standard of living (Zimbalist 1988).

An argument sometimes heard about full employment is that it would be inflationary. The argument seems to be that when everyone is working and incomes are going up, demand for goods climbs and so do prices.

A relevant question might center on the justice of saying to some Americans that they have to be without dollars in the hope that the value of the dollars of other people will be greater. But more to the point, it is not fully demonstrated that high unemployment and inflation are inversely related. In the 1970s, we had high inflation and unemployment at the same time. It is possible to have full employment and price stability (Schiller 1984: 58–59).

It is claimed that inflation means too much money chasing too few goods. But could not the problem be too few goods—that is, the failure to adequately improve productivity? If our productivity were growing faster, more income wouldn't mean higher prices because more goods and services would be produced. And higher wages can improve productivity by motivating workers and by pushing companies to modernize (Lappé 1989: 34).

Further, during much of the post-war period, some countries with the most extensive social programs and relatively low joblessness—West Germany, Austria, and Norway, for example—have enjoyed the lowest inflation rates in the West. Today in Sweden both inflation and unemployment are below 3 percent (Lappé 1989: 34).

Ulmer makes the interesting argument that a zero increase in price level can be combined with a 2 percent unemployment rate. True, inflation is stimulated when the new employees begin to spend their new incomes. New waves of extra income and extra spending will follow one another, but diminish over time. To offset inflationary increased spending, taxes might be raised by the same amount, resulting in a drop in consumer spending.

The country can afford articles produced by private industry, but it cannot afford the various services government might produce, such as effective mass transportation, improved medical care, better protection against street crime, caring for the elderly, mentally ill, and neglected children, cleaning up cities, and protection of the environment (Ulmer 1975). Most of these things, of course, could mean new jobs.

UNIVERSAL PROGRAMS

Several observers have proposed programs that provide at least some benefit to most Americans, including the poor, rather than programs specifically for the poor alone. Waxman argues that the most effective means of breaking the vicious circle, the stigma of poverty, is by creating and implementing policies and programs that will lead to the integration of the poor with the nonpoor, rather than to their further isolation (Waxman 1983: 116). It is hard to rally political support for programs aimed only at the poorest of the poor, because they lack a broad constituency (Schorr 1988: 287).

Our efforts, says Waxman, must involve the creation and expansion of services and income maintenance that are available to all members of the society, thus affording the nonpoor a basis for identifying with and seeing self-interest in these changes. What is called for is the incorporation of social welfare programs within a framework that actively involves the citizenry (Waxman 1983: 126, 133).

Universal programs would de-emphasize categorical aid and means-tested programs. Some think that the time and money spent to determine that clients fit into established categories are unnecessary. And categorical aid denies help to large numbers of needy people who do not meet program specifications and provides incentives for those people to change their status so as to establish eligibility (Walch 1973: 35, 39).

Wilson feels that the more the public programs are perceived as benefiting only certain groups, the less support they receive (Wilson 1987: 118). "The problems of the truly disadvantaged in the United States will have to be attacked primarily through universal programs that enjoy the support and commitment of a broad constituency" (Wilson 1987: 120).

Wilson favors promoting both economic growth and full employment, programs to promote wage and price stability, favorable employment conditions, and development of manpower training programs with educational programs. They would be designed to benefit all segments of society, but the groups that have been plagued by severe problems (like the underclass) would be helped the most (Wilson 1987: 121).

One universal program that has received considerable discussion would replace the current AFDC. A family or child allowance, like those in effect in many western European countries, would provide an annual benefit per child regardless of the family's income. It carries no social stigma and has no built-in work disincentives (Wilson 1987: 152–153). Somewhat surprisingly, Gilder appears to endorse such a system (Gilder 1981: 126).

Haveman's plan is a child-support system to assist children in single-parent families. It would be a unified and universal system to replace the hodgepodge of cash and in-kind benefits, and would have incentives for individuals to save (Haveman 1988: 154). One writer favors child support assistance for all single custodial parents, parental leave and child care assistance for all working families (Skocpol 1991).

While a national standard for AFDC, indexed to inflation, would be a major improvement over the present system, a universal family allowance as discussed above would be one of the major steps this country could take to relieve poverty among its most vulnerable citizens. The cost of administering the program should be much less than AFDC (Chalfant 1985: xxi).

A related issue is child support, possibly as an alternative to a family allowance. Garfinkel and McLanahan propose a child-support tax based on the gross income of parents who live apart from their children. It would function as a wage withholding tax, and any differential between a minimum benefit level and the amount collected would be drawn from general resources (Elesh 1990; Waxman 193: 123). A similar idea is proposed by Danziger (Hughes 1990) and Haveman (1988: 165). Wilson believes this merits serious consideration, and adds that it would be far less stigmatizing than public assistance (Wilson 1987: 152).

A Child Support Assurance System (CSAS) involving custodial families in Wisconsin served as a test case of this idea. Results suggest that CSAS can significantly reduce poverty as well as welfare caseloads. If child support collections increased by one-half of the difference between estimated ability to pay child support and current collections, CSAS will be less costly than the current system (Garfinkel et al. 1990).

Garfinkel suggests that CSAS will lead to an increase in labor supply among custodial parents on AFDC and a decrease in labor supply among custodial parents not on AFDC. In aggregate, then, it should have a neutral effect on labor supply. It should lead to at least a modest decrease in welfare dependency and contribute significantly in a cost-effective manner toward relieving many of the economic pressures facing families having only one parent in the household (Garfinkel et al. 1990).

A different view is that such an idea assumes that male earnings are the only legitimate support for women and children, and strains to improve male "responsibility" without improving men's job prospects (Kornbluh 1991). This does not negate the plan, which appears promising, but does remind us of the crucial importance of good jobs.

Another assessment of the Wisconsin experiments claims that the modest increases in payments to nonmarital children will have little effect on their welfare recipiency. The fathers of these children lack the economic resources to aid their families much in the short term. Expecting the child support system to solve the problem of welfare dependency and poverty among families of never-married mothers is unrealistic. But it is important to send messages to parents that they are expected to assume responsibility for children (Nichols-Casebolt and Klawitter 1990).

One universal program that has received considerable attention is child care. This becomes a critical issue if steps are taken to move single mothers into education and training programs and/or employment. Wilson favors decentralized forms of child care such as child care tax credit and subsidies to the working-poor parents (Wilson 1987: 153). Other countries have effective child care programs (Schorr 1988: 205).

Children of low and moderate-income families have been priced out of the market for high quality preschool care (Schorr 1988: 211). Accordingly, parents need some subsidy in their efforts to purchase such care. One proposal has involved a voucher, requiring people to pay for the voucher according to their ability to pay (Riemer 1988: 143–145).

Another universal program of utmost importance is health care. "Among Western industrialized nations, only the greatest and richest one leaves the allocation of health resources—and therefore the health of its citizens—at the mercy of market forces" (Schorr 1988: 135). Other countries accomplish this at a substantially lower per capita cost than ours. We need universal access to good health care through a universal tax-supported health insurance (Schorr 1988: 138–139; Skcopol 1991: 431).

Other universal services include family planning, which would give the poor the same option as the rest of the population—to choose whether and when they wanted children (Schorr 1988: 37), and a wider range of mental health care, which may deter homelessness among the mentally ill (Elliott and Krivo 1991).

However, exclusive attention to universal programs will not meet the needs of all the poor, particularly the most desperate. In confronting ghetto poverty, it probably makes sense to have policies that focus specifically on the inner city poor (Jargowsky and Bane 1991), as well as poor children and youth in isolated rural areas (Duncan and Tickamyer 1988). Some families and individuals may not be able to benefit from universal programs unless they receive intensive services that help them enter the mainstream economy (Greenstein 1991: 457).

Means-tested benefit programs like Medicaid, SSI, food stamps, EITC, and others have proved durable. It is helpful if a benefit is linked to work and perceived as earned. It is possible to maintain a targeted program structure while incorporating the near-poor and moderate-income working families that are struggling themselves (Greenstein 1991: 450).

Haveman correctly points out that policies must be specifically directed to the particular circumstances of those who have fallen to the bottom of society (Haveman 1988: 87). We need programs responding to the distinct needs of multiproblem families; more resources must flow to population groups at greatest risk (Schorr 1988: 287).

The needs of families with the fewest economic and political resources must receive the highest priority in efforts to make out-of-home child care more widely available (Schorr 1988: 213). After reviewing the success of Head Start, Schorr notes that it contradicts the conventional wisdom that programs targeted to the disadvantaged lack a constituency broad enough to survive political adversity (Schorr 1988: 191).

As Levitan says, we need an integrated approach to reducing poverty, greater hope for advancement and self-support while focusing resources on those areas and groups with the greatest potential or need (Levitan 1985: 138). For example, there is evidence that services offered in adulthood to disadvantaged mothers can make a profound difference (Furstenberg et al. 1987: 152).

Furstenberg and colleagues favor programs for neighborhoods and schools where rates of early childbearing are especially high. Early childhood educational programs are particularly promising (Furstenberg et al. 1987: 153).

Some moderate conservatives have programs for easing poverty that, while hardly adequate to the task, should not be dismissed out of hand. In combination with some proposed solutions listed above, some of them might yield important results.

Glenn Loury stresses leadership and self-help movements for black people; he believes the development of independent black businessmen can be worthwhile (Loury 1986). This approach seems inappropriate for the underclass discussed in chapter 3, for would-be capitalists need capital to launch successful projects. Wilson is probably right in saying that problems of joblessness are so overwhelming that self-help programs seem futile (Wilson 1987: 158). But with other groups and in more favorable circumstances, such ideas might bear some fruit. Another idea favored by many conservatives is tax breaks for businesses that locate in low-income areas and that employ the disadvantaged.

Vouchers for low-cost housing is an idea favored by some conservatives, and it may be worth some consideration. The problem seems to be that without incentives to build low-cost housing or subsidies, there is little likelihood that private developers will construct the massive number of low-cost housing units needed. Existing housing stock could not meet the demand for low-cost housing (Katz 1989: 190).

In summary, building on the current system of welfare would be better than nothing but highly inadequate. Pushing for an increase in the minimum wage, an expansion of EITC, a subsidy program for health insurance, and reduced taxes for the poor would be important steps. The creation of more jobs, using the government if necessary, may be the most significant step of all. And universal programs, such as family allowance, child support, child care, and health care, need to be combined with some targeted programs to effectively deal with the problems. The point is not to accept only one package of reforms. The point is to do whatever can be done.

Chapter 9 discusses political implications, including public support for solutions, the role of government and taxation, and chapter 10 outlines a theory for reform.

9

Political Implications

As we consider proposed solutions to poverty summarized in the previous chapter, a number of questions may come to mind. Is there sufficient support for these reforms among the public? Do these solutions bypass possibly constructive conservative ideas? What about the increasing role for the government most of these solutions imply? Do they make a stronger federal government inevitable? What about a role for local governments and for the private sector? Is there money for these solutions, and if not, will more taxes be required? This chapter speaks to these questions.

Waxman's assessment seems reasonable: "Since a precondition for an effective social policy recommendation is that it have some degree of probability in being adopted and implemented, it is futile to propose directions that go against the very grain of current public sentiment" (Waxman 1983: 135).

There are also problems in translating public sentiment into congressional action. "The public interest groups representing low-income people and focusing on poverty-related issues are among the least well-financed in Washington and must rely heavily on public sources of information" (Primus 1989). The poverty issue is unique in that there are no well-financed producer interests. Members of Congress are not lobbied in the same manner as they are on many other issues. Thus, it takes the conviction of members to keep an issue like this one on the agenda.

Undoubtedly a case could be made that the American public is either unsympathetic to the lot of the poor or unwilling to trust the government to do much about it. Members of the public tend to explain social inequality in an individualistic manner; people are generally deemed responsible for their own socioeconomic fate. This individualistic orientation is especially evident in Americans' beliefs about the causes of poverty. Personal traits (lack of thrift, effort, talent) are considered more important than structural factors (shortage of jobs, inadequate schools, etc.) (Lee et al. 1990).

In 1964, about the time the War on Poverty was being launched, a majority of Americans saw "lack of effort" as the major source of poverty. Feagin found that individualistic reasons were viewed by more of the respondents as important in explaining poverty than the structural reasons. At least 80 percent agreed with the statement, "There are too many people receiving welfare who should be working" (Feagin 1975: 95; Waxman 1983: 73–74).

In 1986, Kluegel and Smith found that individual factors, particularly lack of motivation, were considered much more important than structural ones in causing poverty (Smith and Stone 1989). Kluegel says that beliefs about the causes of poverty and attitudes toward welfare were affected little by the recession of the mid-1970s and early 1980s. There is no evidence that people's personal experience of economic troubles leads them to conclude that broad structural forces are responsible for individual economic outcomes (Kluegel 1987).

But these findings need not lead to pessimism. Most Americans admit to an underlying bias in favor of equality in their social values. They may support inequality if they are convinced it is for the common good, but they believe everyone should have a fair chance to get ahead (Heilbroner and Thurow 1987: 194–195).

Cyclical patterns seem to prevail in the nation every thirty years or so, reflecting an inevitable tension between capitalism and democracy (Haveman 1988: 17; Schlesinger 1986). Americans have been awakened to a dramatic increase in the numbers of long-term unemployed, displaced workers, single black mothers on welfare, and children growing up without traditional family ties. According to an opinion poll, a majority of Americans now believe government should do more to help the poor (Haveman 1988: 18).

While Smith and Stone concede that individualism is still widely accepted as an explanation for poverty, it is but one of several competing metatheories and strong, albeit minority, voices were raised for other views. Individualsim is not as universally supported as is generally assumed (Smith and Stone 1989).

While Kluegel's research did find some negative views, it reported no evidence that the public finds the poor more personally blameworthy, nor that worsening economic conditions engender greater anti-poor sentiment. There was no evidence that the poor are targets of displaced anger or frustration stemming from economic insecurity for racial or other reasons (Kluegel 1987).

A survey of social workers found that a significantly greater proportion in 1984 chose social structural reasons for the existence of poverty than did in 1968. Individualistic views (i.e., that the poor lack motivation) declined from 26 percent to 10 percent. The number believing in the need for basic changes in the political and economic system went from 61 percent to 81 percent (Reeser and Epstein 1987).

Even more encouraging is a recent Gallup poll. While 38 percent list lack of effort as the main cause of a person's being poor, 42 percent named circumstances beyond one's control, whereas in 1984, six years earlier, these reasons drew about equal support. Also, only 37 percent thought most poor people preferred to stay on welfare, while 56 percent thought most poor people would rather earn their own living (The Gallup Report 1990).

There is also some recent dissatisfaction with the way things are going in the country, and the cause appears to be the economy. When asked (May 1991) to name the most important problem in the country, about 46 percent gave answers which relate to economic issues, including the economy in general (21 percent), poverty and homelessness (12 percent, up from 5 percent in late 1990), and unemployment (9 percent) (Gallup and Newport 1991).

And in a study of public beliefs about the causes of homelessness, almost three-fifths attributed the problem to structural forces, while less than two-fifths thought the condition was due to personal choice. Further, healthy support for a wide range of ameliorative measures was reported. Even among residents who saw homelessness as a matter of personal choice, two-fifths felt the community was doing too little on the issue, and two-thirds thought local government should provide additional housing for the homeless. It may be that members of the public are better informed, less prone to stereotype, and able to make finer distinctions than our survey items give them credit for (Lee et al. 1990).

According to a *New York Times*/CBS News poll taken after the Los Angeles riots in 1992, the public was more likely to see violence as a symptom of festering social needs rather than as a simple issue of law and order. Most (60 percent) said the nation was spending too little on urban problems, up from 46 percent in 1988. Further, a majority of the respondents saw a lack of jobs as the root of the trouble ("Americans View Riots . . ." 1992).

While it is important to take public opinion into account, it seems a mistake to limit proposals to those the public is fully ready to accept. I grew up in Alabama in the 1940s and 1950s, and readily recall the hostile climate toward any real change in the pattern of relations between the dominant white group and the black community. The civil rights movement that brought needed changes did not necessarily wait for a public opinion that was completely supportive.

THE ROLE OF GOVERNMENT

It can scarcely be denied that there has been a great mistrust of government in the past few decades. "The government's programs no longer appeared to work successfully, and the government was widely perceived to have been more incompetent than competent in addressing a wide range of issues" (Schwarz 1983: 26). Governmental programs were seen as ineffectual, and the feeling was widespread that the government was wasting large amounts of the public's money.

Accordingly, many conservatives proposed a more diminished role for government. Against the background of mounting skepticism about the government, this argument succeeded in becoming enormously attractive (Schwarz 1983: 27). Fear of concentrated government power is common, of course, among conservatives (Friedman and Friedman 1979: 4; Hazlitt 1973: 188–189).

Interestingly, conservatives are not alone in questioning the role of a strong government. The liberal Schlesinger cautions that the national government, like all tools, is liable to misuse and to abuse. Centralization is not a sovereign remedy. The national government should intervene only when local and private efforts manifestly fail to promote the general welfare (Schlesinger 1986: 245).

The liberal Wilson, in arguing for increased attention to child care, cautions, "it would be better to avoid additional federal bureaucracy" (Wilson 197: 153). Haveman is extremely concerned about economic efficiency, and warns that "it is possible for the government to erode efficiency" (Haveman 1988: 102).

Nevertheless, in the modern era, a government role in helping the poor is widely accepted (Levitan 1985: 17). Many conservatives grant that to some extent government is a form of voluntary cooperation, a way in which people choose to achieve some of their objectives through governmental entities because they believe that is the most effective means of achieving them (Friedman and Friedman 1979: 27). Gilder concedes that the insurance principles of the welfare state reflect a strong bipartisan consensus (Gilder 1981: 110).

When pollsters ask spacious questions, like "Do you think government should stop regulating business?" a sizable majority say yes. But when asked specific questions, like "Do you favor social security? unemployment compensation? Medicare? health and safety standards in factories? government guarantee of jobs for everyone seeking employment?" a sizable majority approves the intervention of the state (Schlesinger 1986: 249).

In the past there was a widespread optimistic belief that the distribution of market incomes would automatically become more equal with growth. The poor would close the gap between themselves and the rich. We know now that this is not the case. From 1948 to 1978 the distribution of earnings grew more unequal (Thurow 1980: 18–19). One study found no statistically significant effect of trickle-down on any poverty group in the period following 1963 (Hirsch 1980). The experience of the 1980s shows that a steadily growing economy will not by itself eliminate the poverty paradox (Peterson 1991: 22). Policies to supplement the benefits of a strong economy are necessary (Osterman 1991: 130).

A writer generally considered conservative himself, Lawrence Mead, points out that there is no reason to suppose that a more small-government, market-oriented society would achieve any particular level of social functioning. Conservatives tend to view human beings as abstractions whose productivity is invariant, but in reality, people differ enormously in their economic capacities (Mead 1986: 86).

> With less government there would surely be a market society of some sort, but the level of economic and other functioning found in it might be below, not above, the relatively high level still usual in the United States. In some societies with weaker governments than in America, the level of cooperation is not far above the warfare of a state of nature; Lebanon and southern Italy are examples. In American cities the atrophy of public authority has produced not harmony and efficiency but crime and economic decline. (Mead 1986: 86–87)

The historian Schlesinger provides a long history of an activist government, noting that the early Congresses assumed that the national authority ought to help any interest significant enough to deserve national attention. Disagreement arose over priorities, not over principles (Schlesinger 1986: 220). In light of the widespread view that early Americans were strictly anti-government, this is an important observation.

At the beginning of chapter 8, I quoted Ackley, who (following John Locke) argued that people have, constitutionally, a guaranteed right to the basic necessities of life. Ackley adds that since individuals are placed in their economic circumstances as the result of state actions such as fiscal policy and tax rates, government has an obligation to provide them with the necessities of life (Ackley 1978).

As governor of New York, Franklin Roosevelt said, "I assert that modern society, acting through its Government, owes the definite obligation to prevent the starvation or the dire want of any of its fellow men and women who try to maintain themselves but cannot" (Schlesinger 1986: 239). FDR felt that in a real community of interests, the public interest must predominate.

Nor did Roosevelt regard affirmative government simply as a temporary expedient in the face of emergency. In 1944 he set forth an Economic Bill of Rights—the right to a job, to wages that assure food and clothing and recreation, the rights to a home, medical care, education, the right to protection against the economic distress of unemployment, sickness, and old age. These were rights to be secured through public action (Schlesinger 1986: 240).

According to Schlesinger, the record shows that the growth of national authority, far from diminishing the individual, has given the majority of Americans more personal dignity and liberty than they ever had before. The individual freedoms destroyed by the increase in national authority have included the freedom to deny black Americans their elementary rights, the freedom to work little children in mills and immigrants in sweatshops, the freedom to pay starvation wages and enforce barbarous working hours and permit squalid working conditions, freedoms we can well do without (Schlesinger 1986: 248).

He argues eloquently that the nation goes through political cycles, with a replacement of private interest by public purpose as the pervading national orientation. Problems, which include the decline of heavy industry, the crisis of cities, the growth of an underclass, and a generation of young people reared in poverty, cannot safely be confided to a deregulated marketplace dominated by great corporations. If the market is incapable, affirmative government becomes a functional necessity in the years ahead (Schlesinger 1986: 249).

Conservatives concede that government has an important role in protecting individuals (as from crime). Lappé asks a very important question: "What is the difference between being beaten up and being deprived of good food, good teachers, and a clean bed to sleep in? Both destroy the body and kill the spirit" (Lappé 1989: 26). Our legal system, she says, is supposed to protect our right to physical security because no other right can be enjoyed without it. "Why doesn't protection of basic economic security—the opportunity to earn a living and access to necessities like health care—warrant the same justification?" (Lappé 1989: 27).

How arbitrary is the line between the maiming of a child by criminal assault and its stunting by malnutrition? Can we maintain that society must prevent one but has little or no responsibility for the other? Loss of a job—undermining economic security—can literally make one sick, even precipitate death. Economic security can't be separated from our physical well-being (Lappé 1989: 57).

Lappé argues brilliantly that a *weak* government may be a great threat to freedom. It is open to manipulation as well as to the public's embrace of authoritarianism, if the public is made desperate by government's lack of responsiveness. It is not that the U.S. government is too strong but that it is too distant, answerable mainly to the most wealthy and powerful. It is not that government does too much, but it answers to too few (Lappé 1989: 26–27).

Halpern shows that the United States has relied inappropriately on services to ameliorate poverty. Americans have been unwilling to acknowledge that many serious problems are products of chosen social and economic arrangements and a general reluctance to use the political process to alter arrangements even when it is acknowledged that they are harmful (Halpern 1991).

There has been great attention recently to the role of the family. But as Schorr points out, to assure that children grow into sturdy adults, the family needs to be buttressed by social institutions, including churches, schools, community agencies—and government. James Q. Wilson now says government has a role in supporting programs to better prepare children for school entry and to help parents cope with difficult children (Schorr 1988: xxviii).

Business leaders and corporate giants are prodding national policy toward greater investment in children. Along with private contributions, they are reaffirming the role of government in helping the poor and the dispossessed. Efforts "cannot be limited to government, but cannot succeed without government" (Schorr 1988: 292–293).

And there is evidence that government efforts have worked in the past (e.g., Lemann 1986). Even conservatives have conceded that New Deal programs like the WPA served a useful function (Friedman and Friedman 1979: 93–94). Keynes's concept of a useful government came to be viewed as inescapable. It became evident how serviceably an increment of income, as from government expenditure, would make up any shortfall in investment spending or consumer borrowing and add to the purchase and production of goods (Galbraith 1987: 246).

World War II showed what Keynes's economics could accomplish through the agency of the state. From 1939 to 1944 the GNP in constant (1972) dollars increased from $320 billion to $569 billion. Personal consumption expenditures increased from $220 billion to $255 billion. Unemployment dropped from 17.2 percent to 1.2 percent. This was the result of upward pressure of public demands on the economy. Federal government purchases of goods and services had increased from $22.8 billion in 1939 to $269.7 billion in 1944 (Galbraith 1987: 246–249).

A strong defense of government policies in the post-Eisenhower years is made by Schwarz. He shows that whatever good results a prosperous private sector and a growing economy realized during these years, they did not address the two main priorities of the time: the reduction of poverty and the control of environmental pollution. "Only through the government and the government's programs could the nation penetrate the surface of either of these complex problems" (Schwarz 1983: 28).

From 1965 through 1972, the real income per American rose, on average, about 3 percent per year, or 24 percent over the seven years. "Real" growth was that which remained in our pockets after subtracting for inflation and most taxes. The growth in real income and the increase in the GNP were much faster than was experienced in the 1950s (Schwarz 1983: 34).

The government's programs to attack poverty during this period frequently were effective. (Recall the defense of the War on Poverty in chapter 5.) The enlargement after 1960 of the many governmental programs to reduce poverty and environmental pollution was associated with solid progress over a broad spectrum of national concerns. The programs led to a diminishing of poverty among Americans by more than half, significantly reduced flagrant malnutrition, lessened inequality in access to medical services, and so on (Schwarz 1983: 76–77).

In Boston, the sharp drop in the incidence of poverty and the high percentage of the poor who are working undercut the idea that an active government social policy is debilitating (Osterman (1991: 130).

In view of the inequities produced by the unregulated market and the horrors produced by total state ownership, the best alternative may be government-business-labor coordination in a free economy. This calls for the restoration of the spirit in which the republic was founded, the spirit of commonwealth, of the public good, of the general welfare. The tradition of affirmative government is quite as authentically American, quite as expressive of American ideas and character, as the competing tradition of self-interest and scrambling private enterprise (Schlesinger 1986: 254–255).

It might be argued that the government indeed has a major role, but it should be concentrated on the state and local level, to obviate the problems of a federal bureaucracy and the building of a dangerous political machine. It may be that the smaller government will understand the local problems more completely.

Schorr suggests that states are more responsive to social issues than the federal government, and she believes that states want to spend more tax money now in ways that would save money in the long run. But she does grant that federal policies are still highly influential and often decisive. She grants the importance of federal funds and leadership in high school and community health centers, of federal funds in compensatory education, of federal funds in the financing of health care. Federal leadership will be essential if the knowledge now available is to be harnessed to change outcomes for the nation's most disadvantaged children (Schorr 1986: 281–282).

There is some evidence, in fact, that this country's highest values, such as aiding the poor, have come from the federal level. There is wide variation in state contributions to welfare payments. "In modern times the expressions of our highest values . . . have come from the national government and from national leadership" (Guzzardie 1982). This function should not be entrusted, Guzzardie says, to fifty little republics with uneven resources, with borders that make no modern sense, and with environments that can narrow minds.

When there has been a decline in federal outlays, states have not taken up the slack, primarily because they are unwilling and unable (in fiscal terms) to do so. Historically, only the federal government has been able to protect the powerless (Beeghley 1983: 44). Similarly, Schlesinger notes, "Historically it has not been local government that has served as the protector of the powerless in the United States; it has been the national government" (Schlesinger 1986: 242).

One writer, arguing that welfare is a national problem, says that federal assumption of state and local shares of welfare and Medicaid would enormously improve the fiscal condition of Frost Belt states and eliminate unwholesome political temptations to compete for new industry by reducing social programs to facilitate tax breaks for business (Lekachman 1982: 92).

The Reagan administration shifted much funding and administration from the federal government to the individual states. This New Federalism appears to have overestimated the states' readiness to assume the burden of administering what had previously been federal programs. There is much variation among the states, with some states creative, others not so (Waxman 1983: 130; Levitan 1985: 20). In most states, state payment levels have fallen far behind inflation in the past fifteen years (Greenstein 1991: 451).

It is not clear that state and local government are more efficient and honest than the federal. (Misuse of political machines, such as political threats or promises to needy voters, have usually been local in character.) As for bureaucracy, duplication, and waste, will there be more or less of it if a single federal agency is replaced by fifty separate state agencies? (Schlesinger 1986: 247).

Poverty and unemployment are widely distributed. Many of the states with the highest poverty rates have the least capacity to raise revenues. Many states with relatively less poverty stand in the best position to raise revenues. Riemer even speaks of a "perverse competition among the states to see who can help the poor the least" (Riemer 1988: 175–176).

However, Riemer does suggest that we need a simpler division of responsibilities between state and federal governments. Many now believe that service program matters are the responsibility of the states, and income security programs that of the federal government. Problems addressed by income and income-substitute programs, such as poverty and unemployment, are intimately connected to the success of the national economy (Riemer 1988: 173–174).

Schorr seems to take a middle position. She argues that while the federal role remains crucial, state and local governments are increasingly competent and many are becoming more concerned about vulnerable populations. Public-private partnerships are pioneering flexible new approaches toward achieving the common good. No one level of government, and certainly no isolated private efforts, can bring nirvana, and a vast array of people and institutions must be enlisted to make progress (Schorr 1988: 282).

A consensus appears to have emerged that private, voluntary organizations can have an important role to play in addressing poverty issues, but are insufficient by themselves. Gilbert (1983), who accepts the broad features of American capitalism, convincingly explains why we should not expect voluntary social aid to fill the gap brought on by the cutbacks in federal funding of social programs (see Harpham 1985).

Even the ultra-conservative Hazlitt admits that private charity operates uncertainly and casually, and systematic provision for the disabled, blind, old, and weak is called for (Hazlitt 1973: 191–192). Typically the private sector cannot be expected to provide cash to low-income people, at least in the long haul (Dear 1989). Dear adds that 46 percent of private charity goes to religious organizations, and only 11 percent to human services.

In a critical comparison, Rosen concludes that privatized services may cost less but they also deliver less, particularly to groups or places that are hard to reach and whose service needs are greatest (Rosen 1988). Clearly churches and other private institutions simply do not have the resources to meet even a small fraction of the sheltering needs of the homeless, for example (Burghardt and Fabricant 1987: 27).

> The earlier views of the private sector's advantages have been shown to be invalid, inadequate, or at least seriously flawed; public baseline provision of benefits and services does not exist in all fields; the private sector is not more innovative than the public sector; competition is not necessarily increased nor is the private sector always more efficient; and pluralism and free choice may be more possible in the private sector but few would be willing to trade off quantitative and qualitative adequacy and accountability for diversity and free choice if access is limited and many are excluded. (Kamerman 1983)

But the important point is not that the public sector is always preferable to the private. The point is that it is becoming increasingly difficult to support the conventional distinction between public and private sectors in the provision of social benefits and services and in their roles in the overall domain of social policy. The conventional dichotomy between public and private sectors can no longer be maintained (Kamerman 1983).

The greatest growth, Kamerman says, and the largest part of social policymaking today is in the hybrid public-private sector, and it is often impossible to distinguish one from the other. A single, uniform model for delivery strategies can no longer be supported. The public's lack of trust in government suggests the importance of diversity; at the same time, the limitations of the market and the continued public insistence on account-ability underscore the need for government involvement, in addition to government money, at all levels (Kamerman 1983). In the previous chapter there was a strong appeal for more jobs. As an example of how public efforts can impinge on the private, the Bureau of Labor Statistics estimates that a million new state and local government jobs will generate about 400,000 additional private sector jobs, through local government pur-chases of supplies and services from local businesses, construction con-tractors, and the like (Harrison et al. 1972).

The government need not do all the administering (e. g., of public jobs). They may contract with private firms to carry out the actual hiring and productive activity. (The government could as well pay Boeing to build sewage treatment plants as to build aircraft frames.) The government can even channel public service funds through community organizations (Schiller 1984: 201).

Waxman urges the incorporation of social welfare programs within a framework that actively involves the citizenry. Government cannot act alone, he says, if real democracy is to prevail. There is a role for voluntary groups and associations. There is increasing need to bolster the role of "mediating structures," "those institutions standing between the individual in his private life and the large institutions of public life," through public policy. We should give greater emphasis to the role of private social welfare in the delivery of services in addition to, but not in place of, existing federal public social service (Waxman 1983: 133–136).

Voluntary organizations have been called the buffer between the individual and government, acting as essential watchdogs and advisors to community-guaranteed services, enhancing and personalizing these services. And because government ensures provision doesn't mean government must itself provide. Some of the most innovative private efforts are sustained by public funds (Lappé 1989: 53).

FINANCING POVERTY SOLUTIONS

A crucial question is the matter of financing proposed solutions to poverty, particularly in a time of budget deficits and a general dislike for new taxes. Some savings might be effected by trimming or eliminating unproductive programs, but that would hardly finance the new initiatives which have been proposed.

Haveman seems to believe that major reforms can be instituted without further tax increases. He thinks there are good prospects for economic growth until the turn of the century, and claims that our society will have both income and output that will enable us to do many things we cannot now afford (Haveman 1988: 90).

Haveman's proposals, some of which were discussed in chapter 8, are based on providing equal opportunities. His emphasis is on the reorientation of policy, which would involve abandoning most existing programs and policies. For example, he would scale back social security benefits for higher earners (Haveman 1988: 153).

While Haveman's ideas are deserving of study, it seems extremely doubtful that they can be implemented with the same money we are now spending. Older Americans are politically powerful, and the idea that social security benefits for higher earners could be scaled back to save money is open to question.

Taxes are an unattractive choice, but they may be the only way to eliminate—or at least significantly reduce—poverty in the United States. "The thought persists that there must surely be some as yet undiscovered way of solving great social problems without pain, but the simple fact is that there is not" (Galbraith 1987: 99). Justice in this country will remain a dream until we face up to the problems (Riemer 1988: 177–178). The imaginative programs discussed by Schorr are not cheap, without sacrifice, without cost to taxpayers (Schorr 1988: 264).

Work incentives are important and it is possible to impose such high taxes that they interfere with work effort; but all of our empirical studies show that our current taxes are far below the levels that create disincentives to work. Repeated studies have shown that highly progressive tax systems do not seem to reduce work effort. Individuals work for a variety of other rewards—power, prestige, promotions, satisfaction (Thurow 1980: 168).

Sample surveys have revealed that professional personnel do not vary their hours of work in response to high tax rates. Historical trends in U.S. labor supply do not suggest that taxes have reduced work effort. Adult males have been reducing their labor supply over the last forty years, largely through earlier retirement, little of which is the effect of tax rates (Pechman 1990).

The strongest conclusion from available evidence is that incentive effects of taxation have been relatively small. The U. S. tax rates were cut sharply in 1981 and 1986, but these cuts had little effect on labor supply and no effect on saving. So long as tax rates are not pushed to punitive levels, incentive considerations do not justify neglect of the distributional objective of tax policy (Pechman 1990).

It is well to remember, Thurow says, that our tax system already taxes capital very lightly, if at all. Great wealth can be generated, controlled, spent, and passed on to one's children without ever being subject to the levels of taxation faced by modest wage earners. U.S. gift and inheritance taxes amount to a tax of only 0.2 percent on net worth (Thurow 1980: 171).

In his 1990 posthumous presidential address to the American Economic Association, Joesph A. Pechman made a strong case for improving the equity of the tax system. This can be done, he said, without punitive tax rates that will hurt economic incentives.

Pechman came to the inescapable conclusion that the well-to-do in our society have had very large reductions in their tax rates in recent years, while the tax rates at the low and middle income levels have not changed much. Inequality has increased even more on an after-tax basis (Pechman 1990).

Ability to pay, he argued, is assumed to increase as incomes rise, and the objective is to impose taxes on a basis that would involve "equal sacrifice" in some sense. If the marginal utility of income declines more rapidly than income increases and the relation between income and utility is the same for all taxpayers, equal sacrifice leads to progression. So the income tax should be used to reduce the great disparities of welfare, opportunity, and economic power arising from the unequal distribution of income (Pechman 1990).

Pechman believed that a minimal goal of federal tax policy in the next several years should be to restore the equalization achieved by the federal tax system in the mid-1970s. He thought we should include in the tax base unrealized capital gains transferred by gift or at death, and that fringe benefits should be taxed at the corporate tax rate (Pechman 1990).

Finally, he claimed that the revenue potential of the income tax has not been exhausted in this country. The tax should be paid by those who have the ability to pay (Pechman 1990).

Many observers have documented the enormous concentrations of wealth in the hands of less than 2 percent of the population with gross assets of over $300,000. Their net worth in 1988 was over $3.3 trillion (Reissman 1991; Phillips 1989). Denny Braun, in a strong presentation of data, demonstrates that income inequality has increased dramatically within the past decade or so, and that increase has meant heavy social, economic, and political costs both for the poor themselves and for the societies they inhabit (see Dietz 1991). Reissman (1991) suggests a wealth tax which would change the outlook for social programs and the expenditures of rebuilding our infrastructure.

Abramovitz favors a restructuring of the tax code as a strategy for active pursuit of distributive justice (Abramovitz (1983). Herbert Gans is more specific: "Since those who benefit from the exclusionary consequences of the economy should subsidize those who suffer from them, the government should levy an income-equalization tax surcharge on the most affluent 20 percent of the population" (Gans 1971). Thurow suggests cutting taxes and raising transfer payments for the bottom three quintiles while raising taxes for the top two quintiles (Thurow 1980: 164).

There seem to be two fears that emerge whenever a tax increase is mentioned. One is that the moderate and low-income family, already burdened, will have to pay more. But it should be clear that we are not talking about raising taxes on this level of income; in fact, as suggested in the previous chapter, taxes for the poor should be eliminated altogether. Those in the middle would have taxes raised only slightly if at all.

The other fear is that the rich will be "soaked," that is, that taxes will be confiscatory. A moderate reform that increased taxes somewhat on the wealthy, without allowing the convenient tax dodges that have been blatant in the past, can raise significant amounts without "confiscating" wealth and still preserving reasonable incentives.

Economist Herbert Stein finds serious deficiencies in the American achievement of important national objectives. Our enormous national output is not being allocated wisely among its possible competing uses. Mentioning increasing poverty among children, he argues for a greater allocation of our national output to neglected purposes. In a significant sentence, he says, "Our failure to devote more of the national output to [domestic programs] . . . or to provision for the future is due to an unexamined argument that we cannot afford to devote the resources" (Stein 1989). What he implies here is that wise investment will be productive in the long run, a theme we shall examine in chapter 10.

Danziger and Weinberg agree that constraints on anti-poverty initiatives are those of ideology and political structure, not economic capacity (Gronbjerg 1987). The cost of eliminating poverty is not so great that our society cannot afford to pay the price (Riemer 1988: 10). Riemer believes that it will take substantially less to eliminate poverty than it now costs to run the Medicare program; far less than social security, defense spending, or interest on the national debt (Riemer 1988: 163).

A recent writer in a business-oriented magazine points out that Americans pay less taxes than citizens of any other major industrial power, including payroll, state, and local taxes. The last time taxes in the United States rose significantly as a share of GNP was in the late 1960s. The federal share of taxes is around 20 percent. The U.S. corporate tax rate is the lowest among industrial nations (Norton 1991).

The drastic tax rate cut of 1981 included generous new incentives to save; instead, the personal savings rate dropped. Norton (1991) suggests ending the deduction for home mortgage interest and taxing fringe benefits. Or if ending the deduction for home mortgage interest does not seem feasible, ending the deduction for a second home would seem appropriate.

Fifteen other countries collect a larger fraction of their GNP in taxes. Nor have our competitors unleashed work effort and savings by increasing income differentials; they have done exactly the opposite. The West Germans work hard with 36 percent less inequality than we, and the Japanese work even harder with 50 percent less inequality (Thurow 1980: 7). Spending and taxing ratios in this country are lower in relation to GNP than those in the democratic states of West Europe (Schlesinger 1986: 246; Lappé 1989: 31).

Agreeing that a smaller percentage of United States national income is spent on redistribution than in most other Western industrialized countries, Morris and Williamson (1987) note that this relatively low level of redistribution does not appear to have led to a relatively high level of economic growth when the United States is compared to these nations.

Gilder claims that the top 1 percent of America's income earners already pay nearly 20 percent of the federal income taxes (Gilder 1981: 171). Another conservative writer claims that the share of federal taxes paid by the wealthy is higher now than ever before. On his figures, the richest 5 percent of families paid 27.1 percent of the total tax burden in 1980, but 30.4 percent in 1990 (Rubenstein 1990). But surely the relevant question is the percentage of income paid in taxes, not the share of the total tax take. The idea that taxes should be paid by those able to pay and should be at least mildly progressive has been generally accepted in this country for many years.

A related point concerns funds becoming available from the apparent end of the arms race. Many believe the Pentagon could easily sustain real cuts of at least 5 percent per year until a new, lower defense floor is reached around the year 2000. The "peace dividend" stands to benefit society in direct proportion to our ability to plan its allocation (Zelnick 1990). A 50 percent cut in military spending would yield $150 billion per year without compromising our national defense (Reissman 1991).

Fortune magazine believes the Pentagon budget can be cut in half by the end of the decade, and military outlays (given economic growth) would amount to a modest 2 percent of GNP in the year 2000. Reducing inventories by two-thirds would strengthen the superpowers' case that nations without nuclear weapons ought to stay that way (Smith 1990b).

A huge military system preempts the skills and talents of our most gifted, best trained scientists, engineers, technicians, and workers (Rosen 1988; Lekachman 1982: 91). Lekachman favors "radical surgery on the Pentagon" as the best way to reduce federal spending and resulting deficits (Lekachman 1982: 18). Even Gilder notes that defense is perhaps the most "inflationary" of all activities, since it pumps money into the economy but produces no domestically consumable goods (Gilder 1981: 209).

Reductions in defense spending give a chance to fill the social gaps that have worsened the conditions of so many. There are great possibilities for changing the texture of American society: reducing inequalities, shifting national objectives, changing the moral tone—as well as redirecting the flows of government spending. Recent public opinion data indicates that sentiment for tax decreases is much less than support for using the peace dividend to deal with pressing social needs (Miller 1990).

Katz believes the defense budget could be reduced by perhaps as much as 60 percent, freeing up billions of dollars for other priorities. Scandinavia and West Germany spend more per capita than the United States on public and private and social services, yet regularly outperform us on every indicator of economic growth and productivity (Katz 1990).

It need not be implied that all savings from the arms race should go directly to anti-poverty programs. Some may be used to reduce the deficit or to help support other programs. All that need be kept in mind is that the the theoretical possibility of significant progress exists.

CONCLUSION

These thoughts about taxation and about funds from the end of the arms race do not mean a more complete attack on poverty will be a simple matter. They do suggest that moving to a more just and fulfilling society is at least a conceivable idea.

Politically, liberals should come to an agreement as to the major solutions that are needed. If fifteen or twenty different proposals exist in the liberal community, the likelihood that any one of them will claim national attention is greatly reduced. Energy will be wasted in defending specific proposals that are so different that a consensus cannot appear.

It is important to keep in mind that there are many different types of poverty, from the underpaid worker to members of the underclass, and no one proposal will solve the entire problem. A strength of Ellwood's proposals is that they recognize this diversity. A series of solutions may well be necessary, and even then they may require supplementing at a later time. There is no perfect solution to any problem.

Liberals should cooperate with moderate conservatives whenever possible. Our point should not be to win arguments or to expand some bureaucracy: our point should be to relieve the suffering and inequity of poverty and to move toward a more just society. If some conservatives have some ideas that can be incorporated into an overall plan, we should at least give them a hearing and not automatically rule them out.

For example, the necessary emphasis on structural reform should not blind us to the need for individuals to take the responsibility for choices made, for people to be held accountable for their actions and decisions (Haveman 1988: 181). Reiman, who stresses the inequities of society, also believes that individuals are responsible for their acts (Reiman 1979: 9).

Some conservatives interpret major proposals against poverty as a radical attack upon the American system. Many of these ideas do imply a critique of aspects of our society, but as Riemer says, job shortages and other problems are not an inevitable consequence of the American system. They can be eliminated by building on the potentially more powerful features of American culture, economy, and government (Riemer 1988: xiii).

A common argument heard from some is that many proposed solutions to the problem of poverty will result in equality of outcome, not opportunity. Most conservatives will grant the idea of equality of opportunity (e.g., Friedman and Friedman 1979: 132), but they object to equality of outcome (Friedman and Friedman 1979: 140; Murray 1984: 233). This concern, however, does not appear warranted.

The liberal Haveman, for example, wants to expand opportunities, maintaining independence and self-reliance. We would not guarantee a certain lifestyle, he says, but provide equal access to that lifestyle (Haveman 1988: 25–28). He seeks an efficient reduction of unwanted economic differences among people, not "global equality" in some Marxian sense (Haveman 1988: 241). Others speak of restructuring our society for people to start with the same opportunities (Segalman and Basu 1981: 4).

And finally, our policies should reinforce fundamental values such as reward for work, opportunities for individual betterment, and family and community responsibility for the care of children and other vulnerable people (Skocpol 1991: 429). Liberals should have no quarrel with ideals of individual responsibility, goals of self-respect and self-reliance, and the values of work and family.

10

A Theory for Reform

Thus far we have not adopted a specific theory with which to address poverty in this country. Conflict and Marxist theories argue that inherent contradictions in the structure of the society inevitably lead to deprivation for many. There are ways to take an interactionist perspective and derive an approach to poverty; an interesting attempt using the concept of stigma is made by Waxman (1983). We do not discuss such theories from lack of space, not because they are undeserving of attention.

While not dismissing any particular theory, this chapter seeks to reason from a structural-functionalist position as outlined by Merton (1968), making two key arguments. The first is the structural point: the major determinants of poverty are found not in the characteristics of the poor themselves, but in the structural elements of the larger society. These include the loss of jobs, the outflow of high-wage industries, insufficient wages, the agricultural crisis, and inflation (Wilkie 1991; Appelbaum 1989; Wilson 1987: 39–55).

To understand why so much poverty exists in the United State, the level of analysis must be shifted away from individuals and to the social structure. Structural variables produce a high rate of poverty by circumscribing the choices available to each person (Beeghley 1988; Chalfant 1985: xiv).

Durkheim, a structuralist and a functionalist, felt that it is in the nature of the society itself that we must seek the explanation of social life. Social structure affects the range of options available to people and such variations produce predictable rates of events. "The lower the social class, then the fewer choices people have and the less effective they are in solving personal problems" (Beeghley 1988).

Beeghley's argument is that the social structure in the United States continually recreates a population of impoverished people. This process occurs primarily because persons located at or near the bottom of the class structure have fewer and less effective choices than those at or near the top.

The rate of poverty in the United States, says Beeghley, is a positive and additive function of several things, including the reproduction of the class structure, the structure of the economy, the vicious circle of poverty, the structure of the electoral process, institutionalized ethnic discrimination, and institutionalized gender discrimination (Beeghley 1988).

That the class structure is reproduced means that most people end up in the same class as their parents. People at each level use their resources to protect their advantages and pass them on to their children. Those who are most vulnerable to poverty, blue-collar families, tend to remain that way over time and across generations. While there is some upward mobility, most people will remain about where they began.

The importance of the structure of the economy is seen in the fact that there are so many employed poor in the United States. Some of these people are poor because they are employed part-time when they would prefer working full-time. Many are caught in a cycle of unstable, low wage jobs punctuated by periods of unemployment (Beeghley 1988).

Haveman makes the same point in a different way. "The causes of inequality among people are systemic. They derive from, among other things, the diversity of individual talents and motivations, individual upbringing, the condition of labor markets, the legacy of bequests, and inequalities of opportunity" (Haveman 1988: 151).

Much of what was said in chapter 3 on the underclass underscored the importance of structural forces. Wilson favors changes in the "structure of opportunities" for the disadvantaged (Wilson 1987: 76), and stresses such structural changes as the loss of manufacturing jobs (1987: 101). In chapter 4 on the homeless, structural factors such as poor economic and social conditions and the lack of low-cost housing were emphasized as causes of this problem (Rossi 1989; Elliott et al. 1991).

If one blames the poor child in a slum school for his or her failure to learn, this overlooks the role of unequal distribution of income, social classes, political struggle, racial group conflict, and inequality of power. Lead paint can kill children. Rather than blame the ravages of lead paint on neglectful mothers, it would more properly be blamed on slum housing and neglectful landlords (Ryan 1970: 22–23).

Working-class women bear the brunt of the institutional and structural changes that constitute the current economic crisis. They experience a special sort of oppression that simply cannot be ameliorated without a fundamental political and economic transformation in both the workplace and the home (Smith 1987).

When examining poverty in Appalachia, a structuralist would not center on the psychological traits of the poor people there, but would ask about the economic, political, and social forces shaping the lives and future of these people (Duncan and Tickamyer 1988).

Motivational factors have only a weak empirical connection to poverty, while social structural variables are much more strongly related (Sherraden 1988). "The circumstances in which stable families develop are in large measure the product of social forces and are therefore amenable to social action" (Schorr 1988: 150).

IMPLICATIONS FROM INTERDEPENDENCE

The second major point in this theory elaborates on an aspect of functionalism that stresses the interdependence of all parts of society (Merton 1968). The point is that what is beneficial (or harmful) to one aspect of the system will be beneficial (or harmful) to the whole system. Our argument, then, is that poverty is harmful not just to the people directly affected but to the nation as a whole, and major reductions in poverty would be beneficial not just to the poor but to us all.

It is often claimed (e.g., Gouldner 1970: 253; Chalfant 1985: xv) that functionalism is an inherently conservative position in that it defends the present order. In responding to this, Merton replies that functionalism doesn't say that all social structures are indispensable for the fulfullment of salient functional needs. He quotes LaPiere, who infers that something is valuable only if it functions to satisfy collective ends (Merton 1968: 93). Merton adds that functional analysis is inherently neither conservative nor radical.

Gouldner (1970: 250) points out that Durkheim was led to a critique of private property, and that if modern functionalism had pursued Durkheim's critique, it would have had to move toward some form of socialism. Later, Gouldner shows how functionalism was led to show how domestic problems can be reduced, and cites functionalist Neil Smelser, who gives special importance to the role of government in addressing social problems (Gouldner 1970: 347–348).

Gans, whose writings on the subject are well-known (1973: 105–113), says that once "a functional analysis is made more nearly complete by the addition of functional alternatives, it can take on a liberal reform cast, because the alternatives often provide ameliorative policies that do not require any drastic change in the existing social order, although radical functional alternatives are also possible" (Gans 1973: 120).

The concept of "dysfunction" implies the existence of strain, stress, and tension on the structural level, an analytical approach to the study of dynamics and change. The accumulation of stresses and strains produce pressure for change in such directions as are likely to lead to their reduction (Merton 1968: 107).

Building on the concept of dysfunctions, functionalism can establish that large inequality and poverty have resulted in vast problems for the society. Thurow (1980:201) shows that vast inequalities are not necessary to keep the economy functioning; they are, in fact, counterproductive.

That poverty is dysfunctional for the poor themselves should be self-evident, though some conservatives try to deny or at least minimize this. The discussion of extensive hardship endured by the poor in chapter 1 should make this clear.

What is equally important, though not quite so obvious, is that widespread poverty is dysfunctional for the society as a whole (Gans 1974: 114). There is significant waste of a relatively unproductive mass of people. The cost to other taxpayers is large not only because of welfare but also because of urban renewal and crime prevention. The entire society would prosper with the elimination (or at least significant reduction) of poverty because of the purchasing power and larger tax base that would result.

Poverty is costly to the whole society. Its ugly byproducts include ignorance, disease, delinquency, immorality, indifference. None of these evils will wholly disappear, but their severity could be markedly reduced, with a coordinated attack on the causes of poverty.

A major plant closing increases unemployment benefits, decreases taxes, including social security taxes, causes a fiscal crisis in the community in which the factory is located, affects all the related businesses that depend on that plant, and leads to an increase in alcoholism, domestic violence, and marital breakdown (Harrington 1984: 241).

A writer in *Fortune* magazine, in discussing the problems of the underclass, notes how troubles there impose costs not just in crime but also in taxes for welfare, drug programs, police, and prisons, not to mention the loss the economy suffers when an able-bodied population produces little (Magnet 1987).

Magnet points out that an increasing fraction of the shrinking pool of new labor force entrants by the year 2000 will be underclass youth, deficient in the skills companies will need in a knowledge-intensive industrial order. There is also the disquieting sense that something is fundamentally wrong in a rich society that allows an underclass to fester.

Wilson agrees with Vivian Henderson, who said that "the economic future of blacks in the United States is bound up with that of the rest of the nation." Americans across racial and class lines continue to be concerned about increasing unemployment, decreased job security, deteriorating real wages, poorer public education, escalating medical and hospital costs, the lack of good child care, and more crime and drug trafficking in their neighborhoods (Wilson 1991b: 477–478).

A do-nothing policy is extremely costly. The recession of the early 1980s cost the nation an estimated $300 billion in lost income and production, and direct outlays for unemployment compensation totaled $30 billion in a single year (study by Levitan and Johnson, cited in Wilson 1987: 164). The costs of the current (1992) recession will surely be as high.

The Carnegie Forum on Education and the Economy declared that the cost of our present failure to educate all American children will be "a steady erosion in the American standard of living," with a growing number of permanently unemployed people seriously straining our social fabric." They warned "it would be fatal to assume that America can succeed if only a portion of our schoolchildren succeed" (quoted in Schorr 1988: 11).

Urban slums cost us dearly. Most cities have to spend a disproportionate amount of their budget for blighted areas in such costs as fire protection, police, and health services (Riemer 1988: 103). Programs to revitalize our cities will help all residents with better schools, parks, clinics, libraries, and other public services.

Lappé has a good discussion of the high price of neglect. Not providing opportunity for everyone and adequately protecting citizens ends up costing government a bundle in what she calls damage control—efforts to salvage people after the destructive fallout of poverty.

> Keeping low-birth-weight babies alive whose mothers were too poor to get good nutrition costs government three-quarters of a billion dollars each year. Supporting just one homeless family in a city shelter can cost over $30,000 a year. Billions go to deal with mounting child abuse, spousal abuse, and alcoholism, all problems exacerbated by poverty. (Lappé 1989: 32)

Basically the same point is made by Schorr, who shows that $20 a day for nourishment for a mother might save $1,500 a day in a hospital neonatal unit. A dollar invested in prenatal care saves up to $3 in hospital costs alone (Schorr 1988: 271).

Poverty's cost to society can also be measured in the loss of potential wealth. Each class of high school dropouts represents roughly $240 billion in lost earnings and tax revenues alone. Joblessness is a huge drain: every unemployed person costs the government about $25,000 a year in lost revenue and direct outlays (Lappé 1989: 33).

If we add up the costs of multiple programs to help a poor child, all the way from prenatal care, through Head Start, special help in school, a summer jobs program, and four years at a public university, the total for one child comes to roughly $39,000. That's about what the public pays now to keep one inmate in prison for just seventeen months! (Lappé 1989: 33). Prison construction costs alone are over $50,000 a bed (Schorr 1986: 4).

We should think of poverty in terms of what is missing. "In every poverty statistic are the shadows of millions of doctors, musicians, journalists, construction workers, artists, engineers, bus drivers, and athletes whose talents and energies have been stolen from us by poverty" (Lappé 1989: 33). Then we can appreciate the real burden, not of ending poverty, but of poverty itself.

There is little question that high rates of poverty are related to the very high crime rates in the country. That crime is a major concern of the nonpoor is seen not only in the taxes paid for the criminal justice system, but in an increase in fear and in elaborate security systems.

A recent study (Huff-Corzine et al. 1991) finds a clear link between economic deprivation and violence. Parker (1989) finds poverty to be a consistent predictor of homicide, and shows a general link between poverty and crime. Messner (1989) shows that economic discrimination has an appreciable effect on national homicide rates, and the effect withstands controls for a wide array of national characteristics. Crime, which is very costly, is linked to the deprivations of poverty (Lappé 1989: 32–33).

Chiricos (1987) finds a positive, generally significant relationship between unemployment and crime. Harrington (1983: 233) believes that a radical drop in the jobless rate will appreciably lower the number of muggings and assaults. Clark (1970: 56–67) persuasively links poverty and crime.

Undoubtedly poverty is also related to other problematic features of our society, such as mental illness. Considerable research has documented higher rates of mental illness, particularly schizophrenia, as the result of features in the lower class situation (Waxman 1983: 12, 39).

ANTI-POVERTY PROGRAMS AS FUNCTIONAL

Granted that poverty is dysfunctional not only for the poor but for society as a whole, does it follow that programs that attack poverty are themselves functional? The answer seems to be in the affirmative.

Modern capitalism cannot function, says Rosen (1988), unless the state is effective and clear in its role of economic management and social support. A welfare state, therefore, is not a drag on the economy. It supplements, controls, directs, and assesses the performance of private power by social criteria. Progressive and humane social policies are not only consistent with one kind of capitalism but are indispensable to its effective functioning.

Cutler (1973) believes that the welfare system allows the federal government to spur business and industry by dropping billions of consumer dollars into the economy. Welfare dollars are spent on food, clothing, housing, and utilities. Lappé believes that government transfer payments stimulate economic growth, probably because they get money into the hands of those most likely to spend it on goods that create jobs (Lappé 1989: 74).

In a defense of the welfare state, Atherton says that it drew from Keynesian economics to provide an economic rationale for state intervention. "Functionalist social theory defined the welfare enterprise as a stabilizing force in the social system" (Atherton 1989). Dear (1989) makes a credible defense of public assistance in general and AFDC in particular, showing that they provide money to millions of low-income people who could not be expected to be served by the private sector.

Schram (1991), as noted in chapter 6, finds an inverse relationship between welfare spending and "dependent" poverty in recent years (the opposite of what many conservatives have claimed). Depriving poor people of needed income, says Schram, "does much to retard their ability to acquire needed resources and impedes their efforts to create the conditions under which they might be able to put their lives on a better footing and begin the process of lifting themselves out of poverty."

According to Haveman (1988: 47–48), welfare reduces poverty and tempers the significant inequality of an unfettered market system; contributes substantially to the economic well-being of individuals by reducing the risks they confront; enables some disadvantaged people to become productive and contributing citizens; promotes economic stability (sustains demand in bad times and tempers it when there is inflation), and facilitates technological change. Public assistance has helped millions of Americans.

Each of us feels better, says Haveman (1988: 142), knowing we live in a society which protects the weak and less able and moderates the extremes in income and economic power that accompany the operation of free markets. Sherraden (1988) claims that social welfare should be viewed as investment in the future: development of the poor is in the economic and social interests of society as a whole.

What about more comprehensive proposals, some of which would replace (or greatly modify) current welfare, that were reviewed in chapter 8? We outlined a major program of economic reform (Wilson 1987: 46), major community-service job creation (Riemer 1988: 9), and a complete restructuring of the welfare state (Ellwood 1988; Haveman 1988). Without reviewing these proposals, we seek to demonstrate that the result would likely be functional or beneficial to the entire society.

Harrington (1984: 231) shows a good understanding of this point: he says that the majority of the people in the United States cannot possibly make themselves secure unless they also help the poor. The very measures that will most benefit the working people and the middle class—the rich will take care of themselves—will also strike a blow against poverty. The programs that are in the self-interest of the majority are always in the special interests of the poor.

Conventional wisdom, says Haveman, is that there is a trade-off between equality and efficiency. But, he says, inequality and poverty can be reduced at the same time that efficiency and growth can be achieved (Haveman 1988: 28).

Haveman directly addresses the fear that additional redistribution carries with it a net efficiency loss. This implies that if we attempt to help the lower class, such as by increasing Medicaid benefits, the rest of society will be heavily burdened. He shows that this is at least misleading, and often wrong in the case of social welfare or redistributionist policy (Haveman 1988: 41–42). The trick, he says, is to identify and implement those policies that simultaneously promote both efficiency and equality. He emphasizes a reorientation of the present policy (Haveman 1988: 44).

Several anti-poverty proposals stress the universal character of the programs; that is, they should be designed for the benefit of all in the society (e.g., Waxman 1983: 121). Recall that Waxman calls for the incorporation of social welfare programs within a framework that actively involves the citizenry. Wilson (1987: 147) urges nonracial solutions such as full employment, balanced economic growth, and manpower training and education.

Wilson urges that the problems of the truly disadvantaged will have to be attacked primarily through universal programs that enjoy the support and commitment of a broad constituency. He adds that these programs should "*improve the life chances of groups such as the ghetto underclass by emphasizing programs in which the more advantaged groups of all races can positively relate*" (Wilson 1987: 120, emphasis in original).

When Gans (1971) recommends a family allowance program, he points out that this would lead to an increase in productivity, an increase in wage rates, and should stabilize family relationships, since the number of intact families increases with higher income. This would be helpful to many in the middle class, because it should reduce their anxiety about losing their jobs. The purchasing power generated in the nation's distressed areas would attract business investment and create additional jobs.

For each rise of one point in the unemployment rate, society loses an estimated $30 billion. Thus a full-employment program would partly finance itself (Harrington 1984: 244). When we discussed the public and private sector in chapter 9, we mentioned that the creation of new state and local government jobs would generate numerous additional private sector jobs.

After recommending some ideas some might call radical, Harrington adds that all of these proposals are not merely compatible with the existence of a private corporate sector; they will help that sector prosper. The New Deal benefitted the entire society including those who most bitterly opposed it (Harrington 1984: 242).

Riemer has an interesting point: he says that when the poor receive medical care, hospitals and doctors who treat them shift costs to insurance companies or self-insured employers that insure most of the rest of us. A more even distribution of health insurance would reduce the necessity of cost shifting (Riemer 1988: 103). The burden of property taxation could also be redistributed. "The establishment of a right not to be poor would benefit American society as a whole" (Riemer 1988: 104).

There would be savings to employers, including the armed forces, in being able to draw on a larger pool of skilled, healthy, and motivated young Americans. There would be savings in the budgets for law enforcement and prisons, as well as other economic effects of a reduction in crime. Savings result when young people are better equipped for parenting: averted dependency, school failure, too early pregnancy, and crime (see Schorr 1988: 272).

Enormous attention has been given to the plight of poor children, not only because one of five American children is poor (Johnson et al. 1991), but because anything that might help poor children in their formative years would mean better, more productive taxpaying citizens later on. All Americans will benefit from the provision of first-class services to children and families living in adversity. All Americans are burdened by the high cost of not making the required investment (Schorr 1988: 294).

It costs us ten times more to care for the physically stunted and mentally damaged victims of malnutrition than it would cost to feed them as babies. When fewer children enter adulthood prepared for work, the economy is less competitive. All of us have a stake in what happens to our children.

Schorr claims that the record is clear that well-organized, comprehensvie health services for poor children have proven to be a cost-effective public expenditure. She adds that universal access to health care for children and pregnant women, coupled with mechanisms to assure that the appropriate services actually reach these groups, represent a sound economic investment (Schorr 1988: 134, 139).

The Committee for Economic Development (1987) said that increasing the prospects of disadvantaged children is "an excellent investment, one that can be postponed only at much greater cost to society" (quoted in Schorr 1988: 273).

The federal government could save countless dollars annually if it took steps to accelerate preventive care and improve prenatal care, and dealt with education problems often incurred by the poor. The absence of early preventive care leads to higher insurance rates and hospital costs for all citizens.

In chapter 5 we reviewed some welfare programs that have established a good record. One such program is Head Start. Writing in *Fortune* magazine, Henkoff (1990) says, "study after study demonstrates that Head Start by and large does what it was designed to do." He adds that one public dollar spent on preschool can generate as much as six dollars in accumulated social benefits, chiefly by reducing expenditures on public assistance and criminal justice. He does note that it serves only 18 percent of today's income-eligible children, and some poor children face problems bigger than Head Start can deal with.

Schorr claims that the long-term effects of Head Start and other preschool programs on participating children and families are today better documented than any of the other interventions discussed in her book. The Committee for Economic Development called the preschool education "an extraordinary economic buy" (quoted in Schorr 1988: 196).

An example of an effective intervention discussed by Schorr (1988: 160) is Homebuilders (a program in Tacoma, Washington). It compared the cost of its intervention with the projected long-term cost of the foster care, group care, or psychiatric hospitalization that was prevented, and found a five- to six-fold return on every dollar invested.

A program of nurses' home visits to pregnant women, new mothers, and infants in depressed Elmira, New York (1978), reduced the incidence of child abuse, neglect, and accidents. They improved the health of mothers and babies, increased the number of teenage mothers returning to school and employment, and reduced welfare dependency (Schorr 1988: 169).

Concerns are often expressed that transfer payments or other means of attacking poverty may have negative consequences for economic growth. Roger Friedland and Jimy M. Sanders provide a strong empirical attack on this proposition. In an analysis of industrially advanced nations, Friedland and Sanders report that transfers to households contribute to economic growth, while transfers to firms and businesses are likely to retard growth (reported in Brown 1989). Economic growth is more likely when all social groups, and not just those at the top, are given a chance to prosper.

Sometimes local businesses may cooperate in anti-poverty programs. Schnall (1989) shows how business leaders came to realize that welfare recipients were unable to purchase their products and services and represented lost customers. She helped involve corporate executives in such a way that they gained greater knowledge of poverty programs from a client's point of view.

Business leaders and corporate giants are prodding national policy toward greater investment in children. Along with private contributions, they are reaffirming the role of government in helping the poor and the dispossed. Big business realizes that out-of-home child care, for example, is too important to the national well-being and too complex to be left to families to grapple with on their own (Schorr 1988: 212).

Haveman shows that redistributionist policies have contributed to the stock of human capital and to productivity. Public education, health care, nutrition, and housing programs lead to economic growth (Haveman 1988: 138–139).

Economic growth is not the same as "trickle down," the belief that the rich save and invest larger portions of their incomes and thus spur economic growth. This reasoning, according to Sherraden (1988), is not generally supported by economic facts. The rates of capital investment since 1981 have been depressed (also see Lappé 1989: 81).

The point is that an entitlement to equality of opportunity need not occur at the expense of economic efficiency (Haveman 1988: 187). If we focus on opportunities rather than outcomes, attend to both incentives and accountability, government policy can support the operation of a more productive and less unequal society and economy.

This chapter has argued that programs that combat poverty can be understood from a structural-functionalist perspective, claiming that the determinants of poverty are most likely to be found in the structural features of the society. Because of the interdependence of all parts of the society, what affects one aspect of the society will have an effect on all of it. In particular, programs to alleviate poverty are to the advantage of the entire nation. Building on the concept of dysfunction, it can be seen that poverty is not only dysfunctional for the poor themselves but also for the rest of society, and programs that help resolve this problem are in the interests of all of us.

Appendix A

1990 Poverty Data

This summarizes the social and economic characteristics of the population below the poverty level in 1990 based on the March 1991 Current Population Survey (CPS). The poverty definition used is that adopted for official government use by the Office of Management and Budget and consists of a set of money income thresholds that vary by family size and composition. Poverty status is based on responses to income questions which in the March CPS refer to pre-tax income received in the previous calendar year.

Families or individuals with income below their appropriate poverty threshold are classified as below the poverty level. Poverty thresholds are updated every year to reflect changes in the Consumer Price Index. For example, the average poverty threshold for a family of four was $12,674 in 1989 but $13,359 in 1990. Average poverty thresholds in 1990 varied from $6,652 for a person living alone to $26,848 for a family of nine or more members. The poverty definition is based on pre-tax money income only, excluding capital gains, and does not include the value of noncash benefits.

The number of persons below the official government poverty level was 33.6, plus or minus (+/-) 0.9 million in 1990, a figure 2.1 million higher than the 31.5 (+/- 0.8) million poor in 1989. The poverty rate was 13.5 (+/- 0.3) percent in 1990, significantly higher than the 12.8 (+/- 0.3) percent in 1989.

Children are overrepresented among the poor, while the elderly are slightly underrepresented. Children under eighteen years were 40.0 (+/- 1.2) percent of the poor and 24.0 (+/- 0.2) percent of the nonpoor, while the elderly were 10.9 (+/- 0.5) percent of the poor and 12.3 (+/- 0.2) percent of the nonpoor.

Source: U. S. Bureau of the Census 1991: 1–13.

Poverty rates for children under eighteen years, persons eighteen to forty-four years and the elderly all increased between 1989 and 1990. The rate for children, 20.6 (+/- 0.7) percent, remains higher than that of other age groups.

Though the poverty rate for the elderly was lower in 1990 than that for children and young adults eighteen to twenty-four years, it was higher than or not significantly different from that for other adult age groups. Furthermore a higher proportion of elderly than nonelderly was concentrated just over their respective poverty threshold (i.e., between 100 percent and 125 percent of their threshold). Consequently, 18.2 percent of the nation's 11.3 million "near poor" persons was elderly, compared with 10.9 percent of persons below the official poverty level.

The poverty rates for whites (10.7 percent) and persons of Hispanic origin (28.1 percent) increased between 1989 and 1990. The poverty rate for blacks (31.9 percent in 1990) did not change significantly, nor did that for Asians and Pacific Islanders as a group (12.2 percent). Non-Hispanic whites represented only about half of the poor in 1990.

About 17.9 (+/- 1.1) percent of the poor were of Hispanic origin in 1990. This fraction was only 10.3 (+/- 1.1) percent in 1973, when such data were first tabulated separately for persons of Hispanic origin.

The poverty rate for the Northeast, while remaining the lowest of the four regions, increased to 11.4 (+/- 0.6) percent, and was the only regional poverty rate to increase between 1989 and 1990. As has historically been the case, the poverty rate was highest in the South (15.8 percent) followed by the West (13.0 percent) and Midwest (12.4 percent). The South continues to have a disproportionately large share of the nation's poverty population: 40.1 percent of the poor lived in the South in 1990, compared with 33.3 percent of U. S. population above the poverty level.

Persons living alone or with nonrelatives only (unrelated individuals) accounted for 22.2 (+/- 1.1) percent of the poor in 1990. The increase in their numbers accounted for one-third of the net increase in the total number of poor between 1989 and 1990.

The average amount of money needed to raise the incomes of each poor family above the poverty level was $5,192 (+/- $105), not significantly different from the 1989 figure.

About 28.6 (+/- 1.3) percent of the poor reported they had no medical insurance in 1990. Persons with income below the poverty level represented 27.7 percent of the 34.6 million persons who reported having no health insurance during 1990. Poor adult males eighteen to forty-four years were the least likely age group to be insured. Among the poor, persons of Hispanic origin were less likely to be insured than blacks or whites.

About 41.8 (+/- 1.4) percent of the poor received cash assistance through such programs as AFDC in 1990. Data on benefits show that about 72 percent of all poor persons were in households in which someone received at least one of the following means-tested noncash benefits in 1990: food stamps, free or reduced price school lunches, Medicaid, and publicly owned or other subsidized housing.

About 28.4 (+/- 1.2) percent of the poor received no assistance of any type, whether in the form of cash or noncash benefits. Some were ineligible because of assets such as a car; some did not know they were eligible; others knew but chose not to accept assistance or felt the effort was not worth the small amount of benefits for which they qualified.

For the fourth consecutive year, there was no significant difference between the farm and nonfarm poverty rates (13.6 percent for nonfarm and 11.2 percent for farm). Typically, the poverty rate has been higher for the farm than nonfarm population.

The number of poor and the poverty rate in the nation's Metropolitan Statistical Areas increased between 1989 and 1990, while the comparable figures for persons living outside metropolitan areas did not change significantly. As has historically been the case the nonmetropolitan poverty rate in 1990 (16.3 percent) was higher than that for metropolitan areas (12.7 percent). The majority of poor metropolitan residents were in central cities (58.2 percent), while nonpoor metropolitan residents were concentrated in suburban areas (64.0 percent).

Poor Hispanic-origin persons were more concentrated in metropolitan areas than the white poor as a whole or the black poor. About 91.9 percent of poor Hispanics lived in metropolitan areas, compared with 78.2 percent of poor blacks and 70.4 percent of poor whites. Within metropolitan areas, 48.8 percent of poor whites lived in central cities compared with 63.9 percent of poor persons of Hispanic origin and 76.3 percent of poor blacks.

About 37.3 percent of the nation's poor in 1990 lived in areas of high poverty concentration (poverty areas), a somewhat smaller fraction than in 1989. While the majority of the 12.5 million poor poverty area residents lived in central cities (59.0 percent), 28.0 percent lived outside metropolitan areas, and 13.0 percent lived in suburban areas. Within such areas, the poverty rate was somewhat higher in large city poverty areas than elsewhere.

Blacks living in cities, regardless of poverty status, were more concentrated in poverty areas than whites or persons of Hispanic origin. About 53.5 percent of blacks living in central cities lived in poverty areas, and 66.9 percent of poor blacks living in cities were concentrated in poverty areas.

White families had a lower poverty rate overall (8.1 percent in 1990), as well as by type of family, than blacks (29.3 percent overall), or families with a householder of Hispanic origin (25.0 percent overall).

The increase in the number of poor families with a female householder accounted for 83.8 percent of the net increase in poor families between 1989 and 1990. Families with a female heading the household and no spouse present accounted for 53.1 (+/- 1.5) percent of poor families in 1990, a figure which was not significantly different from the 1989 proportion. Such families constituted 75.1 percent of all poor black families compared with 46.1 percent of poor Hispanic families and 43.5 percent of poor white families.

Though the poverty rate for families with a female householder and no spouse present did not increase significantly, the number of such families below the poverty level did increase and the change in their numbers accounted for 83.8

percent of the net increase in poor families between 1989 and 1990. Families with a female householder represented 12.7 percent of nonpoor families but 53.1 percent of poor families in 1990.

Female-householder families constituted 75.1 percent of all poor black families compared with 46.1 percent of poor Hispanic-origin families. This difference in demographic composition reflects higher poverty rates for black families and persons.

Poverty rates for families in 1990 decreased with the increasing age of householders up to age forty-five years and then levelled off (from 35.0 percent for those under age twenty-five to 6.8 percent for those with a householder forty-five to sixty-four years and 6.3 percent for those with a householder sixty-five and over). Poverty rates for families also tended to decrease as years of school completed by the householder increased. Poverty rates for families increased as family size increased.

In 1990, 40.3 percent of poor persons fifteen years old and over worked and 9.4 percent worked year-round, full-time. Among poor family householders, 49.8 percent worked in 1990 and 15.2 percent worked year-round, full-time. For comparison, 79.7 percent of nonpoor family householders worked in 1990 and 61.9 percent worked year-round, full-time.

In 59.6 percent of all poor families in 1990 at least one person worked, and in 1.3 million poor families (17.8 percent of all poor families) there were two or more workers in 1990. The majority of the nation's nonpoor families had two or more workers in 1990 (63.2 percent). Poverty rates decreased as number of workers in the family increased.

About 51.8 percent of the poor family householders twenty-five years old and older were high school graduates in 1990, compared with 81.5 percent of nonpoor householders. Although 16.6 percent of poor householders had not completed the eighth grade, a similar proportion had completed one or more years of college. Nevertheless poverty rates decrease dramatically as years of school completed by the householder increases.

Large differences exist among the groups within each education category. For example, 26.2 percent of black family householders who were high school graduates (but had no college) were below the poverty level in 1990, while 15.0 percent of Hispanic householders and only 6.9 percent of white householders with comparable education were poor. Only about one of four poor Hispanic householders was a high school graduate in 1990, compared with about half of both white and black householders below the poverty level.

Of all poor persons, 38.5 percent, or 12.9 million persons, were in families (or were unrelated individuals) whose total income in 1990 was below one-half of their respective poverty threshold. This was not different from the figure for 1989, but remains above the comparable proportion in 1978.

Appendix B

Percentage of Persons in Poverty, by State, 1990

State	Percent	Standard Error
Alabama	19.2	2.0
Alaska	11.4	1.6
Arizona	13.7	1.8
Arkansas	19.6	2.0
California	13.9	0.7
Colorado	13.7	1.9
Connecticut	6.0	1.4
Delaware	6.9	1.4
D.C.	21.1	2.5
Florida	14.4	0.9
Georgia	15.8	1.9
Hawaii	11.0	1.7
Idaho	14.9	1.7
Illinois	13.7	1.0
Indiana	13.0	1.8
Iowa	10.4	1.6
Kansas	10.3	1.5
Kentucky	17.3	2.0

State	Percent	Standard Error
Louisiana	23.6	2.3
Maine	13.1	1.8
Maryland	9.9	1.7
Massachusetts	10.7	0.9
Michigan	14.3	1.0
Minnesota	12.0	1.7
Mississippi	25.7	2.1
Missouri	13.4	1.8
Montana	16.3	1.9
Nebraska	10.3	1.5
Nevada	9.8	1.6
New Hampshire	6.3	1.5
New Jersey	9.2	0.8
New Mexico	20.9	2.1
New York	14.3	0.7
North Carolina	13.0	0.9
North Dakota	13.7	1.7
Ohio	11.5	0.9
Oklahoma	15.6	1.9
Oregon	9.2	1.6
Pennsylvania	11.0	0.8
Rhode Island	7.5	1.6
South Carolina	16.2	1.8
South Dakota	13.3	1.6
Tennessee	16.9	1.9
Texas	15.9	1.0
Utah	8.2	1.4
Vermont	10.9	1.8
Virginia	11.1	1.4
Washington	8.9	1.5
West Virgina	18.1	2.0
Wisconsin	9.3	1.4
Wyoming	11.0	1.9

Source: U.S. Bureau of the Census (1991)

Bibliography

BOOKS

Auletta, Ken. 1983. *The Underclass*, New York: Vintage Books.

Banfield, Edward C. 1968. *The Unheavenly City: The Nature and Future of our Urban Crisis*. Boston: Little, Brown and Company.

Baumann, Donald, and Charles Grigsby. 1988. *Understanding the Homeless: From Research to Action*. University of Texas, Austin: Hogg Foundation of Mental Health.

Beeghley, Leonard. 1983. *Living Poorly in America*. New York: Praeger Publishers.

Bernstein, Blanche. 1986. *Saving a Generation*. New York: Priority Press.

Binford, Shari M., Mark A. Siegel, and Carol D. Foster. 1990. *Social Welfare—Help or Hindrance?* Wylie, Texas: Information Plus.

Brown, R. E. 1977. *Starving Children: The Tyranny of Hunger*. New York: Springer.

Burghardt, Steve, and Michael Fabricant. 1987. *Working Under the Safety Net*. Newbury Park, California: Sage Publications.

Caplovitz, David. 1963. *The Poor Pay More*. New York: The Free Press.

Carouthers, J. Edward. 1966. *Keepers of the Poor*. Nashville, Tennessee: Board of Missions of the Methodist Church.

Chalfant, H. Paul. 1985. *Sociology of Poverty in the United States: An Annotated Bibliography*. Westport, Connecticut: Greenwood Press.

Champagne, Anthony, and Edward J. Harpham (eds.). 1984. *The Attack on the Welfare State*. Prospect Heights, Illinois: Waveland Press.

Clark, Ramsey. 1970. *Crime in America*. New York: Simon and Schuster.

Danziger, Sheldon H., and Daniel H. Weinberg (eds). 1986. *Fighting Poverty.* Cambridge, Massachusetts: Harvard University Press.

Dudley, William (ed.). 1988. *Poverty: Opposing Viewpoints.* St. Paul, Minnesota: Greenhaven Press.

Duncan, Cynthia M. (ed.). 1992. *Rural Poverty in America.* New York: Auburn House.

Ellwood, David T. 1988. *Poor Support: Poverty in the American Family.* New York: Basic Books.

Feagin, Joe R. 1975. *Subordinating the Poor: Welfare and American Beliefs.* Englewood Cliffs, New Jersey: Prentice-Hall.

Foster, Carol D., Mark A. Siegel, and Nancy R. Jacobs (eds.). 1988. *The Information Series on Current Topics: Social Welfare.* Wylie, Texas: Information Plus.

Foster, Carol D., Mark A. Siegel, and Patricia Von Brook (eds.). 1989. *Homeless in America: How Could it Happen Here?* Wylie, Texas: Information Plus.

Friedman, Milton, and Rose Friedman. 1979. *Free to Choose.* New York and London: Harcourt Brace Jovanovich.

Furstenberg, Frank A., Jr., J. Brooks-Gunn, and S. Philip Morgan. *Adolescent Mothers in Later Life.* New York: Cambridge University Press.

Galbraith, John Kenneth. 1987. *Economics in Perspective: A Critical History.* Boston: Houghton Mifflin Company.

Gallup Poll. 1990. *Public Opinion 1990.* Wilmington, Delware: Scholary Resources Inc.

Gans, Herbert. 1973. *More Equality.* New York: Pantheon Books.

Gilder, George. 1981. *Wealth and Poverty.* New York: Basic Books.

Gouldner, Alvin W. 1970. *The Coming Crisis of Western Sociology.* New York: Basic Books.

Harrington, Michael. 1962. *The Other America.* New York: Macmillan.

Harrington, Michael. 1984. *The New American Poverty.* New York: Holt, Rinehart and Winston.

Haveman, Robert. 1988. *Starting Even: An Equal Opportunity Program to Combat the Nation's New Poverty.* New York: Simon and Schuster.

Hazlitt, Henry. 1973. *The Conquest of Poverty.* New Rochelle, New York: Arlington House.

Heilbroner, Robert L., and Lester C. Thurow. 1987. *Economics Explained.* New York: Simon and Schuster.

Jencks, Christopher, and Paul E. Peterson (eds.). 1991. *The Urban Underclass.* Washington, D.C.: The Brookings Institution.

Johnson, Clifford M., Leticia Miranda, Arlos Sherman, and James D. Weill. 1991. *Child Poverty in America.* Washington, D.C.: Children's Defense Fund.

Kaplan, Marshall, and Peggy L. Cuciti. 1986. *The Great Society and its Legacy.* Durham, North Carolina: Duke University Press.

Katz, William. 1989. *The Undeserving Poor.* New York: Pantheon Books.

Kozol, Jonathan. 1988. *Rachel and Her Children: Homeless Families in America*. New York: Crown.

Lappé, Frances Moore. 1989. *Rediscovering America's Values*. New York: Ballantine Books.

Lekachman, Robert. 1982. *Greed is Not Enough: Reaganomics*. New York: Pantheon Books.

Levitan, Sar A. 1985. *Programs in Aid of the Poor*, fifth edition. Baltimore: Johns Hopkins University Press.

Levitan, Sar A., and Isaac Shapiro. 1987. *Working But Poor: America's Contradiction*. Baltimore: Johns Hopkins Press.

Lewis, Oscar. 1965. *La Vida*. New York: Random House.

Lewis, Oscar. 1961. *The Children of Sanchez*. New York: Vintage Books.

Mead, Lawrence M. 1986. *Beyond Entitlement: The Social Obligations of Citizenship*. New York: The Free Press.

Merton, Robert K. 1968. *Social Theory and Social Structure*. New York: The Free Press.

Moynihan, Daniel Patrick (ed.). 1969. *On Understanding Poverty*. New York: Basic Books.

Murray, Charles. 1984. *Losing Ground: American Social Policy 1950–1980*. New York: Basic Books.

Outside the Dream: Child Poverty in America. 1991. New York: Children's Defense Fund.

Phillips, Kevin. 1990. *The Politics of Rich and Poor*. New York: Random House.

Report of the National Advisory Commission on Civil Disorders. 1968. New York: Bantam Books.

Reiman, Jeffrey H. 1979. *The Rich Get Richer and the Poor Get Prison*. New York: John Wiley and Sons.

Riemer, David R. 1988. *The Prisoners of Welfare: Liberating America's Poor from Unemployment and Low Wages*. New York: Praeger Publishers.

Ropers, Richard H. 1991. *Persistent Poverty: The American Dream Turned Nightmare*. New York: Plenum Press.

Rossi, Peter H. 1989. *Down and Out in America: The Origins of Homelessness*. Chicago: The University of Chicago Press.

Ryan, William. 1970. *Blaming the Victim*. New York: Pantheon Books.

Schiller, Bradley R. 1984. *The Economics of Poverty and Discrimination*, fourth edition. Englewood Cliffs, New Jersey: Prentice-Hall.

Schlesinger, Arthur M., Jr. 1986. *The Cycles of American History*. Boston: Houghton Mifflin Company.

Schorr, Lisbeth B. 1988. *Within Our Reach: Breaking the Cycle of Disadvantage*. New York: Doubleday.

Schwartz-Nobel, Loretta. 1981, *Starving in the Shadow of Plenty*. New York: G. P. Putnam's.

Schwarz, John E. 1983. *America's Hidden Sucess: A Reassessment of Twenty Years of Public Policy*. New York: Norton.

Segalman, Ralph, and Asoke Basu. 1981. *Poverty in America: The Welfare Dilemma*. Westport, Connecticut: Greenwood Press.

Thurow, Lester C. 1980. *The Zero-Sum Society: Distribution and the Possibilities for Economic Change*. New York: Basic Books.

The United Methodist Church. 1984. *The Book of Resolutions*. Nashville: The United Methodist Publishing House.

U.S. Bureau of the Census. 1991. *Current Population Reports, Series P-60, No. 175, Poverty in the United States: 1990*. Washington, D.C.: U.S. Government Printing Office.

Valentine, Charles M. 1968. *Culture and Poverty: Critique and Counter-proposals*. Chicago: University of Chicago Press.

Walch, J. Weston. 1973. *Debate Handbook on Reducing Poverty* Portland, Maine: J. Weston Walch.

Wagner, Richard E. 1989. *To Promote the General Welfare Market Process vs. Political Transfers*. San Francisco: Pacific Research Institute for Public Policy.

Waxman, Chaim I. 1983. *The Stigma of Poverty: A Critique of Poverty Theories and Policies,* second edition. New York: Pergamon Press.

Williams, Terry M., and William Kornblum, 1985. *Growing Up Poor*. Lexington, Massachusetts: Lexington Books.

Wilson, William Julius. 1987. *The Truly Disadvantaged*. Chicago: The University of Chicago Press.

Wiseman, Jacqueline P. 1970. *Stations of the Lost*. Englewood Cliffs, New Jersey: Prentice-Hall.

ARTICLES

Abramovitz, Mimi. 1983, November-December. "Everyone is on Welfare: 'The Role of Redistribution in Social Policy' Revisited." *Social Work 28*(6),

Ackley, Sheldon. 1978. "A Right to Subsistence." *Social Policy, 8*(5), 3–11.

"American View Riots as Warning Sign of Racial Friction, Urban Ills, Poll Finds." 1992, May 11. *The Dallas Morning News*, 1A, 6A.

Amidei, Nancy. 1981. "Food Stamps: The Irony of Success." *Public Welfare, 39*(2), 15–21.

Anderson, Elijah. 1991. "Neighborhood Effects on Teenage Pregnancy," pp. 375–398 in Christopher Jencks and Paul E. Peterson (eds.), *The Urban Underclass*. Washington, D.C.: The Brookings Institution.

Applebaum, Richard P. 1989, May-June. "The Affordability Gap." *Society, 26*(4), 6–8.

Atherton, Charles R. 1989, June. "The Welfare State: Still on Solid Ground." *Social Service Review, 63*(2), 170–176.

AuClaire, Philip A. 1979. "The Mix of Work and Welfare Among Long-term AFDC Recipients." *Social Service Review, 53*(4), 586–605.

Bane, Mary Jo, and David T. Ellwood. 1986, Winter. "Slipping Into and Out of Poverty: The Dynamics of Spells." *The Journal of Human Resources, 21*(1) 1–23.

Beeghley, Leonard. 1984, February. "Illusion and Reality in the Measurement of Poverty." *Social Problems, 31*(3), 322–333.

Beeghley, Leonard. 1988. "Individual and Structural Explanations of Poverty." *Population Research and Policy Review, 7*, 201–222.

Bell, Winifred, and Dennis M. Bushe. 1975. "The Economic Efficiency of AFDC." *Social Service Review, 49*(2), 175–190.

Bendick, Marc, Jr. 1980. "Failure to Enroll in Public Assistance Programs." *Social Work, 25*(4), 268–274.

Berk, Richard A., Kenneth J. Lenihan, and Peter H. Rossi. 1980. "Crime and Poverty: Some Experimental Evidence From Ex-Offenders." *American Sociological Review, 45*(5), 766–780.

Berry, Jeffrey M., Kent E. Portney, and Ken Thomson. 1991. "The Political Behavior of Poor People," pp. 357–372 in Christopher Jencks and Paul M. Peterson (eds.), *The Urban Underclass*. Washington, D.C.: The Brookings Institution.

Booker, Betty. 1991, January 13. "Mostly Proud, Mostly Female, 'Genteel Poor' Spurn Charity." *Richmond* (Virginia) *Times-Dispatch*, D1, D3.

Bould, Sally. 1977, May. "Female-Headed Families: Personal Fate Control and the Provider Role." *Journal of Marriage and the Family, 39*, 339–349.

Brown, J. Larry. 1988, March-April. "Domestic Hunger is No Accident." *Social Work, 33*(2), 99–100.

Burt, Martha R., and Barbara E. Cohen. 1989, December. "Differences Among Homeless Single Women, Women With Children, and Single Men." *Social Problems, 36*(5), 508–524.

"Can Handouts Make Better Wage Earners?" 1970, February 28. *Business Week, 2113*: 80–82.

Caputo, Richard K. 1989, February. "Limits of Welfare Reform." *Social Casework, 7*(2), 85–95.

Chambers, Donald E. 1982, July. "The U.S. Poverty Line: A Time for Change." *Social Work, 27*(4), 354–358.

Chernick, Howard, and Andrew Reschovsky. 1990, Fall. "The Taxation of the Poor." *Journal of Human Resources, 25*(4), 712–735.

Chiricos, Theodore G. 1987, April. "Rates of Crime and Unemployment: An Analysis of Aggregate Research Evidence." *Social Problems, 34*(2), 187–212.

Chriss, Catherine. 1991, April 13. "1,900 Homeless Live in Houston, Census Figures." *Houston* (Texas) *Chronicle*, A29.

Chrissinger, Marlene Sonjun. 1980, January. "Factors Affecting Employment of Welfare Mothers." *Social Work, 25*, 52–56.

Clements, Michael. 1991, December 19. "Michigan Leads in Cutting Benefits to Poor." *Detroit* (Michigan) *News*.

Conover, Patrick. 1989, April 19. "Welfare and Work: A Dispute." *The Christian Century, 108*(13), 403–406.

Corcoran, Mary, Greg J. Duncan, Gerald Gurin, and Patricia Gurin. 1985, Summer. "Myth and Reality: The Causes and Persistence of Poverty." *Journal of Policy Analysis and Management, 4*(4), 516–536.

Corcoran, Mary, Roger Gordon, Deborah Laren, and Gary Solon. 1990, May. "Poverty and the Underclass." *The American Economic Review, Papers and Proceedings*, 362–366.

Crane, Jonathan. 1991a. "Effects of Neighborhoods on Dropping Out of School and Teenage Childbearing," pp. 299–341 in Christopher Jencks and Paul E. Peterson (eds.), *The Urban Underclass*. Washington, D.C.: The Brookings Institution.

Crane, Jonathan. 1991b, March. "The Epidemic Theory of Ghettos and Neighborhood Effects on Dropping Out and Teenage Childbearing." *American Journal of Sociology, 96*(5), 1226–1259.

Cuciti, Peggy L. 1990. Review of *Divided Opportunities*, eds. Gary D. Sandefur and Marta Tienda. *Journal of Policy Analysis and Management, 9*(1), 105–108.

Cutler, Ira M. 1973, Summer. " 'Regulating the Poor' Revisited: Testing the Model Against the Reality of Events." *Public Welfare, 31*(3), 29–33.

Dallas Times-Herald. 1990, (September 5).

Danziger, Sheldon. 1982. "Measuring Poverty and Cutting the Federal Budget." *Social Work, 27*(4), 369–372.

Danziger, Sheldon, and Peter Gottschalk. 1987, May. "Earnings Inequality, the Spatial Concentration of Poverty, and the Underclass." *The American Economic Review, Papers and Proceedings*, 211–228.

Danziger, Sheldon, and Robert D. Plotnick. 1986, March. "Poverty and Policy: Lessons of the Last Two Decades." *Social Service Review, 60*(1) 34–51.

Darden, Joe T. 1989, July. "The Status of Urban Blacks 25 Years After the Civil Rights Act of 1964." *Sociology and Social Research, 73*(4), 160–173.

Davidson, Chandler. 1976, Fall. "On 'the Culture of Shiftlessness.' " *Dissent, 23*, 348–356.

Dear, Ronald B. 1989, June. "What's Right With Welfare? The Other Face of AFDC." *Journal of Sociology and Social Work, 16*(2), 5–43.

Devault, Marjorie L., and James P. Pitts. 1984, June. "Surplus and Scarcity: Hunger and the Origins of the Food Stamp Program." *Social Problems, 31*(5) 545–557.

Devine, Joel A., and William Canak. 1986, June. "Redistribution in a Bifurcated Welfare State: Quintile Shares and the U.S. Case." *Social Problems, 33*(5), 391–406.

Devine, Joel A., and James D. Wright. 1990, July-August. "Minimum Wage, Maximum Hokum." *Society, 27*(5), 50–54.

DeViney, Stanley. 1988, November. Review of *The Economics of the Welfare State*, by Nicholas Barr. *American Journal of Sociology, 94*(3), 669–671.

DeViney, Stanley. 1989, September. Review of *Remaking the Welfare State: Retrenchment and Social Policy in America and Europe*, ed. Michael K. Brown. *American Journal of Sociology, 95*(2), 501–503.

Dickinson, Nancy S. 1986, July-August. "Which Welfare Work Strategies Work?" *Social Work, 32*(4), 266–272.

Dietz, Henry. 1991, September. Review of *The Rich Get Richer*, by Danny Brawn. *Social Service Quarterly, 72*(3), 639–640.

Donovan, Rebecca, Nina Jaffe, and Viola M. Pirie. 1987, July-August. "Employment of Low-Income Women: An Exploratory Study." *Social Work, 32*(4), 301–305.

Duncan, Cynthia M., and Ann R. Tickamyer. 1988, Fall. "Poverty Research and Policy for Rural America." *The American Sociologist, 19*(3), 243–259.

Duncan, Gregory J., and Saul D. Hoffman. 1991. "Teenage Underclass Behavior and Subsequent Poverty: Have the Rules Changed?" pp. 155–174 in Christopher Jencks and Paul E. Peterson, (eds.), *The Urban Underclass.* Washington, D.C.: The Brookings Institution.

Duncan, Gregory J., and Willard L. Rodgers. 1988, November. "Longitudinal Aspects of Childhood Poverty." *Journal of Marriage and the Family, 50*(4) 1007–1021.

Eberstadt, Nick. 1988, Winter. "Economic and Material Poverty in the United States." *The Public Interest, 90*, 50–65.

Ehrenreich, Barbara. 1985, February 14. "Welfare is Not the Lap of Luxury." *New York Times*, C2.

Eig, Jonathan. 1992, February 9. "New Poor Swelling State's Welfare Rolls." *The Dallas Morning-News*, A1.

Elesh, David. 1990, December. Review of *Poverty and Social Welfare in the United States*, ed. David Tomaskovic-Devey. *Social Forces, 69*(2), 655–657.

Elliott, Marta, and Lauren J. Krivo. 1991, February. "Structural Determinants of Homelessness in the United States." *Social Problems, 38*(1), 113–131.

"A Family Down and Out." 1987, January 12. *Newsweek*, 44–46.

Farber, Naomi. 1989, December. "The Significance of Aspirations Among Unmarried Adolescent Mothers." *Social Service Review, 63*(4), 518–532.

Farley, Reynolds. 1991. "Residential Segregation of Social and Economic Groups Among Blacks, 1970–1980," pp. 274–298 in Christopher Jencks and Paul E. Peterson (eds.), *The Urban Underclass.* Washington, D.C.: The Brookings Institution.

Feagin, Joe T. 1988, July. Review of *The Truly Disadvantaged*, by William Julius Wilson. *American Journal of Sociology, 94*(1), 179–182.

Fernandez, Richard. 1988, April 8. "Poor But Honest." *Christianity and Crisis, 48*(6), 141–143.

Ferree, Myra Marx. 1989, March. Review of *Bitter Choices: Blue Collar Women In and Out of Work*, by Ellen Israel Rosen. *American Journal of Sociology, 94*(5), 1234–1236.

Fierman, Jaclyn. 1990, July 30. "Why Women Still Don't Hit the Top." *Fortune*, 40–62.

First, Richard J., and Beverly G. Toomey. 1989, March. "Homeless Men and the Work Ethic." *Social Service Review, 63*(1), 113–126.

Foster, Dick. 1991, December 15. "Economy Prosperity Still Elusive for Many Coloradans." *Denver* (Colorado) *Rocky Mountain News*, 112.

Freeman, Richard B. 1991. "Employment and Earnings of Disadvantaged Men in Labor Shortage Economy," pp. 103–121 in Christopher Jencks and Paul E. Peterson (eds.), *The Urban Underclass*. Washington, D.C.: The Brookings Institution.

Gallup, George Jr., and Frank Newport. 1991, June. "As Memories of Gulf War Fade, Dissatisfaction at Home Increases." *The Gallup Poll Monthly, 309*, 46–48.

Gans, Herbert J. 1971, March 7. "Three Ways to Solve the Welfare Problem." *New York Times Magazine,* 99–100.

Gans, Herbert J. 1981, Winter "What Can Be Done About Poverty?" *Dissent, 28*(1), 40–46.

Gans, Herbert J. 1990, April 20. "Effects of Welfare." *Commonweal, 117*, 117–118.

Garfinkel, Irwin, Philip K. Robins, Pat Wong, and Daniel R. Meyer. 1990, Winter. "The Wisconsin Child Support Assurance System." *The Journal of Human Resources, 25*(1), 1–31.

Gideonse, Sarah K., and William R. Meyers. 1988, January-February. "Why 'Workfare' Fails." *Challenge, 31*(1), 44–49.

Gifford, Bernard R. 1986. "War on Poverty: Assumptions, History, and Results, a Flawed but Important Effort," pp. 60–72 in Marshall Kaplan and Peggy L. Cuciti (eds.). *The Great Society and Its Legacy*. Durham, North Carolina: Duke University Press.

Glazer, Nathan. 1984. "The Social Policy of the Reagan Administration: a Review." *Public Interest, 75*: 76–79.

Goodwin, Leonard. 1972, August. "Welfare Mothers and the Work Ethic." *Monthly Labor Review, 95*(8), 35–37.

Goodwin, Leonard. 1981, Fall. "Can Workfare Work?" *Public Welfare, 39*(4), 19–25.

Gottlieb, Alan. 1991, March 31. "Shelter's Demise Shuts Another Door on the Homeless." *Denver Post,* 1B.

Gottschalk, Peter. 1990, May. "AFDC Participation Across Generations." *The American Economic Review, Papers and Proceedings*, 367–376.

Greenstein, Robert. 1989, March 6. "Making Work Pay." *Christianity and Crisis, 49*(3), 57–59.

Greenstein, Robert. 1991. "Universal and Targeted Approaches to Relieving Poverty: An Alternative View," pp. 437–459 in Christopher Jencks and Paul E. Peterson (eds), *The Urban Underclass*. Washington, D.C.: The Brookings Institution.

Greenstone, J. David. 1991. "Culture, Rationality, and the Underclass," pp. 399–408 in Christopher Jencks and Paul E. Peterson (eds.), *The Urban Underclass*. Washington, D.C.: The Brookings Institution.

Griffiths, Martha W. 1975. "Of Government and Welfare." *Human Ecological Forum, 6*(1), 1–8.

Gronbjerg, Kirsten. 1987, September. Review of *Fighting Poverty*, eds. Sheldon H. Danziger and Daniel H. Weinberg. *Social Forces, 66*(1) 275–277.

Gruber, Murray. 1972. "The Nonculture of Poverty among Black Youths." *Social Work, 17*(3), 50–58.

Guzzardie, Walter, Jr. 1982, June 28. "Who Will Care for the Poor?" *Fortune, 105*(13), 34–32.

Halpern, Robert. 1991, September. "Supportive Services for Families in Poverty: Dilemmas of Reform." *Social Service Review, 65*(3), 343–364.

Harpham, Edward J. 1985, March. Review of *Capitalism and the Welfare State: Dilemmas of Social Benevolence*, by Neil Gilbert. *American Journal of Sociology, 90*(5), 1112–1113.

Harrison, Bennett, Harold L. Sheppard, and William J. Spring. 1972, November 4. "Public Jobs, Public Needs." *The New Republic, 167*(20), 18–21.

Henkoff, Ronald. 1990, Spring. "Now Everyone Loves Head Start." *Fortune*, 35–43.

Higgins, Joan, 1982, April. "Public Welfare: The Road to Freedom?" *Journal of Social Policy, 11*(2), 177–200.

Hill, Michael. 1983. "Poverty and Welfare Dependence Across Generations." *Economic Outlook U.S.A., 10*, 61–64.

Hirsch, B. T. 1980, January. "Poverty and Economic Growth: Has Trickle Down Petered Out?" *Economic Inquiry, 18*(1), 151–158.

Holthaus, Terry. 1991, April 10. "Cuyahoga Fears $130 Million Loss in State Welfare." *Cleveland* (Ohio) *Plain Dealer*, B3.

Horowitz, Daniel. 1989, December. Review of *Middle American Individualism: The Future of Liberal Democracy*, by Herbert J. Gans. *Social Forces, 68*(2), 680–682.

Howell, Leon. 1988, November 7. "The Poor Grow Poorer." *Christianity and Crisis, 16*(17), 388–390.

Huff-Corzine, Lin, Jay Corzine, and David C. Moore. 1991, March. "Deadly Connections: Culture, Poverty, and Direction of Lethal Violence." *Social Forces, 69*(3), 715–732.

Hughes, Mark Alan. 1990, Fall. Review of *Welfare Policy for the 1990s*, by Phoebe Cottingham and David T. Ellwood. *Journal of Policy Analysis and Management, 9*(4), 581–590.

Hyde, Henry J. 1990, November 5. "Morals, Markets and Freedoms." *National Review, 42*(21), 52–54.

Jargowsky, Paul A., and Mary Jo Bane. 1991. "Ghetto Poverty in the United States, 1970–1980," pp. 235–273 in Christopher Jencks and Paul E. Peterson (eds.), *The Urban Underclass*. Washington, D.C.: The Brookings Institution.

Jauden, Brian. 1988, July. "U.S. Hunger Crisis Intensifies." *Sojourners, 17*(7), 9.

Jencks, Christopher. 1991. "Is the American Underclass Growing?" pp. 28–100 in Christopher Jencks and Paul E. Peterson (eds.), *The Urban Underclass.* Washington, D.C.: The Brookings Institution.

Johnson, Alice K., and Larry W. Kreuger. 1989, November. "Toward a Better Understanding of Homeless Women." *Social Work, 34*(6), 537–540.

Jones, Brian. 1984, April. "Towards a Constructive Theory for Anti-Poverty Policy." *American Journal of Economics and Sociology, 43*(2), 247–256.

Kamerman, Sheila B. 1983, January-February. "The New Mixed Economy of Welfare: Public and Private." *Social Work, 28*(1), 5–10.

Kane, Thomas J. 1987, September "Giving Back Control: Long-Term Poverty and Motivation." *Social Service Review, 61*(3), 405–419.

Katz, Wallace. 1990, February 9. "The Flawed Triumph of Social Democracy." *Commonweal, 117,* 77–80.

Kaufman, Marc. 1991, January 15. "Study: Poverty, Inadequate Care Afflict City's Elderly." *The Philadelphia* (Pennsylvania) *Inquirer,* B1.

Kaus, Mickey. 1986, July 7. "The Work Ethic State." *The New Republic, 195*(1), 22–33.

Kaus, Mickey, 1992, May 18. "Yes, Something Will Work: Work." *Newsweek,* 38.

Keefe, David E. 1983, June. "Governor Reagan, Welfare Reform, and AFDC Fertility." *Social Service Review, 57*(2) 234–253.

Keigher, Sharon M. 1988, March. Review of *The Faces of Homelessness,* by Marjorie Hope and James Young. *American Journal of Sociology, 93*(5), 1280–1282.

Kemper, Vicki. 1986, March. "Poor and Getting Poorer." *Sojourners, 15*(3), 15–18.

Kemper, Vicki. 1988, December. "Welfare Reform: Helping Whom?" *Sojourners, 17*(11), 5–7.

Kilson, Martin. 1981, Summer. "Black Social Classes and Intergenerational Poverty." *The Public Interest, 64,* 58–78.

Kirschenman, Joleen, and Kathryn M. Neckerman. 1991. " 'We'd Love to Hire Them But . . . ': The Meaning of Race for Employers," pp. 203–232 in Christopher Jencks and Paul E. Peterson (eds.), *The Urban Underclass.* Washington, D.C.: The Brookings Institution.

Kluegel, James R. 1987, February. "Macro-Economic Problems, Beliefs about the Poor and Attitudes Toward Welfare Spending." *Social Problems, 34*(1), 83–99.

Kondratas, S. Anna. 1988. "Hunger is Not Epidemic," pp. 50–54 in William Dudley (ed.), *Poverty: Opposing Viewpoints.* St. Paul, Minnesota: Greenhaven Press.

Kornbluh, Felicia. 1991, Spring. "Subversive Potential, Coercive Intent: Women, Work, and Welfare in the '90s." *Social Policy, 21*(4), 23–39.

LaGory, Mark E. 1990, March. Review of *New Homeless and Old: Community and the Skid Row Hotel*, by Charles Hoch and Robert A. Slayton. *American Journal of Sociology, 95*(5), 1329–1331.

LaViest, Thomas A. 1989, July. "Linking Residential Segregation to the Infant-Mortality Race Disparity in U.S. Cities." *Sociology and Social Research, 73*(4), 160–173.

Lee, Barrett A., Sue Hinze Jones, and David W. Lewis. 1990. "Public Beliefs About the Causes of Homelessness." *Social Forces, 69*(1), 253–265.

Lemann, Nicholas. 1986, September 8. "Ghettos: What Has to Be Done." *Washington Post*, A15.

Lerman, Robert I. 1988, Spring. "Middle Class and Underclass." *The Public Interest, 91*, 111–116.

Leusner, Donna. 1991, April 22. "Advocates Call Welfare Housing Program Unfair to Poor and Taxpayers." *The Newark* (New Jersey) *Star-Ledger*.

Levitan, Sar A., and Clifford M. Johnson. 1986. "Did the Great Society and Subsequent Initiatives Work?" pp. 72–90 in Marshall Kaplan and Peggy L. Cuciti (eds.). *The Great Society and Its Legacy*. Durham, North Carolina: Duke University Press.

Lewis, Oscar. 1969. "The Culture of Poverty," pp. 187–200 in Daniel P. Moynihan (ed.), *On Understanding Poverty*. New York: Basic Books.

Lichter, Daniel T. 1988, January. "Racial Differences in Underemployment in American Cities." *American Journal of Sociology, 93*(4), 771–792.

Lichter, Daniel T. 1989, June. "Race, Employment, Hardship, and Inequality in the American Nonmetropolitan South." *American Sociological Review, 54*(3), 436–446.

Liebow, Elliott. 1970, April 5. "No Man Can Live With the Terrible Knowledge That He Is Not Needed." *New York Times Magazine*, 132.

Lipka, Mitch, 1991, April 16. "Lower 48 Job Hunters Swell Welfare Rolls." *Anchorage* (Alaska) *Times*.

Lissner, Will. 1985, October. "Homelessness and Poverty in Affluent America." *American Journal of Economics and Sociology, 44*(4), 389–390.

Loury, Glenn C. 1986, April 30. "A Prescription for Black Progress." *The Christian Century*, 434–438.

Lynn, Laurence E. 1990a, Summer. "Rejoinder to Mead." *Journal of Policy Analysis and Management 9*(3), 405–408.

Lynn, Laurence E. 1990b, June. "The Rhetoric of Welfare Reform: An Essay Review." *Social Service Review 64*(2), 175–188.

Magnet, Myron. 1987, May 11. "America's Underclass: What to Do?" *Fortune, 115*(10), 130–150.

Mare, Robert D., and Christopher Winship. 1991. "Socioeconomic Change and the Decline of Marriage for Blacks and Whites," pp. 175–202 in Christopher Jencks and Paul E. Peterson (eds.), *The Urban Underclass*. Washington, D.C.: The Brookings Institution.

Mason, Jan, John S. Wodarski, and Jim Parham. 1985, May-June. "Work and Welfare: A Reevaluation of AFDC." *Social Work, 33*(3), 197–203.

Massey, Douglas, and Mitchell L. Eggers. 1990, March. "The Ecology of Inequality: Minorities and the Consequences of Poverty." *American Journal of Sociology, 95*(5) 1153–1188.

Matthews, Richard. 1991, April 28. "Room at the Inn." *Providence* (Rhode Island) *Journal-Bulletin,* M14.

Mayer, Susan E., and Christopher Jencks, 1989, Winter. "Poverty and the Distribution of Material Hardship." *Journal of Human Resources, 24*(1), 88–113.

McLanahan, Sara. 1985, January. "Family Structure and the Reproduction of Poverty." *American Journal of Sociology, 90*(4), 873–901.

McLanahan, Sara, and Karen Booth. 1989, August. "Mother-Only Families: Problems, Prospects, and Politics." *Journal of Marriage and the Family, 51*(3), 557–561.

Mead, Lawrence M. 1987, June. "Author's Response to Reviewer." *Social Service Review, 61*(2) 373–377.

Mead, Lawrence M. 1989, Fall. "The Limits of Structural Analysis." *The Public Interest, 97*, 105–111.

Mead, Lawrence M. 1990, Summer. "Should Workfare Be Mandatory? What Research Says." *Journal of Policy Analysis and Management, 9*(3), 400–404.

Messner, Robert G. 1991, July. "Annual Estimates of California's Poor: 1959 Through 1990." *American Journal of Economics and Sociology, 50*, 299–312.

Meyer, Madonna Harrington. 1990, November. "Family Status and Poverty Among Older Women: The Gendered Distribution of Retirement Income in the United States." *Social Problems, 37*(4), 551–563.

Miller, Dorothy C. 1983, December. "AFDC: Mapping a Strategy for Tomorrow." *Social Service Review, 57*(4), 599–613.

Miller, S. M. 1990, Spring. "A Sea Change Around the World." *Social Policy, 20*(4), 21–33.

Mincy, Ronald B. 1990, July. "Raising the Minimum Wage: Effects on Family Poverty." *Monthly Labor Review, 113*(7), 18–25.

Mogull, Robert d. 1991, July. "Annual Estimates of California's Poor: 1959 through 1990." *American Journal of Economics and Sociology, 50*, 299–312.

Moore, Thomas S., and Aaron Laramore. 1990, June. "Industrial Change and Urban Joblessness: An Assessment of the Mismatch Hypothesis." *Urban Affairs Quarterly, 25*(4), 640–658.

Monsma, Stephen. 1987, June 12. "Should the Poor Earn Their Keep?" *Christianity Today, 31*, 28–31.

Morris, Michael. 1989, Summer. "From The Culture of Poverty to the Underclass: An Analysis of a Shift in Public Language." *The American Sociologist, 20*(20), 123–133.

Morris, Michael, and John W. Williamson, 1987, Summer. "Workfare: The Poverty/Dependence Tradeoff." *Social Policy, 18*(1), 13–16, 49–50.

Murray, Charles A. 1982, Fall. "The Two Wars Against Poverty: Economic Growth and the Great Society." *Public Interest, 69*, 3–16.

Murray, Charles. 1988, October 28. "What's So Bad About Being Poor?" *National Review, 40*(21), 36–39, 59.

Nasar, Sylvia. 1986a, May 26. "America's Poor: How Big a Problem?" *Fortune, 113*(11), 74–80.

Nasar, Sylvia. 1986b, May 26. "What Should Government Do for the Poor" *Fortune, 113*, (11) 82–85.

Nichols-Casebolt, Ann M. 1988, July-August. "Black Families Headed by Single Mothers: Growing Number and Increasing Poverty." *Social Work, 33*(4), 306–313.

Nichols-Casebolt, Ann, and Marieka Klawitter. 1990, September. "Child Support Enforcement Reform: Can It Reduce the Welfare Dependency of Families of Never-Married Mothers?" *Journal of Sociology and Social Work 17*(3), 23–54.

Norman, Jane. 1991, December 18. "Conditions Worse for Rural Children Than Those in Cities." *Des Moines* (Iowa) *Register.*

Norton, Robert. 1991, March 25. "What Ought to Be Done About Taxes." *Fortune, 123*(6), 100–106.

Oliver, Gordon. 1991, April 28. "Too Little Too Late: The Children Suffer." *The Portland* (Oregon) *Oregonian*, 1, 20–21.

Oliver, Melvin L., and Thomas M. Shapiro. 1990, April. "Wealth of a Nation: A Reassessment of Asset Inequality in America Shows At Least One Third Of Households Are Asset Poor." *American Journal of Economics and Sociology, 49*(2), 129–152.

Osterman, Paul. 1991. "Gains from Growth? The Impact of Full Employment on Poverty in Boston," pp. 122–134 in Christopher Jencks and Paul E. Peterson (eds.), *The Urban Underclass*. Washington, D.C.: The Brookings Institution.

Ozawa, Martha N. 1983. "Income Security: The Case of Nonwhite Children." *Social Work, 28*(5), 347–353.

Panetta, Leon E. 1984, May. "Hunger in America." *USA Today, 112*, 38–41.

Parker, Robert Nash. 1989, June. "Poverty, Subculture of Violence, and Type of Homicide." *Social Forces, 67*(4), 983–1007.

Pechman, Joseph A. 1990, March. "The Future of the Income Tax." *The American Economic Review, 80*(1), 1–20.

Peterson, Paul E. 1991. "The Urban Underclass and the Poverty Paradox," pp. 3–27 in Christopher Jencks and Paul E. Peterson (eds.), *The Urban Underclass*. Washington, D.C.: The Brookings Institution.

Petrie, Laurie. 1991, March 27. "For Many Youngsters, Cupboards Are Always Bare." *Cincinnati Post.*

Plotnick, Robert D. 1990, August. "Welfare and Out-of-Wedlock Childbearing: Evidence From the 1980s." *Journal of Marriage and the Family, 52*(3), 735–746.

Phillips, Cabell. 1971, February 6. "Why Not Another WPA?" *The New Republic, 164*(19), 19–20.

Popkin, Susan J. 1990, February. "Welfare: Views From the Bottom." *Social Problems, 37*(1), 64–79.

Porter, Louis. 1991, April 22. "Middle-Class People Finding Themselves in Welfare Lines." *St. Paul* (Minnesota) *Press-Dispatch.*

Presser, Harriet, and Linda S. Salsberg. 1975, December. "Public Assistance and Early Family Formation: Is There a Pronatalist Effect?" *Social Problems, 23*(2), 226–241.

Primus, Wendell E. 1989, Winter. "Children in Poverty: A Committee Prepares for an Informed Debate." *Journal of Policy Analysis and Management, 8*(1), 23–34.

Quigley, John M. 1990, Winter. "Does Rent Control Cause Homelessness? Taking the Claim Seriously." *Journal of Policy Analysis and Management, 9*(1), 89–93.

Randall, Gail. 1991, January 13. "Record Number of Area Families Now on Welfare." *The Colorado Springs* (Colorado) *Gazette-Telegraph*, A1, A10.

Rank, Mark R. 1987, February. "The Formation and Dissolution of Marriages in the Welfare Population." *Journal of Marriage and the Family, 49*(1), 15–20.

Rank, Mark R. 1988, June. "Racial Differences in Length of Welfare Use." *Social Forces, 66*(4), 1080–1101.

Rank, Mark R. 1989, April. "Fertility Among Women on Welfare." *American Sociological Review, 54*(2), 296–304.

Ready, Tinker. 1991, April 13. "States, Counties Feeling Strain of Expanding Welfare Rolls." *Raleigh* (North Carolina) *News and Observer*, A1.

Rector, Robert, Kate Walsh O'Beirne, and Michael McLaughlin. 1990. "How 'Poor' Are America's Poor?" Printed position paper. Washington, D.C.: The Heritage Foundation.

Reeser, Linda Cherrey, and Irwin Epstein. 1987, December. "Social Workers' Attitudes Toward Poverty and Social Action: 1968–1984." *Social Service Review, 61*(4), 610–622.

Rein, Mildred. 1982, June. "Work in Welfare: Past Failures and Future Strategies." *Social Service Review, 56* (2), 211–229.

Reissman. Frank. 1991, Summer. "Time for a Wealth Tax." *Social Policy, 22*(1), 49–50.

Rhoads, Brian J. 1991, April 25. "Too Many Poor Crowd Alameda County's Shoe." *Hayward* (California) *Daily Review*, A3.

Rome, Linda. 1989, March. "There's No Place Like Home." *National Association of Social Workers, Texas Network, 14*(2), 1.

Rosen, Sumner. 1988, January-February. "The Economy and the Welfare State." *Social Policy 5*(5), 7–12.

Rosenbaum, James E., and Susan J. Popkin. 1991. "Employment and Earnings of Low-Income Blacks Who Move to Middle-Class Suburbs," pp. 342–

356 in Christopher Jencks and Paul E. Peterson (eds.), *The Urban Underclass*. Washington, D.C.: The Brookings Institution.

Rosenman, Mark. 1988, Spring. "How the Poor Would Remedy Poverty." *Social Policy, 18*(4), 61–62.

Rubenstein, Ed. 1990, December 31. "Decade of Greed?" *National Review, 42*(25), 37–38.

Rubiner, Betsy, and Veronica Fowler. 1991, April 21. "Study: Welfare Benefits Too Low." *Des Moines* (Iowa) *Register*, 1A.

Schnall, Sandra Maley. 1989, Summer. "How Big Business Can Help the Human Services—and Vice Versa." *Public Welfare, 47*(3), 6–17.

Schram, Sanford F. 1991, April. "Welfare Spending and Poverty: Cutting Back Produces More Poverty, Not Less." *The American Journal of Economics and Sociology, 50*(2), 129–141.

Schram, Sanford F., J. Patrick Turbett, and Paul H. Wilken. 1988, October. "Child Poverty and Welfare Benefits: A Reassessment with State Data of the Claim That American Welfare Breeds Dependence." *American Journal of Economics and Sociology, 47*(4), 409–422.

Schram, Sanford F., and Paul H. Wilken. 1989, April. "It's No 'Laffer' Matter: Claim that Increasing Welfare Aid Breeds Poverty and Dependency Fails Statistical Test." *Journal of Economics and Sociology, 48*(2), 203–217.

Sherraden, Michael. 1988, Winter. "Rethinking Social Welfare: Toward Assets." *Social Problems, 18*(3), 37–43.

Shulman, Steven. 1990, December. "The Causes of Black Poverty: Evidence and Interpretation." *Journal of Economic Issues, 24*(4), 995–1016.

Sigelman, Lee, and Albert D. Karnig. 1977, March. "Black Education and Bureaucratic Unemployment." *Social Science Quarterly, 57*(4), 858–862.

Simon, Paul. 1987, June 12. "Work Over Welfare." *Christianity Today, 31*(9), 28.

Simon, William E. 1990, November 5. "The Morality of Economic Freedom." *National Review, 42*(21), 52–54.

Skocpol, Theda. 1991. "Targeting Within Universalism: Politically Viable Policies to Combat Poverty in the United States," pp. 411–436 in Christopher Jencks and Paul E. Peterson (eds.). *The Urban Underclass*. Washington, D.C.: The Brookings Institution.

Smeeding, Timothy M. 1977. "The Antipoverty Effectiveness of In-Kind Transfers." *The Journal of Human Resources, 12*(3), 360–378.

Smith, Joan. 1987, December. "Transforming Households: Working-Class Women and Economic Crisis." *Social Problems, 34*(5), 416–436.

Smith, Kevin B., and Lorena H. Stone. 1989. "Rags, Riches, and Bootstraps: Beliefs about the Causes of Wealth and Poverty." *The Sociological Quarterly, 30*(1), 93–107.

Smith, Lee. 1990a, December 31. "The Face of Rural Poverty." *Fortune, 122*(16), 100–110.

Smith, Lee. 1990b, June 4. "What We Really Need for Defense." *Fortune, 121*(13), 161–168.

Snow, David A., Susan Baker, and Leon Anderson. 1986, June. "The Myth of Pervasive Mental Illness Among the Homeless." *Social Problems, 33*(5), 407–423.

Snow, David A., Susan G. Baker, and Leon Anderson. 1989, December. "Criminality and Homeless Men: An Empirical Assessment." *Social Problems, 36*(5), 532–549.

Sokoloff, Natalie. 1988, February. "Evaluating Gains and Losses By Black and White Women and Men in the Professions, 1960–1980." *Social Problems, 37*(1), 36–50.

Sosin, Michael. 1987a, May. Review of *Beyond Entitlement: The Social Obligations of Citizenship*, by Laurence M. Mead. *Social Service Review, 61*(1), 156–159.

Sosin, Michael. 1987b, June. "Reviewer's Reply." *Social Service Review, 61*(2), 377–379.

Spolar, Christine. 1991, January 8. "Food Stamp Fraud." *The Washington* (District of Columbia) *Post*, 10–13.

Spring, Beth. 1989, April. "Home, Sweet Home." *Christianity Today, 33*(7), 15–18.

Stein, Herbert. 1989, Fall. "Problems and Non-Problems in the American Economy." *The Public Interest, 97*, 56–70.

Strout, Richard L. 1970, February 21. "Cash Incentives Spur Poor to Work." *Christian Science Monitor*, 1–2.

Sullivan, Mercer L. 1987, May. Review of *Growing Up Poor*, by Terry Williams and William Kornblum. *American Journal of Sociology, 92*(6), 1570–1571.

Swanstrom, Todd. 1988, May-June. "The Limits of Social Research." *Society, 26*(4), 21–23.

"This Land is My Land." 1992, May 18. *Time, 139*(24), 30–33.

Tienda, Marta, and Haya Stier. 1991. "Joblessness and Shiftlessness: Labor Force Activity in Chicago's Inner City," pp. 135–154 in Christopher Jencks and Paul E. Peterson (eds.), *The Urban Underclass*. Washington, D.C.: The Brookings Institution.

Tobin, James. 1967, June 3. "It Can Be Done." *The New Republic, 156*(15), 14–18.

Treas, Judith. 1983, August. "Trickle Down or Transfers? Postward Determinants of Family Income Inequality." *American Sociological Review, 48*(4), 546–549.

Ulmer, Melville J. 1975, January-February. "Full Employment Without Inflation." *Social Policy, 5*(5), 7–12.

van Vliet, William. 1989, May-June. "The Limits of Social Research." *Society, 26*(4), 16–20.

Weir, Margaret. 1987, September. Review of *Beyond Entitlement: The Social Obligations of Citizenship*, by Lawrence M. Mead. *American Journal of Sociology, 93*(2), 495–497.

"Welfare is Work." 1990, March. *Hunger Action Forum 3*: 1.

West, Paul. 1991, January 3. "31 States Lack the Funds for Health, Welfare Costs." *The Baltimore* (Maryland) *Sun*, 1A.

Whitman, David. 1991, Summer "The Great Sharecropper Success Story." *The Public Interest, 104*, 3–19.

Wilkie, Jane Riblett. 1991, February. "The Decline in Men's Labor Force Participation and Income and the Changing Structure of Family Economic Support." *Journal of Marriage and the Family, 53*.(1), 111–122.

Wilson, William Julius. 1991a, February. "Studying Inner-City Social Dislocations: The Challenge of Public Agenda Research." *American Sociological Review, 56*, 1–14.

Wilson, William Julius. 1991b. "Public Policy Research and the Truly Disadvantaged," pp. 460–481 in Christopher Jencks and Paul E. Peterson (eds.), *The Urban Underclass*. Washington D.C.: The Brookings Institution.

Wodarski, John S., Jim Parham, Elizabeth W. Lindsay, Barry W. Blackburn. 1986, July-August. "Reagan's AFDC Policy Changes: the Georgia Experience." *Social Work, 31*(4), 273–279.

"The Problem of Homelessness is Exaggerated," pp. 105–111 in William Dudley (ed.), *Poverty: Opposing Viewpoints*. St. Paul, Minnesota: Greenhaven Press.

Wright, Sonia R., and James D. Wright. 1975. "Income Maintenance and Work Behavior." *Social Policy, 6*(2), 24–32.

Zelnick, C. Robert. 1990, Spring. "We Could Easily Save $350 Billion." *Public Welfare, 48*(2), 4–5.

Zick, Cathleen, and Ken R. Smith. 1991, May. "Marital Transitions, Poverty, and Gender Differences in Mortality." *Journal of Marriage and the Family, 53*(2), 327–336.

Zimbalist, Sidney E. 1988, January-February. "Winning the War on Poverty: The Swedish Strategy." *Social Work, 33*(1), 46–49.

Name Index

Abramovitz, Mimi, 84, 86, 87, 144
Ackley, Sheldon, 113, 136
Amidei, Nancy, 80
Anderson, Elijah, 48, 49
Anderson, Leon. *See* Snow, David A.
Appelbaum, Richard P., 44, 67, 68, 149
Atherton, Charles R., 78, 87, 135
AuClaire, Philip A., 33, 36
Auletta, Ken, 39

Baker, Susan. *See* Snow, David A.
Bane, Mary Jo, 81, 90, 92. *See also* Jargowsky, Paul A.
Banfield, Edward C., 10, 11, 13, 24
Barr, Nicholas, 85
Bassuk, Ellen, 66
Basu, Asoke. *See* Segalman, Ralph
Baumann, Donald, 57, 63, 66, 67
Beeghley, Leonard: assistance helps the nonpoor, 86–87; "beaten-down" effect of poor, 43; coping behavior of poor, 29; desire for equality, 2; desire of poor to

work, 35–36; federal government, 139; income guarantees,
114; in-kind benefits, 9; poverty
line too low, 6, 9, 10; problems
in school, 32–33; public assistance, 79, 83, 86; role of structure, 149–150; unemployment,
120; vulnerable poor, 11, 26;
War on Poverty, 73, 75
Bell, Winifred, 9
Bendick, Marc, Jr., 8
Bernstein, Blanche, 91, 100, 101, 107, 109
Berry, Jeffrey M., 23
Binford, Shari M.: black unemployment, 44; minimum wage, 117;
various federal programs, 99,
100, 102, 103, 104, 116; welfare
defined, 71
Black, Fred, 94
Blackburn, Barry W. *See* Wodarski, John S.
Booker, Betty, 17, 18
Booth, Karen. *See* McLanahan, Sara

Bould, Sally, 91
Braun, Denny, 144
Brown, J. Larry, 13, 85, 159
Brown, Richard, 13
Burger, Stephen, 61
Burghardt Steve: affront of poverty, 2; Americans, rich and poor, 2; cuts in assistance programs, 84, 85; insufficiency of private institutions, 141; loss of low-cost housing, 68; poor record of "workfare," 105, 107; on welfare dependency, 96
Burt, Martha R., 59, 61, 62, 63, 65, 66
Bushe, Dennis M. *See* Bell, Winifred

Canak, William. *See* Devine, Joel A.
Caplovitz, David, 43
Caputo, Richard K., 100, 102, 108, 110
Carouthers, J. Edward, 73
Chalfant, H. Paul: dire straits of poor, 11; food plan for poor, 6; ideas on functionalism, 151; national standard for AFDC, 126; poverty opposed to our ideals, 2; role of structure, 149; War on Poverty, 73
Chambers, Donald E., 6, 9
Champagne, Anthony, 77
Chernick, Howard, 118
Chiricos, Theodore G., 154
Chriss, Catherine, 57
Clark, Ramsey, 40, 43, 154
Clements, Michael, 19, 65
Coe, Richard D., 92
Cohen, Barbara E. *See* Burt, Martha R.
Conover, Patrick, 92, 106
Corcoran, Mary, 22, 27, 31, 38, 42, 90, 92
Corzine, Jay. *See* Huff-Corzine, Lin

Crane, Jonathan, 48, 55
Cuciti, Peggy L., 51
Cutler, Ira M., 156

Danziger, Sheldon H., 16, 47, 77, 82, 126, 145
Darden, Joe T., 48, 52
Davidson, Chandler, 25, 35
Dear, Ronald B., 8, 80, 116, 140–141, 155
Devault, Marjorie L., 121
Devine, Joel A., 79, 80, 115, 117, 118
Deviney, Stanley, 85
Dickenson, Nancy S., 101, 102, 103, 106, 109, 110
Dietz, Henry, 144
Donovan, Rebecca, 100, 109
DuBois, W.E.B., 40, 81
Dunbar, Leslie, 1
Duncan, Cynthia M.: culture of poverty, 26, 37–38, 40; the poor work, 34; role of structure, 151; rural poverty, 14, 127; sociological views on poverty, 3; the underclass, 42
Duncan, Greg J., 15, 32, 53, 81, 94, 97. *See also* Corcoran, Mary
Durkheim, Emile, 149, 151

Eberstadt, Nick, 10, 16, 72
Edelman, Peter, 80
Eig, Johathan, 20
Elliott, Marta, 67, 68, 121, 127, 150
Ellwood, David T.: conflict in welfare, 71; dependency, 98; expenditures in welfare, 79; frustrations of welfare, 78, 79; minimum wage, 118; the poverty line, 10; proposals on welfare, 119, 147; single-parent families, 2, 109; stress on working women, 109; struggle of poor families, 11; two-parent families,

8; War on Poverty, 73; welfare and illegitimacy, 82–83; welfare defended, 79–80. *See also* Bane, Mary Jo

Epstein, Irwin. *See* Reeser, Linda Cherrey

Fabricant, Michael. *See* Burghardt, Steve

Farber, Naomi, 22, 27–28, 31, 37

Farley, Reynolds, 47, 48

Feagin, Joe R., 53, 132

Ferree, Myra Marx, 109

Fierman, Jaclyn, 109

First, Richard J., 59, 60, 63

Foster, Carol D.: AFDC employment, 103, 106; changing population of the homeless, 59; characteristics of the homeless, 59; education of the homeless, 60; the elderly, 60; homelessness defined, 57; increase in homelessness, 58; training programs, 102; veterans, 60; women, 61; youth, 62. *See also* Binford, Shari I.

Foster, Dick, 19

Fowler, Veronica. *See* Rubiner, Betsy

Freeman, Richard B., 54, 121

Friedland, Roger, 159

Friedman, Milton: concern about equality, 148; concern for poor, 3; fear of government power, 134; high assistance payments, 78; housing distributed well, 57–58; Negative Income Tax, 114–115; New Deal programs, 137; numbers of poor overestimated, 7; opposes minimum wage, 117; poor uninterested in work, 33; welfare dependence, 90; welfare fraud, 72

Friedman, Rose. *See* Friedman, Milton

Galbraith, John Kenneth, 6, 71, 80, 137–138

Gallup, George, Jr., 133

Gans, Herbert J.: cultural and situational views of poverty, 38; defends welfare, 93–94; family assistance, 82, 157; few options of the poor, 31; government intervention, 79; poverty and functionalism, 152; private jobs, 121; tax surcharge, 144

Garfinkel, Irwin, 26, 82, 126

Gideonse, Sarah K., 100, 105, 106, 107, 111

Gifford, Bernard R., 73

Gilbert, Neil, 140

Gilder, George: AFDC reforms in California, 91; culture of poverty, 25; defense is inflationary, 146; denies racism, 53; family allowance, 126; government fringes for jobs, 118; income maintenance experiments, 115; poor do not work hard, 33, 46; public jobs, 122; some welfare appropriate, 71, 134–135; top earners pay high tax, 146; value of welfare, 7, 72, 78; welfare and family breakdown, 81, 90, 109; welfare dependence, 81, 90, 98

Glasgow, Douglas, 40

Glazer, Nathan, 72, 77, 118

Gold, Steven, 19

Goodwin, Leonard, 26, 36, 37, 105, 106, 114

Gordon, Roger. *See* Corcoran, Mary

Gottlieb, Alan, 65

Gottschalk, Peter, 91, 97. *See also* Danziger, Sheldon H.

Gouldner, Alvin W., 151

Greenstein, Robert, 74–75, 76, 80, 127–128, 140

Greestone, J. David, 95

Grigsby, Charles. *See* Baumann, Donald

Gruber, Murray, 26
Gurin, Gerald. *See* Corcoran, Mary
Gurin, Patricia. *See* Corcoran, Mary
Guzzardie, Walter, Jr., 139

Halpern, Robert, 137
Harpham, Edward J. *See* Champagne, Anthony
Harrington, Michael: culture of poverty, 21; employment reduces crime, 154; full employment, 120, 157; interdependence of the poor and nonpoor, 156; poor get sicker, 12; problems of plant closings, 152; War on Poverty, 73, 74, 76
Harrison, Bennett, 141
Haveman, Robert: American beliefs about the poor, 132; child support, 126; earnings for females, 109; economic efficiency, 134; elderly poor, 8, 17; equal opportunity, 148; importance of schooling, 32; individual responsibility, 147; poverty and the national conscience, 2; proposals, 142; redistribution, 78; structural unemployment, 45; targeted programs, 128; universal assistance, 114; value of work, 36; War on Poverty, 75, 76; welfare, 83, 84, 87; welfare helps the nonpoor, 86
Hazlitt, Henry: minimum wage, 117; poor should try harder, 24, 33–34; poverty estimates high, 10; poverty is individual, 24; role of government, 134; some welfare needed, 140; status of blacks, 13; unemployment, 46; welfare and cheating, 85; welfare and children, 78; welfare dependence, 89, 90
Heilbroner, Robert L., 132
Henderson, Vivian, 153

Henkoff, Ronald, 84, 158
Hennholtz, Hans F., 12–13
Higgins, Joan, 113
Hill, Michael, 92
Hirsch, B. T., 136
Hirschman, Charles, 51
Hoch, Charles, 57
Hoffman, Saul D. *See* Duncan, Greg J.
Hope, Marjorie, 69
Howell, Leon, 107
Huff-Corzine, Lin, 154
Hyde, Henry J., 24, 89

Jacobs, Nancy R. *See* Foster, Carol D.
Jaffe, Nina. *See* Donovan, Rebecca
Jargowsky, Paul A., 47, 50, 127
Jencks, Christopher, 24, 34, 39, 40, 42, 82, 96
Joe, Tom, 77, 84, 93, 100, 103
Johnson, Alice K., 61
Johnson, Clifford M.: cuts in programs for poor, 11, 84; difficult choices for poor, 11, 12; limited benefits for poor, 8, 9; poor children, 1, 12, 15, 16; rural poverty, 14. *See also* Levitan, Sar A.
Jones, Brian, 25–26
Jones, Sue Hinze. *See* Lee, Barrett A.

Kamerman, Sheila B., 141
Kane, Thomas J., 30, 31, 37, 107
Karnig, Albert D. *See* Sigelman, Lee
Kasarda, John, 44
Katz, Wallace, 65, 75, 80, 147
Kaufman, Marc, 17
Kaus, Mickey, 24, 81, 89, 94, 101, 104, 123
Keefe, David E., 82
Keigher, Sharon M., 69
Kemper, Vicki, 93, 104, 105, 108
Keynes, John Maynard, 137–138

Kilson, Martin, 40
Kirschenman, Joleen, 46, 50, 52
Klawitter, Marieka. *See* Nichols-
  Casebolt, Ann
Kluegal, James R., 85, 132–133
Kondratas, S. Anna, 10
Kornbluh, Felicia, 71, 106, 115, 126
Kornblum, William. *See* Williams,
  Terry
Kozol, Jonathan, 58, 60, 61, 64, 65,
  68
Kreuger, Larry W. *See* Johnson,
  Alice K.
Krivo, Lauren J. *See* Elliott, Marta
Kuttner, Robert, 79

LaGory, Mark E., 59
LaPiere, Richard, 151
Lappé, Frances Moore: capital in-
  vestment, 159; economic secu-
  rity, 136–137; high cost of
  neglect, 153, 154; minimum
  wage, 117; productivity, 124; proposals, 124; public-private efforts, 142; rights of poor
  violated, 42; unemployment, 94,
  120, 124; War on Poverty, 73
Laramore, Aaron. *See* Moore,
  Thomas S.
Laren, Deborah. *See* Corcoran, Mary
LaViest, Thomas A., 53
Lee, Barrett A., 67, 132, 133
Lekachman, Robert, 73, 79, 80,
  109, 139, 146
Lemann, Nicholas, 40, 114, 137
Lerman, Robert I., 51
Leusner, Donna, 18
Levitan, Sar A.: culture of poverty,
  24; high cost of neglect, 153; limited dependence, 92; minimum
  wage, 117; the poor work, 4, 35,
  108, 111, 117; poverty line, 6; tar-
  geted programs, 119, 128; War

on Poverty, 73, 74; welfare, 4,
  116, 134
Lewis, David W. *See* Lee, Barrett,
  A.
Lewis, Oscar, 21–22, 24, 31, 37
Lichter, Daniel T., 14–15, 40, 45,
  46, 49, 51
Liebow, Elliot, 29
Lindsay, Elizabeth W. *See*
  Wodarski, John S.
Lipka, Mitch, 19
Lissner, Will, 69
Locke, John, 113
Lowry, Glenn C., 128
Lynn, Laurence E., 9, 107, 108, 120

Magnet, Myron, 153
Marck, Carolyn, 104
Mare, Robert D., 23
Mason, Jan, 100
Matthews, Richard, 18, 60
McLanahan, Sara, 44, 107, 110. *See
  also* Garfinkel, Irwin
McLaughlin, Michael. *See* Rector,
  Robert
Mead, Lawrence M.: behavioral
  problems of poor, 25; his work
  reviewed, 94; permissiveness,
  101; the poor and work, 34, 101,
  102, 106–107; role of govern-
  ment, 122, 135; welfare depen-
  dence, 90
Merton, Robert K., 149, 151
Messner, Robert G., 154
Meyer, Daniel R. *See* Garfinkel,
  Irwin
Meyers, William R. *See* Gideonse,
  Sarah K.
Miller, S. M., 146
Mincy, Ronald B., 117
Miranda, Leticia. *See* Johnson, Clif-
  ford M.
Mogull, Robert D., 18
Monsma, Stephen, 101

Moore, David C. *See* Huff-Corzine, Lin

Moore, Thomas S., 33, 47

Morris, Michael, 21, 24, 40, 95, 111, 146

Morris, Norval, 41–42

Moynihan, Daniel P., 26, 40, 72–73

Murray, Charles: AFDC, 78; community isolation, 49; concern over poverty, 3; failure of War on Poverty, 72, 75, 76, 77; income maintenance experiments, 115; irresponsible poor, 25, 32, 34; poverty not destitution, 10–11; problems of the urban poor, 14; role of benefit programs, 7; welfare dependence, 90, 91

Nasar, Sylvia: AFDC, 8, 116; difficulties of the poor, 11; food stamps, 6, 7; poverty defined, 5; reduced low-cost housing, 68; War on Poverty, 76

Neckerman, Kathryn. *See* Kirschenman, Joleen

Newport, Frank. *See* Gallup, George, Jr.

Nichols-Casebolt, Ann, 29, 35, 46, 82, 110, 127

Norton, Robert, 145

O'Beirne, Kate Walsh. *See* Rector, Robert

Oliver, Melvin L., 6

Orshansky, Mollie, 6

Osterman, Paul, 50, 54, 120, 135, 138

Ozawa, Martha N., 115

Parham, Jim. *See* Mason, Jan; Wodarski, John S.

Parker, Robert Nash, 43, 154

Pechman, Joseph A., 118, 143–144

Peters, Charles, 122

Peterson, Paul E., 16, 38, 51, 74, 96, 135. *See also* Jencks, Christopher

Phillips, Cabell, 19

Phillips, Kevin, 144

Pirie, Viola M. *See* Donovan, Rebecca

Pitts, James P. *See* Devault, Marjorie L.

Plotnick, Robert D., 81. *See also* Danziger, Sheldon H.

Popkin, Susan J., 31, 91, 111. *See also* Rosenbaum, James E.

Porter, Louis, 18

Portney, Kent E. *See* Berry, Jeffrey M.

Presser, Harriet, 82

Primus, Wendell E., 131

Quigley, John M., 69

Rainwater, Lee, 22–23

Randall, Gail, 18

Rank, Mark R., 30, 32, 38, 81, 96

Ready, Tinker, 19

Reagan, Ronald, 6, 84, 91, 103

Rector, Robert: behavioral poverty, 24; "luxuries" owned by poor, 13; number of poor overestimated, 7, 10; the poor cold in winter, 12; the poor do not work, 34; poverty worse in other countires, 13; welfare dependence, 89, 115; welfare spending up, 78

Reeser, Linda Cherrey, 133

Reiman, Jeffrey H., 12, 43, 147

Rein, Mildred, 102

Reissman, Frank, 144, 146

Reschovsky, Andrew. *See* Chernick, Howard

Rhoads, Brian J., 18–19

Ribicoff, Abraham, 86

Riemer, David R.: the American system, 148; attacking poverty benefits the country, 157; community jobs, 123; the cost of urban slums, 153; importance of structure, 28, 34, 45, 108, 123; need to face problems, 143, 145; our problems solvable, 55; poverty hurts country's self-image, 2; poverty line too low, 6, 8; problems with states, 140; role of discrimination, 53; scarcity of jobs, 119–120; vouchers, 127; wage supplement, 118

Roberts, Paula, 110

Robins, Philip K. *See* Garfinkel, Irwin

Rodgers, Willard L. *See* Duncan, Greg J.

Rogers, Cheryl. *See* Joe, Tom

Rome, Linda, 62, 65

Roosevelt, Franklin, 136

Ropers, Richard H., 63, 69

Rosen, Sumner, 1, 141, 146, 155

Rosenbaum, James E., 49

Rosenman, Mark, 18, 45, 123

Rossi, Peter H., 58, 66, 150

Rubenstein, Ed, 146

Rubiner, Betsy, 19, 84

Russell, Carol Crill. *See* Sari, Rosemary C.

Ryan, William, 150–151

Salsberg, Linda S. *See* Presser, Harriet

Sampson, Robert J., 43, 54

Sanders, Jimy M., 96. *See also* Friedland, Roger

Sari, Rosemary C., 95

Schiller, Bradley R.: culture of poverty, 22, 28, 30; destitution of the poor, 8, 17; discrimination, 50; employment, 122, 123, 124, 142; expectancy of the poor, 35; limits of assistance, 116, 119; low assistance levels, 85, 95; the poor and jobs, 36, 121; poor can't afford

education, 32; public criticism of the poor, 34; subemployment, 45; WIN program, 102

Schlesinger, Arthur M., Jr., 98, 122, 134, 135, 136, 139, 140, 145

Schnall, Sandra Maley, 159

Schorr, Lizabeth B.: against dependency, 96; ambiguity of helping poor, 113; child care, 127, 159; cost of programs, 143; family planning, 127; futility of poor, 32, 41; Head Start, 83–84, 158; health care, 127; Hispanics, 52; intervention with children, 55, 113–114, 137, 158; the poor in school, 43; poor not covered by Medicaid, 8; risk factors of the poor, 41; role of government, 137, 139, 140; role of structure, 151; savings from programs, 157–158, teenage births, 23, 32, 81, 82; universal programs, 125; value of federal programs, 77, 83; weakness of the ghettos, 42, 50

Schram, Sanford F., 74, 75, 76, 84, 93, 95, 96

Schwarz, John, 72, 75, 134, 138

Segalman, Ralph, 23, 91, 117, 120, 148

Shapiro, Isaac. *See* Levitan, Sar A.

Shapiro, Thomas M. *See* Oliver, Melvin L.

Sheppard, Harold L. *See* Harrison, Bennett

Sherman, Arlos. *See* Johnson, Clifford M.

Sherraden, Michael, 6–7, 36, 107, 120, 151, 156, 159

Shulman, Steven, 120

Sidel, Ruth, 93, 100, 109

Siegel, Mark A. *See* Binford, Shari M; Foster, Carol D.

Sigelman, Lee, 33

Simon, Paul, 106

Skocpol, Theda, 73, 74, 126, 127,
    148
Slayton, Robert E. *See* Hoch,
    Charles
Smeeding, Timothy M., 7
Smelser, Neil, 151
Smith, Joan, 14, 91, 146
Smith, Ken R. *See* Zick, Cathleen
Smith, Kevin B., 132
Smith, Lee, 80, 146
Snow, David A., 58, 66–67
Sokoloff, Natalie, 51
Solon, Gary. *See* Corcoran, Mary
Sosin, Michael, 25, 93, 94, 102
Spolar, Christine, 86
Spring, Beth, 60, 61, 67
Spring, William J. *See* Harrison,
    Bennett
Stack, Carol B., 29
Stein, Bruno, 86
Stein, Herbert, 145
Stier, Haya. *See* Tienda, Marta
Stone, Lorena H. *See* Smith, Kevin
    B.
Strout, Richard L., 116
Sullivan, Mercer L., 27
Sumner, William Graham, 77
Suttles, Gerald, 73
Swanstrom, Todd, 60, 63–64, 65, 68

Taylor, Paul, 85
Testa, Mark, 52
Theobold, Robert, 114
Thomson, Ken. *See* Berry, Jeffrey
    M.
Thurow, Lester C.: distribution is
    unequal, 135, 152; jobs program,
    122–123; the rich stay rich, 87;
    shortage of jobs, 45; tax policies,
    143, 144, 145; War on Poverty,
    76. *See also* Heilbroner, Robert L.
Tickamyer, Ann R. *See* Duncan,
    Cynthia M.
Tienda, Marta, 25, 34, 51, 108

Tobin, James, 14, 114
Tomaskovic-Devey, David, 121
Toomey, Beverly G. *See* First, Rich-
    ard J.
Treas, Judith, 77
Tucker, William, 68–69
Turbett, J. Patrick. *See* Schram, San-
    ford F.

Ulmer, Melville J., 124

Valentine, Charles M., 25
van Vliet, William, 61

Wagner, Richard, 90
Walch, J. Weston, 2, 74, 86, 114,
    125
Waxman, Chaim I.: culture of pov-
    erty, 22, 37, 38; economic re-
    form, 43; educational
    deprivation, 32; importance of
    public sentiment, 131; minimum
    subsistence, 115; poor not receiv-
    ing assistance, 7; poverty and
    mental illness, 154; proposals,
    125, 156; role for voluntary
    groups, 142; stigma theory, 149;
    variation among states, 140
Weill, James D. *See* Johnson,
    Cliffrod M.
Weinberg, Daniel H. *See* Danziger,
    Sheldon H.
Weir, Margaret, 73, 107
West, Paul, 18
Whitman, David, 112, 175
Wilkie, Jane Riblett, 11, 41, 149
Wilkin, Paul H. *See* Schram, San-
    ford F.
Williams, Terry, 36
Williamson, John W. *See* Morris,
    Michael
Wilson, James Q., 137
Wilson, William Julius: black moth-
    ers, 32; child allowance, 125–

126; child care, 127, 134; child support, 126; concentration effects, 47, 48, 49; criticism of "workfare," 107–108; culture of poverty, 25, 30, 38; economic deprivation increased, 14, 41; family problems, 23, 41, 48–49; futility of self-help programs, 12; income maintenance experiments, 116; joblessness, 44, 45, 51, 52, 76, 121; low-income blacks, 41, 51; minorities in the underclass, 50, 53; need new initiatives, 119; poverty line low, 6, 7; poverty line useful, 10; problems in schools, 43, 44, 53; social isolation, 30, 45–46, 47, 49, 50; structural changes, 150, 156; theory assessed, 54; *The Truly Disadvantaged*, 40; the undercalss, 41, 53, 54; universal programs, 121, 125, 153, 156–157; War on Poverty, 73, 75, 76; welfare and illegitimacy, 83

Winship, Christopher. *See* Mare, Robert D.
Wiseman, Jacqueline P., 64
Wodarski, John S., 100, 108, 183, 184. *See also* Mason, Jan
Wong, Pat. *See* Garfinkel, Irwin
Wooster, Martin Morse, 57
Wright, James D., 58, 61, 63, 65, 66. *See also* Devine, Joel A.; Wright, Sonia R.
Wright, Sonia R., 115

Young, James. *See* Hope, Marjorie

Zeinick, C. Robert, 146
Zick, Cathleen, 8, 12
Zimbalist, Sidney E., 124

Subject Index

adaptive responses, 22, 29, 42
adolescent mothers, 27–28, 31, 48–49, 96
advisory group on poverty, 121
agricultural crisis, 149
Aid to Families With Dependent Children: caseloads higher, 18, 19, 20; creates dependency, 91, 96–97; cuts in, 84, 100; defended, 80–81, 116, 155; eligible for Medicaid, 100, 110; fraud in, 86; history of, 99–100; need for minimum standard, 115; not received by all poor, 7; recipients had rather work, 36–37; can be reduced, 103; reforms in, 101, 125–126; relation to efficacy, 91; relation to workfare, 102–103, 111; role in chilbearing, 78, 81–83; study of recipients, 33; value declined, 75, 76, 82, 96, 99–100
Alabama, 8, 134
Alaska, 19, 100

alcohol problems, 66. *See also* Skid Row alcoholic
American Public Welfare Association, 18
American system, 55, 138, 147–148. *See also* capitalism
Anchorage, 119
Angola, 15
Appalachia, 14, 43, 151
Arizona, 86
Arkansas, 65
arms race, 146–147
Atlanta, 41
Austin, 58
automobiles, 13, 110

Biafra, 13
blacks: compared to blacks in other countries, 13; concentrated in poverty, 47–48; earnings, 51; education insufficient, 33; falling behind, 51; future of, 153; isolated, 49; problems with marriage, 52; rural, 14–15; self-help

programs, 128; in school, 50; students, 50; in underclass, 50–53; unemployment, 44, 45, 46, 47–48, 51; women, 29, 35, 52, 96
"blaming the victim," 23
Boston, 50, 54, 120, 138
Bureau of Labor Statistics, 141
bureaucracy, 78, 115, 134, 139, 140
Bush administration, 121
business, 121–122, 124, 135, 137, 155, 159

California, 18, 82, 91, 103, 105
California Community Work Experience Program, 103
Cambodia, 15
Canada, 16, 82
capital gains, 87, 143
capitalism 77, 132, 155
Carnegie Forum on Education and the Economy, 153
Carter administration, 99
census, 1, 7, 9, 10, 17, 58
Center for Law and Social Policy, 110
Center on Budget and Priority Policies, 15, 19, 119
charities, 86, 141
Chicago, 23, 48, 52, 59, 108
"Chicago school," 40
child care, 87, 101, 104, 105, 109–110, 153, 159
child care vouchers, 127
child support, 100, 126
Child Support Assurance System, 126
children: black, 90; controversy about relation to welfare, 78, 81–83; costs of helping, 154; dependent, 98; difference by race, 52–53; homeless, 62, 66; impact of workfare on, 105, 109; inherit advantages, 150; middle-class, 43; need assured support, 116;
need for intervention, 55, 113–114, 157–158; not helped by workfare, 105; number of and social class, 22–23; problems among, 12, 105, 157–158; report on poverty among, 15–17; risk factors among, 41; in schools, 43–44, 150–51; welfare, 80, 84, 92–93, 95, 96, 97. See also fertility; infant mortality
Children's Defense Fund, 15, 16, 62
churches, 137, 141
cities, 39, 44, 46, 58, 135, 153. See also inner city
civil rights movement, 49, 134
Colorado, 19
Committee for Economic Development, 158
Community Childhood Hunger Identification Project, 15
Community Work and Training Program, 102
Comprehensive Employment and Training Act (CETA), 75
conservatives: against equality of outcome, 148; anti-poverty programs, 128, 147; claim the poor do not want to work, 33–34; claim the poor own luxuries, 13; claims of dependency, 9, 95; critical of welfare, 77–78, 85, 90, 155; defend the American system, 147–148; duck the question of jobs, 123; interpretation of the culture of poverty, 24, 30, 32; meaning of the term, 2–3; mistrust of government, 134, 135, 136; poor in other countries, 12–13; poor underreport income, 9; seek to minimize poverty, 10–11, 152; want to count "in-kind" benefits, 7

Dallas, 61

day care. *See* child care
death, 12, 136. *See also* infant mortality
Declaration of Independence, 113
Denmark, 82
Denver, 65, 115
dependency, 24, 89–98
depression, 94. *See also* mentally ill
deviance, 43
disabled poor, 18, 79, 106
discrimination, 46, 51, 52, 53, 94, 109, 150
dysfunctions, 152

Early and Periodic Screening, Diagnostic, and Treatment program, 83
Earned Income Tax Credit, 99, 103, 118, 127
Economic Bill of Rights, 136
economic efficiency, 85, 134, 156, 159
economic growth, 76, 95, 125, 138, 142, 146, 155, 159
economic mobility, 28, 92, 150
Economic Opportunity Act, 73, 102
economic security, 137
economy, 44, 51, 67, 133, 135, 138, 152. *See also* economic growth; recession; trickle-down
education, 27, 32–33, 60, 106, 123, 153
efficacy scale, 91
elderly, 17–18, 60, 76, 79
Elmira, New York, 159
employers (in urban areas), 46, 50, 52
employment, 17, 63–64; among the underclass, 40–41; of black men, 45; full, 120, 121, 124, 125; may not raise out of poverty, 84; and minimum wage, 118; of the poor, 35; programs, 101; and a strong

job market, 121. *See also* jobs; unemployment; work
Employment and Training choices, 104
environmental pollution, 138
"epidemic" theory of ghetto, 48
equal opportunity, 142, 148, 159
Equal Opportunity Act, 102
equality, 2, 132
expectations, 23, 27, 30, 35

families: abuse in, 11, 61, 152, 159; background in underclass, 42, 43; black, 29, 81; homeless, 59, 61; income constant, 117; lack of cultural differences, 28; lack only education, 26; limited benefits for, 8, 19, middle-class, 49, 50; problems with, 11, 12, 23, 30, 95; relation to unemployment, 52; role of, 137; two-parent, 11, 18, 59, 60, 85; weak structure in, 22; welfare for, 77, 78, 84, 95, 96; young, 16. *See also* female-headed familes; single-parent families
family allowance, 114, 116, 125–126, 157
family planning, 127
Family Support Act, 104–105
federal government, 68, 138, 139–140, 155, 158. *See also* government
federal training programs, 75
female-headed families: black, 32, 52; homeless, 59, 61, 68; income disparities in, 77; increase in poverty among, 63; increasing numbers, 52; often poor, 23; in the underclass, 109; weak benefits for, 18; in welfare, 82–83. *See also* single-parent families
fertility, 81–83, 116
food, 65

food plan, 6
food stamps: cuts in, 19, 85, 103; do
    not reach many poor, 15; fraud
    in, 86; most do not get full
    amount, 6; not counted as in-
    come, 7; numbers up, 20; small
    allowance, 18, 100; valuable, 76,
    80, 127; value of declined, 75
Fortune magazine, 11, 76, 109,
    146, 152, 158
France, 82
fraud. *See* welfare, fraud in
Frost Belt states, 139
functionalism, 149, 151–152, 155

Gallup poll, 133
General Accounting Office, 103
Georgia, 11, 95, 100
Germany, 16, 82, 124, 145
ghetto, 41, 48, 50, 119, 127. *See
    also* cities; inner city, underclass
government: active policy of, 54,
    120; conservative attitudes about,
    3, 78, 89, 90; government jobs,
    122–123; people want to do more,
    132; role in guaranteed income,
    114–115; role of, 71, 134–142,
    151. *See also* federal governme-
    ment; local government; states
Government Accounting Office, 85
Great Britain, 13, 16, 82
Great Society, 72, 77. *See also* War
    on Poverty
Guaranteed Annual Income, 114, 179

habits, 30
Haiti, 15
handicapped, 18, 79, 106
hardship, 11, 80
Harvard School of Public Health, 15
Head Start, 83–84, 128, 154, 158
health, 12, 17, 62, 65–66, 83, 159.
    See also health care; health insur-
    ance

Health and Human Services, 159
health care, 76, 80, 11, 127, 136, 157
health insurance, 69, 157. *See also*
    Medicaid
health services, 158
Heritage Foundation, 2, 10, 12, 13
Hispanics, 18, 47, 52, 61, 68, 81,
    116
home mortgage interest, 145
home ownership, 13
Homebuilders, 158
homeless, the, 18, 47, 57–70, 94,
    133, 150
homicide, 43, 154
housing, 42, 57–58, 67, 68, 69, 80
housing assistance, 8, 68, 72, 79,
    81, 128–129
housing vouchers, 128–29
Houston, 41, 58
hunger, 10, 15, 80, 121

immigrants, 46–47, 136
income taxes, 86. *See also* taxation
India, 13
individual characteristics, 24
individual responsibility, 24, 27,
    147, 148
individualism, 24, 132
industries, loss of, 44, 45, 67
inequality 48, 53, 143, 144, 150,
    152, 156
infant mortality, 16, 53, 75, 76
inflation, 117, 124, 149, 155
inheritance taxes, 98
"in-kind" income, 7–9, 72
inner city, 34, 40, 46, 48, 49–50, 51,
    110. *See also* cities; ghetto; un-
    derclass
interactionism, 149
interdependence, 151
intervention, 55, 113–114, 135, 157–
    158
investment, 55, 145
Iowa , 19

Iowa State University, 19
isolation. *See* social isolation; spatial isolation

Japan, 145
job corps, 73
job training, 104, 105, 124
Job Training Partnership Act, 100, 104, 106
jobs: dead-end, 35, 36; difficult for homeless to find, 64–65; government, 122–123, 141; imbalance of, 28, 45; lack of as cause of riots, 133; low-paying, 34, 64, 67–68, 102, 108; measure of status, 97; not assured with education, 33; of the books, 9; outflow of, 44, 48; poor opportunity for, 30; public, 73–74, 102, 103, 122–123, 141; safeguards for, 111; shortage of, 36, 45, 107, 119–120; as solution to poverty, 119–125; transfer to high-tech, 67; for welfare recipients, 107–108. *See also* employment; work
joint survivorship, 17

liberals, 2, 25, 78–79, 122, 147, 148, 152
life style, 21, 25, 148
local government, 139, 140, 157
Los Angeles, 58
Los Angeles riots, 1, 14, 54, 133
low-birthweight babies, 16, 65, 153
lower class, 22, 23, 24, 32, 39, 52. *See also* underclass

Maine, 14
Maine Health Bureau, 12
malnutrition, 137, 158. *See also* hunger
Manpower Demonstration Research Project, 39
marriages, 23, 52, 115, 116

Marxist theory, 149
Massachusetts, 61, 62, 104, 105
maternal and child health clinics, 83
Medicaid: concern to AFDC recipients, 100, 110; cuts in, 103; helped the poor, 76, 83; many ineligible, 8, poor receive no money, 79; has proved durable, 127; recent explosion, 18
Medicare, 135, 145
Memphis, 85
men, 41, 44, 51, 52
mentally ill, 25, 63, 66, 67, 94, 154
Mexican Americans, 116
Mexico, 13, 21
Michigan, 11, 19, 95
Michigan Institute of Social Research, 93
Michigan Panel Study of Income Dynamics, 28, 92
migrant workers, 14
Milwaukee, 85
minimum wage, 102, 105, 117–118, 123
minorities, 9, 50, 51, 82. *See also* race
Mississippi, 13, 14
motivational factors, 22, 27, 31, 132, 151

Nashville, 67
National Academy of Sciences, 62
National Advisory Commission on Civil Disorders, 47
National Alliance to End Homelessness, 58
National Association of Home Builders, 68
National Conference of Catholic Bishops, 1
National Longitudinal Studies, 27
National Review, 2
National School Lunch program, 116

Native Americans, 14
Negative Income Tax, 114–115
neighborhood health clinics, 76, 83
neighborhoods, 48, 50, 110, 128
networking (for minorities), 51
New Deal, 122, 137, 157
New Federalism, 139–140
New Jersey, 18, 115–116
New Jobs Tax Credit, 123
New York City, 60, 61, 62, 85, 86,
    105
noncash benefits. *See* "in-kind" in-
    come
nonpoor, 9, 25, 26, 50, 64, 86–87
North, 41
North Carolina, 19
Northeast, 44
Norway, 16, 124
nurse home visting, 159
nutrition, 10, 12, 66, 80. *See also*
    malnutrition

Ohio, 19
Oklahoma, 65
Omnibus Budget Reconciliation
    Act, 101, 103
opportunities, lack of, 29, 30, 32,
    38, 40, 42, 47, 49, 53
options, lack of, 26, 29
Oregon, 20
outmigration of nonpoor, 49–50

Pakistan, 13
peace dividend. *See* arms race
Pennsylvania, 14
Philadelphia, 17, 81
Philadelphia Negro, The, 40
Phoenix, 58
Physician Task Force on Hunger in
    America, 14
political implications, 131–148
poor: apathy among, 31; attack on,
    24–25; behavior of, 12, 26, 29,
    31, 42; benefits for, 7–8; budget

of, 5–6, 11; case histories of, 27,
    29; coping mechanisms of, 26,
    27; defense of, 25–33; destitution
    of, 9; frustration of, 26, 31, 32,
    34; luxuries of, 13–14; near poor,
    17; unemployable, 35; vulnerabil-
    ity of, 11–12, 26
poverty: absolute definition, 10; be-
    liefs about, 131–133; costs to so-
    ciety, 152–154; culture of,
    21–38; defined, 5, 7; different
    types of, 147; extent of, 10–20;
    measurement of 5–10; in other
    countries, 12–13, 16; rate of, 1,
    74, 150; relative definition, 10;
    reports on, 15–17; rural, 14–15,
    29, 34, 40, 110, 127; spells of,
    12, 40, 90, 92; spur of, 90, 98; as
    subject of inquiry, 1; theories of,
    149; transmission of, 21, 22, 128–
    129; trends in, 10, 18, 76; types
    of, 119, 147
prenatal care, 154. *See also* low-
    birthweight babies
prisons, 66, 154
private services, 138, 140–141, 142,
    202, 207, 212–113, 218, 244
productivity, 157
progressive tax, 146
psychological characteristics, 27, 31
public assistance. *See* welfare
public jobs, 73–74, 102, 103, 122–
    123, 141
public opinion, 25–26, 67, 131, 133–
    134, 147
public-private partnerships, 140, 141
public services, 125, 141, 142. *See
    also* public jobs
Puerto Rico, 21

race, 30, 47, 50–53. *See also* minor-
    ities
Reagan administration, 68, 82, 139
recession(s), 80, 153

references for homeless people, 64
rent allowances, 68
rent control, 68–69
rental units, 65, 68
returning to society (for homeless or underclass), 64–65
rich, 86, 98, 144, 145. *See also* wealth
rights, 2, 42, 113, 136
role models, 49, 50, 98
runaways, 62
rural homeless, 63

Sacramento, 65
San Antonio, 65
San Francisco, 61
Scandanavia, 147
School Breakfast program, 116
school dropouts, 50, 154
schools, 12, 32–33, 42, 43–44, 50, 98, 150
Seattle, 61, 115
segregation, residential, 47–48
self-help, 128
sharecroppers, 14, 40
shelters, 58, 59, 60, 61, 62
shiftlessness, 25
single individuals, 59–60, 65, 80
single-parent families, 16, 23, 78, 82, 108, 126. *See also* female-headed families
single room occupancy, 68
situations faced by poor, 29, 38
Skid Row alcoholic, 59, 64
social class, 22, 42, 150. *See also* lower class
social institutions, 42, 49, 137
social insurance programs, 72
social isolation, 30, 47–50
social policy, 141
social security, 72, 78, 79, 86, 135, 142, 152
Social Security Act, 99
social workers, 114, 133

socialism, 151
sociological imagination, 3
solutions to poverty, 38, 113–129, 147, 156
Somalia, 15
South, 14, 40
Southwest, 59
spatial isolation, 47–49
spatial mismatch, 49
Special Milk Program, 116
starvation, 86
states, 18, 82, 85, 95, 104, 139, 140
stigmatization of poverty, 37, 67, 91, 106–107, 115, 125, 149
streetcoter men, 29
structure, 38, 45, 67, 77, 132, 133, 149–151
subculture, 22, 38
subemployment, 45
subsidized housing, 68
suburbs, 20, 45, 49, 61
Summer Food Service program, 116
Supplemental Security Income, 5, 8, 17, 74, 127
Sweden, 16, 82, 124
Switzerland, 16

targeted programs, 127–128
tax breaks, 128
Tax Reform Act of 1986, 118–119
tax surcharge, 144
taxation, 124, 143–146
taxes for the poor, 118–119, 144
teachers, 44
teen pregnancy/births, 23, 27, 32, 41, 48, 96
Temporary Emergency Food Assistance program, 116
Texas, 19–20, 65, 100
time orientation, 22
Title II (JOBS), 104
transients, 58, 59, 60
transitional support, 119
transportation, 110

trickle-down, 135, 159
Truly Disadvantaged, The, 40

underclass, 21, 30, 39–55, 100, 153, 157
underreporting of income, 9
unemployment: of blacks, 15, 44, 45, 46, 48, 49, 51, 52; cause of homelessness, 67, 69; cause of poverty, 45, 76, 95, 121; controversy over, 49; cost to society, 120, 157; dropped in 1940s, 138; hidden, 15; low in Sweden, 124; needs among homeless, 64; relation to marriage, 52; relation to problems, 41, 46, 153; relation to welfare, 94; relation to workfare, 107–108
unemployment compensation, 36, 72, 80, 94, 101, 152
United Kingdom, 13, 16, 82
United Methodist Church, 110–111
United States, 2, 10, 15, 79, 121, 146, 150
United States Conference of Mayors, 59, 60, 62
United States Department of Agriculture, 6, 15
universal programs, 69, 121, 124–127, 156–157
University of Michigan Institute for Social Research, 93
urban poverty, 14, 30, 133, 153. *See also* cities; ghetto; inner city; underclass
urban renewal, 72, 75, 152
Utah, 20, 105

values, 21–22, 23, 25, 28, 37, 148
Vermont, 18
veterans among the homeless, 60
veterans programs, 78, 79
violence, 25, 39, 43, 79, 96, 154
Virginia, 17

voluntary organizations, 140, 142
volunteers (in the War on Poverty), 77
Volunteers in Service to America, 73

wage supplement, 118, 123
wages, 16, 34, 51, 68, 75, 92
War on Poverty, 72–77, 138
Washington, D.C., 58
wealth, 6–7, 143, 144
wealth tax, 144
welfare, 71–87; attack on, 77–79; benefit levels fallen, 76, 94; and child-bearing, 7, 81–83; covers fewer poor children, 84; cuts in, 19, 84–85; decline in value, 65; defense of, 79–87, 155–156; demands for up, 18, 20; dependency, 89–98, 107; fraud in, 72, 85–86; helps the nonpoor, 86–87; most use for short time, 7, 92, 93; not rescue from poverty, 8–9, 16, 19; programs involving citizens, 142; proposal to replace, 119; should not be reduced, 87, 111; stigma of, 106–107; variations in payments, 85; and work, 96, 110
West, 59
Western Europe, 16, 145
whites, 29, 35, 43, 44, 52, 61, 92, 93
Wisconsin, 18, 126–127
women: affected by Family Support Act, 105; aspirations of, 37; black, 29, 35, 52, 96; earn less, 109; forced into poverty, 18; higher unemployment rate, 109; homeless, 59–60, 61–62; hurt by low minimum wage, 118; lack of skills, 106; limited marital choices, 23; single, 65, 110; stress from working, 109; struggle for survival, 96, 151; and wel-

fare, 96; and work, 101, 115. *See also* female-headed families

Women, Infants, and Children's formula, 76, 83

work: incentive, 114; may work and be poor, 108–109; poor avoid work, 22, 25, 33–34; poor desire work, 27, 34–37; related to welfare benefits, 94, 96–97; value of, 28, 100–101, 120. *See also* employment; jobs

Work Incentive Program, 101, 102

work study program, 74

workfare, 99–111; case for, 100–102; history of, 102–105; questions about, 105–111

working poor, 84, 103, 108, 117, 118, 123, 150

Works Progress Administration, 122, 137

World War II, 138

young people, 16, 26, 36, 43, 44, 92, 157

About the Author

C. EMORY BURTON is Associate Professor of Sociology at Richland Community College, Dallas, Texas. He has authored chapters for several textbooks and has published articles in *Teaching Sociology* and the *Journal of Nursing Administration*.